RACIAL FOLLY

A TWENTIETH-CENTURY
ABORIGINAL FAMILY

RACIAL FOLLY

A TWENTIETH-CENTURY ABORIGINAL FAMILY

Gordon Briscoe

Published by ANU E Press and Aboriginal History Incorporated
Aboriginal History Monograph 20

This title is also available online at: http://epress.anu.edu.au/racial_folly_citation.html

National Library of Australia
Cataloguing-in-Publication entry

Author: Briscoe, Gordon, 1938-

Title: Racial folly : a memoir of a twentieth century family / Gordon Briscoe.

ISBN: 9781921666209 (pbk.) 9781921666216 (pdf)

Series: Aboriginal history monograph ; 20.

Notes: Bibliography.

Subjects: Briscoe, Gordon, 1938-
            Aboriginal Australian intellectuals--Australia--Biography.
            Intellectuals--Australia--Biography.
            Aboriginal Australian historians--Biography.
            Historians--Australia--Biography
            Political activists, Aboriginal Australian--Australia--Biography.
            Political activists--Australia--Biography.
            Aboriginal Australians--Politics and government.
            Aboriginal Australians--Northern Territory--Removal--Biography.
            Children, Aboriginal Australian--Institutional care--South Australia--Biography.

Dewey Number: 994.007202

Aboriginal History Incorporated

Aboriginal History is administered by an Editorial Board which is responsible for all unsigned material. Views and opinions expressed by the author are not necessarily shared by Board members.

The Committee of Management and the Editorial Board
Kaye Price (Chair), Peter Read (Editor), Robert Paton (Treasurer and Public Officer), Anne McGrath (Deputy Chair), Karen Smith (Secretary), Isabel McBryde, Niel Gunson, Luise Hercus, Harold Koch, Christine Hansen, Tikka Wilson, Geoff Gray, Jay Arthur, Shino Konishi, Dave Johnson, Ingereth Macfarlane, Brian Egloff, Lorena Kanellopoulos, Serene Fernando, Richard Baker, Peter Radoll, Samantha Faulkner, Sophie Collins.

Contacting Aboriginal History
All Editorial enquiries: Editor, Aboriginal History, Australian Centre for Indigenous History, Coombs Building, ANU 0200. Sales and subscriptions thelma.simms@anu.edu.au

Aboriginal History Inc. is a part of the Australian Centre for Indigenous History, Research School of Social Sciences, The Australian National University and gratefully acknowledges the support of the History Program, RSSS and the National Centre for Indigenous Studies, The Australian National University.

WARNING: Readers are notified that this publication may contain names or images of deceased persons.

ANU E Press: All correspondence should be addressed to:
ANU E Press, The Australian National University, Canberra ACT 0200, Australia
Email: anuepress@anu.edu.au, http://epress.anu.edu.au

Cover image: Sleeping arrangments for half-caste children. Jay Creek, Northern Territory, 1929. From Dr WD Walker Report on Aborigines N Aust (1928-1929), NAA: CRS A1 1928/10743. Courtesy of National Archives of Australia.

Cover design and layout by ANU E Press

Apart for any fair dealing for the purpose of private study, research, criticism or review, as permitted under the Copyright Act, no part of this publication may be reproduced by any process whatsoever without the written permission of the publisher.

This edition © 2010 ANU E Press and Aboriginal History Inc

Contents

Illustrations xi
Foreword xv
Preface xix
1. My family background, 1890 to 1941 1
2. Evacuation, Mulgoa to Semaphore, 1938 to 1945. 17
3. Racial theory and a religious solution, 1920s to 1945 31
4. Pembroke Street to St Francis House, 1946 to 1949. 47
5. Educated men or Christian misfits? 1950 to 1956 77
6. Life after St Francis House, 1957 to 1964 91
7. Race relations, work and education, 1964 to 1968 103
8. University and Aboriginal politics, 1969 to 1971 119
9. Redfern and the early 1970s. 151
10. The Northern Territory, 1972 165
11. A new era in Aboriginal politics, 1974 to 1981. 177
12. The education years: 1980s 191
13. The 1990s and beyond 203
Epilogue. 215
References. 221

For my brother Bill (1944 to 2003) who served his country well.

'I have had many dealings with adversity,
but the want of parental affection has
been the heaviest of my trials'

Edgar Allan Poe

Illustrations

All photographs in author's possession unless otherwise indicated.

Cover Illustration: Sleeping arrangments for half-caste children. Jay Creek, Northern Territory, 1929.From Dr WD Walker Report on Aborigines N Aust (1928-1929), NAA: CRS A1 1928/10743. Courtesy of National Archives of Australia.

Figure 1: Map showing route of Overland Telegraph and railway including place names mentioned in the text.

Figure 2: School children at first 'Bungalow', Alice Springs, 1914. Courtesy of National Archives of Australia.

Figure 3: [original caption:] Half-caste children sleeping arrangements, Jay Creek, 1929-32. NAA: 1928/59. Courtesy of National Archives of Australia.

Figure 4: Meal time at the first 'Bungalow', Alice Springs, 1929-32. NAA: 1928/59. Courtesy of National Archives of Australia.

Figure 5: Building new dormitories at Iwaputarka (Jay Creek) 1929-32. See *wiltja* in foreground. NAA: 1928/59. Courtesy of National Archives of Australia.

Figure 6: St Francis House on day of inspection for proposed purchase, 1947. NAA: A431/1. Courtesy of National Archives of Australia.

Figure 7: Father Smith and Frank Moy inspecting St Francis House for proposed purchase, 1947. NAA: A431/2. Courtesy of National Archives of Australia.

Figure 8: St Francis House, late 1940s: from rear left to right, Jim Foster, David Woodford (in hat), Laurie Bray, Peter Tilmouth, Malcolm Cooper, (front) Gerry Hill, Tim Campbell and Vince Copley.

Figure 9: Mulgoa boys in cowshed, 1947: from left to right John Hampton milking cow while Tom Campbell and Ken Hampton look on. Courtesy of National Archives of Australia.

Figure 10: Mulgoa, New South Wales, 1949: from left to right James Stirling, Wally McArthur, Cyril Hampton and James Foster. Courtesy of National Archives of Australia.

Figure 11: Alice Springs railway station, 1952: self, my mother, Millie Glenn, Billy and Dennis at front.

Figure 12: Reunion of Amy Tennant, Millie Glenn and Mary Woodford at Rainbow Town, Alice Springs, 1951. These three girls were evacuated to Mulgoa at the same time as me.

Figure 13: My mother holding Sam, and Sandra on lawn at Administrator's Residence, Alice Springs, 1952.

Figure 14: Christmas 1952 at St John's Alice Springs: from back to front Jacky Campbell, Billy Briscoe (with hat), Phillip Bray in centre with Les Nayda and Harold Thomas (creator of Aboriginal flag).

Figure 15: St Francis House boys camping at Goolwa, 1953: from left to right Des Price, John Spencer, Denis Wickham (obscured), Jacky Campbell and Les Nayda (front).

Figure 16: St Francis House boys, 1953.

Figure 17: My brothers Billy and Dennis, at St Francis House in 1957.

Figure 18: Port Lincoln Soccer Representative side 1957. Self back row, second from left.

Figure 19: Croatia team 1960. Charlie Perkins back 3rd left, self 4th left.

Figure 20: Charles Perkins with President of Croatia North Adelaide club, John Moriarty and self, 1960.

Figure 21: Our wedding, Apsley Church, United Kingdom, 1962.

Figure 22: Herb and Ruth Simms at their Sydney home, 1965. Herb was the Director of the Foundation for Aboriginal Affairs in the mid 1960s.

Figure 23: Norma's parents, Beatrice and Ernest Foster visiting Australia, 1966.

Figure 24: Picnic at Wattamolla, Sydney, 1967: Eileen, Charlie and Hetti Perkins, Vincent Copley, me, John Moriarty and my son Aaron in front.

Figure 25: My mother at Melanka Hostel, Alice Springs, about 1970.

Figure 26: My Mardu family, circa 1970: my mother's two brothers Percy and Intji are on the far left, and Uncle Cydika Warri.

Figure 27: Charlie Perkins and me at apartheid demonstration at Australia v South African Rugby match Sydney Cricket Ground, 1971.

Figure 28: St Francis House reunion, 1967: Father Smith second row, second from left.

Illustrations

Figure 29: Djabangardi. My Australia Party campaign photograph 1972. Authorised by PJ Graham, Mitchell Street, Darwin.

Figure 30: Federal election, 1972: George Bray and family and my campaign manager Len Smith in shorts.

Figure 31: Briscoe and Perkins family on holidays at Malua Bay, New South Wales, 1978: back row, from left to right Adam, Eileen, Aaron, Hettie, Norma, John, front row, Charlie, Rachel (my goddaughter), Lisa and me.

Figure 32: Farnham House, my son Aaron, Gary Foley and Kelly (Farnham House resident), 1983.

Figure 33: Self and Fred Hollows at the time of his Australian of the Year award, 1990.

Figure 34: My sons Aaron and John, mid 1990s.

Figure 35: My son Aaron and his partner Meredeth Taylor, 1993.

Figure 36: My daughter Lisa and self at her acceptance as ACT Barrister, 1996.

Figure 37: My PhD Conferral, Canberra, 1997: from left to right Sam (Jupurulla) brother, self, Michael Johnson, Norma, Roz and John Moriarty, Gabi Hollows, Mike Lynskey and John Balazs.

Figure 38: My grandson Mitchell Taylor-Briscoe and me on a cricket break, Canberra, 2001.

Figure 39: My brother Bill and Gerry Hill, Canberra, 2001.

Figure 40: My cousin Mary Ross (nee Swan) and Aaron, 2000.

Figure 41: My sister Jennifer Summerfield at Umuwa Pitjantjajara Homelands where she is a health worker and traditional artist, 2004.

Figure 42: Launch of my book *Counting, Health and Identity: A history of Aboriginal health and demography in Western Australia and Queensland 1900-1940* at the Sydney Writers Festival, 2004: from left to right Julia Moriarty, Rosa (my goddaughter), Norma, Anna and Ruth Hollows and Kate Balazs.

Figure 43: Australia Day AO Award with my son Aaron on lawns of Government House, Canberra, 2004.

Figure 44: Australia Day AO Award 2004 at Government House, Canberra 2004: from left to right Governor General Michael Jeffrey, Dr Tom Gavranic, Millie Glenn, me, Norma and Mara Gavranic.

Figure 45: My brother Sam with his sons Sam and Leeroy, 2008.

Figure 46: My daughter Lisa, partner Shaun Wilde, and baby Jack at Glen Helen, 2005.

Figure 47: My eldest grandson Mitchell, 2009.

Figure 48: My grandson Jack and me at Malua Bay, New South Wales, 2008.

Figure 49: This is where it all began for me – Pembroke Street. I still recall my mother leaving me here in 1945. Self with friends Elaine and Geoff Ziersch, 2009.

Foreword

Gordon Briscoe is one of the most remarkable and successful Australians of his generation. He has had a profound impact, over more than 40 years, on what has happened in public affairs. But his real impact has been on people's thinking on significant public policy issues, particularly Aboriginal affairs. And yet many people who have been influenced by his ideas and his actions, or by structures he has helped put into place, scarcely know him. Or if they do, fail to recognise how important he has been not only in what has happened but how we understand what has happened and what we think about it.

This is Gordon's story, as told, all too modestly, by himself. It is a remarkable story, even for fellow citizens now more or less familiar with tales of the Australian frontier, the role and place of Aboriginal Australians, including women, in the Central Australian economy, the story of the Bungalow, of the impact of the Second World War on Aboriginal people and policy in the Northern Territory, and of wholesale dislocations of individuals and families. Gordon is one of a group of people who were taken, on understandings that were never really honoured, to South Australia with the St Francis home. Gordon, Charles Perkins and John Moriarty are three of the best known, but several dozen others were to play important local, regional and national roles in Aboriginal affairs. The boys who became men there were among the most significant leaders of a new generation of Aboriginal men and were to have a profound impact on policy and programs from the mid-1960s. That so inadequate a place punched so significantly above its weight invites real questions of what might have happened if those sent there had been given access to real education, as well as more love and nurturing. There are and were other important activists of their like – and from all parts of Australia. One could, however, write a general history of the past 50 years and somehow forget to mention some players. One could not write such a history without frequent reference to the influence of the boys of St Francis.

For some, including Charlie, Gordon and John, sport and travel and marriage played a very significant role in helping them get to points at which they could begin to influence others, then further their educations and ultimately nag the national conscience. Gordon, like Charlie, first became known in NSW. He played a leading role in the establishment of the first Aboriginal legal service, not least in mobilising the goodwill of a number of sympathetic and liberal lawyers, including Professor Hal Wootten. Briscoe was to be the service's first field officer. Not long after, he was the most significant figure in helping to mobilise the resources, including the help of sympathetic white doctors such as Professor Fred Hollows, to establish Australia's first Aboriginal medical service. Later, Briscoe, now a Commonwealth public servant, helped conceive and carry into effect a plan which, with Fred Hollows, became the National Trachoma and Eye Health Program. Over three years, it visited all parts of rural Australia to look at, and do something about, the state of poor Aboriginal eye health. Hollows always made clear how much he had depended on Gordon not only for the development and funding of the program, but for its innovative and critical focus on engaging with and creating something real and lasting for Aboriginal people. Quite apart from the services directly delivered, the program played midwife to scores of new Aboriginal medical services around Australia. As one who worked with the program myself, having been more or less recruited by Big O, I can testify to the centrality of his ideas, his focus and his nagging about and insistence on the fundamentals.

It was just that focus on ideas that took him in his next directions. Briscoe became a student again, a historian and a leading, and by no means uncritical intellectual, of Aboriginal history, policy and programs. His work was in new fields. His ideas were not usually popular ones, sometimes even (or especially) in Aboriginal circles. The irritating but basic questions he was asking about some things – for example, about whether the very legal and medical services in whose establishment he had played such a role were living up to their charters – made him quite unpopular in some quarters, often with old colleagues. That has led to his foundation roles being significantly underplayed in the early histories of Aboriginal affairs over the past 50 years. That is a deficiency which he will not have to redress; it is in part because he has led a charge in Aboriginal involvement in writing their own history that he can be assured that his role will never ultimately be forgotten.

But if Gordon's story can be – should be – seen as a triumph, one should not forget the adversity against which it was achieved, and the sadness of many of the circumstances of his life. He wears the scars. He's had his pleasures, not least in a lovely and successful family and some acknowledgment of how a man can make a difference, but he is also highly conscious of what he has lost, of promises unkept, of linkages which have slipped, and of a liberation yet to be achieved. But it is not only a matter of the light on the hill being far, far ahead, with many certain disappointments on the way, because Gordon has always had a forward optimism and hope in the perfectibility of man that has ever astonished me. It is much more an appreciation of how much of his achievement has been at a cost of the anguish of separation, emotional detachment, big and little betrayals and ever-present pebbles in his shoes. Even in telling his own story, Gordon rejects any notion of presenting it as romance and triumph – though some could see it that way. Even less any sort of excuse-mongering or wallowing in self-pity. It's a narrative, a story, a history. He can tell a story. And the truth. It has been a slog for him, and a sorrow. A hard one, and one that has worn on him hard. I sometimes wish that he understood better that even if the love and the respect and the admiration of his family, his friends and his followers cannot entirely paint over the lines on his brows, they can stand out too.

Jack Waterford is editor at large of the Canberra Times and has been a friend and colleague of Big O for 40 years.

Preface

In part, my Aboriginal identity has shaped my life; in part too, my life has been shaped by the race laws straddling the twentieth century under which my family lived. In this memoir I bring my Aboriginal origins as a Marduntjara person to life revealing both events I have been involved in together with some of the people who shared the journey with me. The story begins in the late nineteenth century and leads to: my grandmother Kanaki's move from traditional life to Lilla Creek for the birth of my mother; my mother's subsequent removal from Larapinta to Stuart in 1927; my birth in 1938, and onwards through my institutionalised childhood; the raising of my political consciousness and experiences, and finally, a life in academia.

Why did I write this memoir? The driving idea behind this memoir was the need to document the history of a group of Aborigines who were institutionalised from birth but saw liberty, equality and fraternity as more important than notoriety. Most of my contemporaries grew up in the boys' home, neither returning to their parents nor their homelands. Moreover, some died at their own or other people's hands and were pushed into an unattainable conformity that forced us all to have a distorted perspective of Australian nationalism. But to begin at the beginning, this memoir is about aspects of my life, what I learnt and memorised and what I was told about the lives of my Aboriginal and non-Aboriginal relatives.

Unlike many people of Aboriginal descent, I believe that if we do not write factually about ourselves we face the tragedy of letting others monopolise us as a people. This monopoly was an ideological goal of the Commonwealth and states' 'assimilation policy', and as such they took away Aboriginal peoples' heritage, their lands, along with their long term family relationships and inheritances. It first dawned on me to articulate my background in the 1980s, while working as the history officer at the Australian Institute for Aboriginal Studies in Canberra. During this time I worked in the field of reconstructing people's past and studying the discipline of history at the Australian National University.

The traditional way of retaining the Aboriginal past and culture was by telling stories, using dance and creative thinking like recounting dreams and drawing patterns on the ground. Today, these traditional techniques have to be meshed with new ways of thinking. This process, however, is unacceptable to most Australian scholars because it lacks a recorded capacity to critique one's self, to have an acceptable common language, a way of storing material to enhance, and to evaluate the narrative. However, sometime later, following completion of my own research and writings for higher degrees, the conviction was still with me. I still believed that the Aboriginal past had to be written and not created out of the remnants of an alienated or secret society built on stories alone. Secret societies are anathema to history for obvious reasons and this in some way explains why anthropologists do not understand history. Modern history is derived out of principles emerging from the political and epistemological ideas of the French Revolution, most notably the now familiar notions of liberty, equality and fraternity.

The idea to write this memoir was cemented in my mind after talking to a number of American scholars following a study tour of the Northern Territory. They were adamant that I was possibly the best person to reconstruct this narrative. It would be about the children I grew up with and their experiences, through my eyes, and would probably not be written unless I did so. Although there are many boys that have survived and gone on to lead fruitful lives, many have perished. By doing this work I have made a start but have left much to be done by other younger Aboriginal scholars and I hope they will accept the challenge.

It will come as a revelation to some readers that nearly 100 years after Captain Cook landed and claimed New South Wales as a British possession my ancestors had had no contact with Europeans. This fact gave me confidence to tell the story about how slow and tortuous the expansion into the centre of Australia really was. It is not surprising, then, that many of my people were born of people who could remember seeing the first whites when they entered Marduntjara and Arrernte lands. Aboriginal relatives of my generation can recall their fathers, mothers, brothers and sisters telling them stories about Europeans such as John McDougall Stuart passing through Larapinta, or what was later renamed the Finke River, in the 1860s. And later the coming of the telegraph line followed by sheep and cattle, pastoralists, and the rail extension in the 1890s from Oodnadatta reaching Stuart, later renamed Alice Springs, in 1929. My mother Eileen was about nine years of age during this later period of colonial expansion.

This memoir also hopes to capture the essence of what was happening in the broader sense in Aboriginal affairs. I use significant landmark issues in Aboriginal social and political history as a way of weaving these events into the fabric of my own personal narrative. By definition, although this memoir focuses on my actions, experiences and memories, I have been inspired by other peoples' deeds and biographies. I am indebted to two other Aborigines in particular, with whom I have had life-long social and political relationships and who have written autobiographies.[1] There have been a number of ghosted biographies or novels written about special events involving Aborigines, but possibly only one is based on primary documentation. It is therefore one of my

---

1   Perkins C 1975. See also Read 1990; Moriarty 2000.

challenges to draw on primary, secondary and oral sources. Additionally, it is as important to record the primary oral sources and memories passed on to me by my relatives when they were alive.

This book reflects on my, and my family's background, involving the making of aspects of Aboriginal political and social history during the period from the late nineteenth through to the twentieth century and beyond into the new millennium; a past beginning in the Northern Territory, moving to other states, although never gaining liberty from 'race laws'. As the reader might appreciate, my reflections on such laws and the way they were administered, are both personal and subjective. For all my objectivity as a historian, I am angered to reflect on the way such legislation impacted on the lives of people like me who were once classified 'half-castes', and worse. (I won't use the inverted commas around 'half-castes' again.) Somehow – as this book elaborates – I survived the experiences of growing up half-caste but many of my relatives, inmates and friends did not; and that for me is the well-spring of an enduring bitterness.

The story opens with a short narrative on my Aboriginal and white ancestors. Then, because I believe the Christian religion became a tool of racial folly, I examine how this 'bad faith' affected my and my family's lives. It continues with my birth in 1938 at the 'Old Telegraph Station' but also discusses other half-caste institutions in and around Alice Springs. There were three different sites for what people referred to as 'the Bungalow' and 'my' Bungalow was the former Alice Springs Telegraph Station in the 1930s. The 'renovations' had added dormitories, converting it into a Native Institution. Over time, these dormitories housed thousands of children from 1914 until Paul Hasluck and Menzies introduced their 'New Assimilation' program during the period 1951-1952.

I use oral and documentary source material to build the historical narrative of events in the early chapters. As a historian I am fortunate because a lot of documentary evidence about Aborigines is available. Before 1972 most people identifying as Aborigines were wards of the state or federal governments and subject to government race laws, and, as such, records were kept of their movements. This record keeping, while not perfect, was even more diligently kept on Aborigines who came under Commonwealth control; those Aborigines born or living in institutions or reserves, in the Northern Territory, entered the records. In 1911 the South Australian government handed over all its administrative records to the Federal government when it became responsible for the Northern Territory. The National Archives either in Canberra or their state branches hold a substantial amount of the documentary sources from that era to the present. All of these data are available to researchers. I also tap into scholarly material held by national and state libraries and archives on Mardu traditional and material culture.

The availability of secondary sources means that I have drawn on a stock of sources written by scholars as well as novelists and political writers. Since the 1960s a large number of important works and special collections, indexes and encyclopaedias have been discovered or published. The Australian National University, in particular, hosted a series called 'Aborigines in Australian Society' through the Social Science Research Council of Australia. In 1964, Professor CD Rowley was appointed Director of the project. Rowley's objective was to:

> Elucidate the problems arising from contact between Aborigines and non-Aborigines and formulating policy implications from these; drawing together existing knowledge in various parts of Australia and underlying such further original research as can be carried out over a period of three years.[2]

Rowley used demographic methods to identify the components of the Aboriginal population and, in doing so, identified modern Aborigines. He linked historical records with journals of everyday life with anthropological studies. Rowley mostly drew on secondary writings by anthropologists and archaeologists when he wrote his trilogy because he was unaware of the primary source documents. Covering a new perspective, Rowley narrated 200 years from the first British colony at Botany Bay and Sydney Cove to the failed operations of both the 'protection' and 'assimilation' policies of the late-1960s. The funding of Rowley's project came from the Myer Foundation and was completed in the early 1970s with a three-volume study. The project produced many more publications from which I draw too.

The final point that I want to raise is the question of the use of human memory as a historiographical tool. I do not think many would argue with the view that the human memory is notoriously bad, and in many instances deteriorates with age, but it can be both a bane and a boon! Some historians, and many Aborigines, have had to draw on memory to reconstruct their accounts of the past, making them vulnerable to attacks by people like Windschuttle, and others.[3] Oral sources or what some call 'oral history' is in my view, really a term depicting what we might call the writing of a history of everyday people. Normally, these everyday people neither write biographies nor write about past events and so their past is collected by oral source material. As colonial invaders took lands and material objects they ignored the Aboriginal past. More than this, British historiography confined the past to whatever Britons wrote or thought about their pasts. This trait has been adopted by Australians, whose political history

---

2   Rowley 1970.
3   Windschuttle 1994.

reflects their narcissism. For these reasons it is understandable that Aborigines want to reconstruct their own past from which they can learn in a qualitatively different way.

Because of these notions, the uses of historiography in the reconstruction of Aboriginal history, has had to be borrowed from progenitors sometimes unable or unwilling to pass on their knowledge. So it has had to be reinvented by adopting general ideas and expressions of concrete feelings. Memory is something at hand, easily used to recount and reconstruct anyone's past. In particular Aborigines have come to use the past as a way of focusing on a fascinating new way of using it through their adaptations of the European cultural past: that is history.

The traditional Aboriginal past is still reliant on memory conjured up by dance, bark and ground painting together with simple and deeply complex story telling of peoples' *Tjukurrpa* (in the Pitjantjatjara language, this is either an unexplainable event or an object like a body wart or dreaming) as well as through common and sacred ceremonies. In doing so Aborigines reconstruct their complex past that shifts and changes in the process of interpreting events they know happened: but that comes from what they remember and from what older custodians have passed on to them; recorded on sacred objects and once held in sacred places.

In this way some historians have seen memory as unreliable in recalling ideas and facts, thereby, calling the Aboriginal past into question or branding Aboriginal ideas as doubtful information. Keith Windschuttle, for example, criticises Aboriginal accounts of massacres and the ill-effects of Liberal and National Party 'assimilation policies' as fabrications of the past. Windschuttle refutes Aboriginal people whose relatives where killed by police or by illegal means as having an unacceptable perspective on what happened.[4] Therefore, because many Europeans see the written word as fact they have dismissed the idea that many documents are indeed subject to interpretation. Colonial administrations and even Australian government agencies have, in some instances, either omitted or tended to skew records in favour of their own view of the past. Consequently, Aboriginal voices have been either dismissed or ignored, or included as abstractions and shadowy figures.

Some believe the past is another country, and as a historian I accept this proposition as a metaphor, but there are many Aborigines upon whom the past has left terrible scars. I hope to be able to reveal some of these events but, at the same time, soothe some, especially those too young to have been directly

---

4 Windschuttle 2000: 8-16.

involved, but who have felt the pain of the stories. Historians are builders of narratives in that their work is always a work in progress and I hope this narrative is accepted in this way.

I owe many thanks to a great many people for the help, guidance and inspirational advice that have been given so generously in bringing this memoir to completion. By its very nature in a work such as this there are many more in the text than can ever adequately be thanked. My first debt is to my colleagues in the Department of History program at the Research School of Social Science, Professors Barry Higman, Barry Smith and Anne McGrath who helped me find the genre and to shape the narrative of this work; the greatest part evolving out of morning and afternoon teas in the Coombs refectory. I would also like to thank the Australian Institute of Aboriginal and Torres Strait Islander Studies who gave me a Fellowship that included an office and access to primary and secondary sources, found nowhere else. I am also indebted to the Australian Archives Authority (Australian Capital Territory) staff that helped me find my way around their Aboriginal records collection and other government primary sources.

On an individual basis I owe a sincere debt of gratitude to my friend and colleague Dr Ian Howie-Willis. I am grateful to him for inspiring me to write in an informal narrative genre for this memoir. I also thank him for editing later drafts to his usual professional and polished standard. Similarly, I have a debt of gratitude to Drs John Clanchy and Brigid Ballard of the Australian National University for reading and commenting on the final draft. Their words of wisdom have been invaluable because, like other writers, I looked for critical evaluation and an analytical perspective that they gave willingly. I would be remiss if I did not acknowledge my great friend and colleague Dr Leonard Smith. I thank him for his intellectual inspiration over the last 40 years and for introducing me to the discipline of historical demography; together with linking the narrative to historical theory in this work. I shouldn't forget to thank Father Smith's son John Smith for his writings and showing an interest in my work. I would also like to thank Professor Peter Read and the board of the Aboriginal History Journal for their encouragement.

And finally, as always, my family, and in particular my greatest debt goes to my wife Norma whose unbounding love, dedication and hard work has bought this memoir to fruition. I am indebted to my children Aaron, Lisa and John and their partners, Meredeth and Shaun for their unquestioning loyalty. Much of the inspiration behind this memoir has been so that my grandsons Mitchell and Jack know something of their heritage. To my family for their undying support I have a debt that even after presenting this book to them I think I will never be able to repay.

Chapter 1
My family background, 1890 to 1941

My first encounter with my grandmother Kanaki was during the early 1950s. She would travel into Alice Springs every fortnight in the white station manager's truck from Maryvale cattle station along with other family members to collect her pension money. Maryvale is a place Mardu people call Titjikala (meaning land of the eagle). The station truck would collect stores and generally stay one or two days in Alice Springs for weekend recreation of one kind or another. The bush camp was in an area west of the Rainbow-town cottages and south of Connellan's airstrip, close to the MacDonnell Ranges. Every fortnight Kanaki would bring in bags of *mingulpa*, or native tobacco, from out-bush, for my mother. What sticks in my mind is that, during these visits, she would tell me stories about her past.

Kanaki told me that her father, a Marduntjara man was born at Kulkara (called Kulgera by Europeans) at a time when only a few Europeans had passed through the region. Kanaki was born some distance west of Kulkara at a water hole called, Puntu tjapa (or ground lizard) a native well north of Uluru; an important location on the southern part of the Gibson Desert. As a young girl in the early 1890s, my grandmother moved around the western deserts, then east to her father's birthplace at Kulkara. This was about the time the Horn Expedition went through the region and she remembered Spencer's trek through the Mardu lands to Uluru and Kata Tjuta. At the age of about four or five, she remembered the story of a small group of white men with a policeman called Cowle from Illamurta, on McMinn's Creek, travelling through Mardu and Arrernte lands from Illamurta to Uluru, returning then to Glen Helen Gorge.[1] They made the trek, there and back, on horseback and went up through King's Canyon, crossing Lake Amadeus, the southern part of the Gibson Desert, the Petermann Ranges and then returning to Hermannsburg through to Glen Helen Station.[2]

Kanaki grew up migrating around Mardu lands. In doing so, Kanaki participated in traditional ceremonies, foraged in favoured food collection grounds as well as engaging in meeting obligations made to others. Such commitments meant attending funerals of relatives as well as keeping meeting arrangements made with both close and distant relatives. She attended initiation ceremonies that included fulfilling obligations made many years before and acted as cultural custodian to younger brothers and sisters. In later years the small bush family

---
1 Spencer 1896.
2 Mulvaney 2000: 20-21.

travelled east to Lilla Creek (*Lil* means in Mardu, place where the water disappears and the suffix *-la* indicates the adverb), for ceremonial reasons and Kanaki stayed with relatives while her traditional husband (Wati Kunmanara, meaning dead man) went to ceremony at Ooraminna. At the time camels were the main form of trade-transportation and Lilla Creek, a tributary to the Finke River, became one of the most reliable watering depots. While at Lilla Creek Kanaki conceived my mother; her biological father was a white man named William (Billy) Briscoe.

It was around October of 1918 that my mother was born. Kanaki named her Eileen. They were inseparable as they travelled as far south to Aprawatatja and Puntu Tjapa, the birthplace of Kanaki. They travelled together with other family around the edges of the Western, Gibson and Great Victoria deserts for ceremonial reasons. This region stretched from the edge of the Simpson Desert to Lilla Creek, north to Illamurta, and as far south as Oodnadatta west to Aprawatatja, deep into Yunguntjatjara and Pitjantjatjara country. This is a huge area, and relates more to traditional relationships rather than land ownership in the European sense.

Billy Briscoe was a rouseabout and acted as a station manager on short term arrangements, he also worked for Afghan cameleers as a camel transport shepherd. Later in the 1920s, Briscoe moved north to manage Randal Stafford's Coniston lease. Fredrick Brooks who was later speared by 'Bullfrog' Japanunga as 'payback' also worked for Stafford.[3] All these white men knew each other from their pastoral, dogging and transport activities around the western side of Lake Eyre.[4] Stafford and Brooks also knew Briscoe from his days camel shepherding from Oodnadatta to Stuart (now Alice Springs). The route from Oodnadatta to Lilla Creek is mainly dry mesa country with sand hills, saltpans, gibber, low growing desert flora and sparsely littered desert oak trees (in Mardu language *kulka* or *karlka*).

Mardu lands, likewise, are distinguished by weathered mesa, low lying hills of mulga scrub, *kulka* and sandy desert on the western side of the Finke River. This is land belonging to Marduntjara peoples. The country begins in an area called Larapinta, and goes south to Apatula and north to Illamurta, then across the southern part of the Gibson Desert westwards of the Petermann Ranges. It then goes west, taking in lands shared by Yunguntjatjara, and Pitjantjatjara peoples, including the Pintubi, Antekerintja and Arrernte peoples. Bush people were attracted to Lilla Creek by railway-building activities and the convenience of

---

3   Wilson and O'Brien 2003: 59-72.
4   Hill 2003: 153.

the many waterholes along the camel transport route. Lilla Creek was also on a ceremonial migratory route from Uluru to Ooraminna, and its permanent water made it a guaranteed camping site.

The itinerant European, Afghan and Chinese men – who were cameleers, rail workers, pastoral labourers, telegraph station workers and casual tourists – came with alcohol and often left leaving the women pregnant and their children destitute. Some Mardu women were very young and left their children in the camps. Others were either already burdened with too many children or had left to meet ceremonial obligations in distant communities. In many instances Aboriginal women were raped thus exacerbating the population explosion of unwanted children of mixed descent, most of whom were abandoned by their white fathers. The workers like the cameleers would leave the camps and return in 12 months only to see their mixed blood offspring as babies in the camps. Many Mardu people were killed by pastoralists and brutal marauding police. Some Aborigines were killed at will and others for spearing for food cattle and sheep that crossed their traditional hunting lands. In particular, the struggle was over water resources on the Aboriginal side and killing and disturbing stock on the European pastoralist's side.[5] Equally Mardu peoples had to cope with European population influxes that meant conceding to the ravages of stock that took over waterholes dispersing native game. Moreover, Mardu people were forced into conceding their land through the influx of stock, as well as their culture because antiquarian collectors removed sacred objects from ceremonial grounds, mostly never to be returned. For me, the history of Aboriginal politics begins in central Australia, and, as many Aborigines will discover as they research their historic past, it appears that concessions were made in only one direction: a direction favouring colonists.

The cultural implications in this upheaval also meant that Mardu peoples were forced to leave their traditional lands that had become occupied by strange animals such as cattle and sheep; their waterholes were poisoned; bush women were being lured to telegraph stations; and bush men were dislodged from their ceremonial obligations and practices. The culture, seemingly unchanged for millennia, crumbled in mostly material ways because of the imposition of a new mode of production. Cultural practices that had continued for 1000 or more years were lost. Animal game, so much a staple diet of hunter-gatherers, was soon changed as sheep and cattle meat entered the Mardu diet. What began as a strange phenomenon ended up as everlasting death or perdition.

From our grandmothers, who lived through this brutal past, and from our mothers, who were born of it, we learned that most of the white men, who ventured into the Tywerentye, Western MacDonnell Ranges, and the river

---

5   Mulvaney 2000: 10-30.

regions of Leratupa and Umbarntuwa, came alone, without wives. They came to build and operate the telegraph stations, the pastoral leases, the small stores and the railway stations. Slowly, between the 1890s and 1914, a few white women began migrating from South Australia and other colonies, and many learnt that their white husbands had black children whom they had abandoned to Aboriginal camps. As the half-caste population grew, the small number of white women residing in the service towns dotted along the arterial route from Oodnadatta to what is now Darwin began to panic. They panicked not only because they saw the presence of half-caste children in the same classrooms as disadvantaging their white children, but also because their white husbands had sired these same children.

The increasing presence of half-caste children aroused deep-seated fears and anxieties in the settler women. Their men were equally intent on denying the existence of these offspring. Each morning when these men washed their faces and looked out across the creeks in service towns, they would see their abandoned children in the Aboriginal fringe camps running around before their very eyes, barely existing. Meanwhile, the children themselves were forced to rely on these same belligerent, brutal and racist males, their fathers, for food, occasionally supplemented by bush food, although for the most part government rations were their only form of economic support.

Horseshoe Bend was a pastoral lease owned by consecutive white owners: the first owners were a British company, followed by a man named Breaden who purchased the lease from British pastoralists following the severe droughts of the 1890s. The next was Gus Elliott who came up from the Flinders Ranges to work in the burgeoning pastoral industry.[6] Both these latter white men had numerous Aboriginal female sexual partners who produced many children of mixed descent. In 1926, at the age of about seven, Eileen and Kanaki left Lilla Creek for Horseshoe Bend, where Eileen went to her first school lessons conducted by Gus Elliot's European wife Ruby.

Gus Elliot fathered at least four children of mixed descent from Mardu and Arrernte women, like Lil. One of the children was Michael Gus Elliott who was raised at Hermannsburg, the other three Bert, Sonny and Jim had their names changed from Elliott to Swan when Elliott married the European woman, Ruby, whom he brought to the station.[7] Lil was a Marduntjara woman and sister to my grandmother Kanaki. My mother Eileen became a sister to Lil and her offspring who in turn became a sister to my mother's two traditional brothers, Intji and

---

6   Strehlow 1969.
7   Hill 2003: 653-654.

Percy Summerfield, who were born in the early 1930s.[8] Traditional relationships were complex between the Swan and Briscoe families and were made more so as Europeans moved into the region.

Kanaki and Eileen both stayed at Horseshoe Bend before moving, in 1927, to New Crown Station. During that year an Aboriginal census was taken across what might now be called the settled pastoral areas of the Northern Territory.[9] Eileen was identified as a young person to be removed by Mounted Constable Sergeant Stott of the Northern Territory Police, and was about nine when taken. There were about ten other girls, of roughly the same age in this group, who were moved with my mother via Illamurta to the native ration depot at Alice Springs.

It is difficult to determine the exact ages of these girls because it took nearly 20 years to register all Aboriginal half-caste births, a long time after the Commonwealth's takeover in 1910. Aboriginal and half-caste births were not routinely registered until the Territory began funding Native Institutions in the late 1920s and 1930s. Even then registration was never fully completed in the Territory, until well after the Second World War.

I discuss briefly the journey from Crown Point cattle property to Alice Springs following my mother's removal by Sergeant Stott. The protector's party travelled from Larapinta to Urapitchira, on to Hermannsburg to deliver the mail, then to Alice Springs, a distance of over 300 kilometres by camel. The country was as hazardous then as it is now with its mountainous terrain; trekking was arduous along the dry sandy river beds, and through rocky gullies and canyons. My mother's journey by camel took about six days because during the trip up from Larapinta, the older Breaden girls from Itikawara, escaped and the progress of the camel caravan was halted for about 48 hours. What may have appeared then as a relatively uninteresting family group travelling to Alice Springs was in reality a sinister exercise of removing children from their blood relatives. For example, my mother's traditional grandfather, Kanaki's brother Paddy Stuart (father of Rupert Max Stuart) and his wife Nada were part of the contingent. Paddy was employed by Sergeant Stott as a 'police tracker' tracking cattle spearers. Like most employed Aboriginal people Paddy also tended the police stock of camels and horses, as well as goats, donkeys, pigs and cows. Paddy's wife Nada went with him to cook for the whole group. It was often the case that girls escaped the camel trains for the bush and trackers were necessary to help police hunt down the 'fleeing youths'.

---

8 'Half-Castes in Northern Territory re Training and Employment of', CRS A1, 1926/5350, National Archives of Australia (NAA), Canberra. See Fraser 1993 as guide to National Archives of Australia.
9 'Half-Caste Home, Alice Springs, NT', CRS A659, 1939/1/996, NAA, Canberra.

In Alice Springs my mother became an inmate under the control of Sergeant Stott and Ida Standley. Standley's role was that of matron, appointed by both police and other whites. Her teaching appointment was through the South Australian Education Department. The Aboriginal girls were taken to the police ration depot, also called 'The Bungalow' and the surname Briscoe was added soon after arriving. Because my mother's first language was Marduntjara she was unable to say who her father was. However, other older girls informed the Matron that her father's name was Billy Briscoe. So after 1928 Eileen became Eileen Briscoe in all the institutional records. Ida Standley adopted the custom that if children were unable to either remember or answer questions put by her, the children were simply named after the place from which they were removed if no other information was available. Most children were given European names; for example, those who came from Tennant Creek were given the name Tennant. Those who came from either the Plenty or the Palmer River were registered as Plenty or Palmer.

At first my mother was confined in a collection of tin sheds located at the rear of the Stuart Arms Hotel in Todd Street. After about two years older males and females, including my mother, were moved 40 kilometres west to Jay Creek, to a second 'Bungalow'. The sleeping quarters were not rooms but a large concrete slab covered with a second hand galvanised iron roof. Throughout the period my mother was there this structure was without walls: rain, hail or shine.

The Native Institutions were originally created because of what was perceived as the growing 'half-caste problem'. The population explosion was mainly the result of enforced and sometimes casual sexual relationships between European, Asian and Afghan men and Aboriginal women of all ages. Many of these transport camps created around freshwater were without governance and the children and women suffered throughout their lives as a result of living in places where there was no 'rule of law'. Specific events such as the coming of pastoralists into Central Australia and the railway from Oodnadatta during the period 1880-1929, greatly exacerbated the problem. Some Afghan cameleers did care for their children, by giving money to their mothers or older siblings. To meet their responsibilities some Afghan fathers took their partners and children to the harem-like camps at Marree. The exploding half-caste population, in turn, put pressure on camel depots like Lilla Creek, telegraph stations like Charlotte Waters and rail depots such as Rumbalara, as well as the fringe camps on route to Alice Springs.

Whatever the morally legal and illegal practices of those responsible, Ida Standley moved the children from Mbartuwarintja, Alice Springs to Iwaputarka (Jay Creek), in December of 1929. Illnesses caused by exposure and sedentary living in filth and squalor followed the children to Jay Creek. This shameful situation was highlighted by the Reverend W Morley of the Association for the Protection of Native Races of Australia and Polynesia who wrote to the Minister for Home Affairs Arthur Blakeley about the conditions that the half-caste children lived under. Morley wrote in November 1929 of

> The ... bad conditions ... at the temporary hostel for Half-caste children at [Jay Creek]'. Ida Standley had left for Sydney three months earlier and as: [d]isgraceful as are the conditions under which Mr and Mrs Thorne have had to exist [nothing compares] with the conditions under which the fifty or so Half-caste children have to exist.[10]

Morley's report was written in such a way that he tried to articulate the pain and suffering of the children. It must be remembered, however, that Morley's report captured only the moral and political aspects of what he observed. For a man of religion like Morley, his interests were admirable but he and the Thornes were there to do the bidding of the Protestant Church. Nevertheless, Morley was interested in conveying the Thornes' most important role, which was to keep the children within the boundaries of the institution. Morley believed the Thornes were doing Christian acts, but in keeping with the Department of Native Affairs' edicts. It behoves the historian, however, to put himself in the skins of those children as well as to glean Morley's unspoken feelings.

How did these children cope with the deplorable situation in which they found themselves? There were 48 boys and girls ranging in age from one to 16 years, sleeping in the one room, 24 by 50 feet. To verbalise the answer to this question was impossible for my mother beyond saying: 'that it was a terrible place'. Similarly, many of the older children who had to cope with these conditions were unable to articulate their pain and suffering in later life. The children were prevented from speaking their own languages and were forced to learn English. This meant that most of the younger girls could only communicate by speaking 'pidgin' while the older ones spoke in broken English.

The children had no power at all, apart from Morley's and the press's interest, to resist what was happening to them. Morley pointed to the appalling conditions by reporting that the children slept on burnt lime floors, in buildings of rough wooden frames with dilapidated sheets of corrugated iron for the roof, and suffered exposure at night. Children were issued with only two blankets each, meaning they slept on one while using the other as cover. The food was extremely poor so the children killed wild game and stored it close to the camp, out of sight of staff. Similarly, while hunting for wood they were able to collect wild honey and yams to supplement their meagre diets. After dark two hurricane lamps were the only lighting provided and as such the girls' security was threatened by desperate men. During the day school lessons were equally chaotic with no

---

10 'Half-Caste Home, Alice Springs, NT', CRS A659, 1939/1/996, NAA, Canberra.

text books or school supplies. This farrago of shifting the children so far out of town in such poor circumstances was premised on the need to protect half-caste girls from marauding rail and pastoral workers.[11]

The children's plight was exacerbated by the loss of their association with relatives; this alienation in turn affected the children's capacity even more to manage their everyday lives. The children's isolation from their relatives was made worse because relatives were forbidden by law to determine what could or would happen to their children – the basic right that their European overlords enjoyed. Some reservations had been exercised by Dr Cecil Cook[12] over what Davies and Morley had written to Minister Blakeley. Nevertheless he acted positively and instead of being over critical of these two missionaries he tended to use them as a way of finding out the children's health conditions while at the same time gaining everyone's confidence. Minister Blakeley ordered Cook to carry out a medical survey in 1928 at the Bungalow hovel operated by Ida Standley. After the children had been at the Jay for a few years, Davies and Morley complained once more, which prompted Cook to carry out an additional medical survey around these new claims of mistreatment. In this new report Cook recorded that my mother Eileen Briscoe was listed as being treated for an unnamed complaint. I suspect that most of the children suffered from either mild or more serious sexually transmitted infections. Moreover, the survey noted a total of 48 children, 26 girls and 22 boys.

Cook reported on the children's health after reading Davies's article and Morley's letter of complaint, and produced a still more damning health report than either of them.[13] Cook described to the Minister in a more technical way what Davies and Morley had written, yet at the same time, covered up the missionaries' criticisms by claiming that they had made 'careless statements'.[14] Cook was mindful of the poor conditions under which the children lived and supported the government's intention to renovate the old telegraph station as a half-caste institution. In 1933, Eileen along with the other inmates was moved to the renovated 'Old Telegraph Station', the third of the Bungalows. This Bungalow in Alice Springs acted as a holding place for babies and new arrivals, while the Jay Creek institution was mainly for older boys, pregnant women and pubescent girls.

In spite of the moral outrage by the Church and institutions like the press, the white administration held the upper hand everywhere along the arterial route from Port Augusta to Darwin. It erected a system of control to benefit and

---

11   'Half-Caste Home, Alice Springs, NT', CRS A659, 1939/1/996, NAA, Canberra.
12   Cook 1925.
13   Article 'Scandal of North', *The Adelaide Mail*, see also, Letter from Rev Morley to A Blakeley MP, 23 November 1929, CRS A659, 1939/1/996, NAA, Canberra.
14   'Half Caste Home, Alice Springs. NT', CRS A659, 1939/1/996, folios 174-182, NAA, Canberra.

reward itself socially, politically and financially. The white population was only a fraction of the combined Aboriginal and part-Aboriginal populations, yet they dominated daily lives and built racial barriers. What this meant was that the children's culture was changed to that of a new European set of beliefs, practices and behaviour by institutional control and education. The 'caste system' was more damaging because the children were segregated from their relatives and forced only to be with their teachers. This caste system left behind by the British was easily adapted and intensified by European civil society established in 'the centre'. This brutal and inhuman class structure had worked in all the colonies since first contact. Europeans held the positions of control, they managed the food, they held the leased lands and they also controlled the water, and regulated the transport system through Afghans and Asians. Finally, these colonists worked closely with the police and co-operated with them to remove as many of the half-caste children as possible thus exonerating themselves from crimes against the laws of the land and the inhumanity they had heaped upon Aboriginal women and children, for the term of their lives. Many Aboriginal women tried desperately to hide or rub charcoal on their babies to make them darker but even this failed to save many from removal.

Thus the design of this system excommunicated half-castes, quarter-castes, quadroons and lastly, 'near-whites'. But what was the origin of this monstrous conspiracy? At Federation in 1901 the Commonwealth government was able to legally by-pass the federal constitutional constraints regarding Aborigines; putting all power over them in the hands of the Northern Territory administration.[15] Special laws were created to allow the Northern Territory to be directly governed by the Governor General. This method of governance meant that delegated responsibilities allowed the Northern Territory administrator to create 'ordinances for wards'. All people governed under these Ordinances (whether black, near-white or white) could be regarded as wards, if declared as such. Legislators were then able to omit the word 'Aborigines' enabling the Commonwealth to legally manage the daily lives of 'wards'.

The application of the 'removal policy' centred on the three Bungalows, as everyone called them. The bungalow system, essentially holding-institutions, allowed white pastoralists and town people across the Northern Territory to either illegally remove or detain Aborigines as they thought fit. By 1918, the Ordinance was renewed, redefining Aborigines and giving,

> the Chief Protector [powers] to undertake the care, custody or control of any Aboriginal or half-caste, if in his opinion, it [was] necessary or desirable in the interests of the Aboriginal or half-caste for him to do so.[16]

---

15 McCorquodale 1987: 9.
16 McCorquodale 1987: 27.

In reality the term 'in the interest of the Aboriginal or half-caste' meant removing children whom the state preferred to refer to as 'unwanted'. What made it easier for white people in the Northern Territory to carry this policy to its ultimate conclusion was that it was administratively divided into two regions, north and south. After 1918 administrators in collaboration with leaseholders began incarcerating half-castes at greater distances from towns. White people have always argued they acted out of moral imperative. To me it was blatant barbarianism.

By April of 1932, as I explained earlier, the Commonwealth Treasury approved the renovations of the Old Telegraph Station for use as a half-caste institution.[17] The changes were soon completed and the children were moved once more to the renovated 'Native Institution'. More changes followed by June of the same year as the Thornes were replaced by other managers. The storm of criticism continued. The strategy of changing the children's culture, ethics, thinking and daily behaviour did not totally pass without notice and comment. Aborigines across Australia suffered from these kinds of colonial policies and as control fell into the hands of Australian rather than British administrators, the practice continued with greater insensitivities. Church bodies took over without legal sanction and without transparent government control. The total absence of any form of reporting system as well as the complete lack of political action in civil society, revealed the nation-wide indifference. In the 1920s and 1930s Ernestine Hill, a white journalist and adventurer, told readers across Australia that libertarianism had become an 'art form' in the hands of 'white male trash' imperialising the Northern Territory under Commonwealth control.[18]

Some of these white people were related by blood to me but I reluctantly discuss my European biological forbears because they, for the most part, rejected and despised Aborigines. I never knew until much later in my life that my father was a white man named Ron Price. Price was the son of a white telegraph station manager and a female pastoralist. The Northern Territory press reported his death in early November 1938, a few days before I was born. As a young person I did sometimes see Alf Price, Ron's brother, who lived with an Aboriginal woman named Annie. Much later Annie's son Desmond and I were at St Francis House together. Yet at the time I never really appreciated, or knew, just how close a relative Desmond was to me. It was to be many years later that I learnt that he was my first blood cousin! However, I have been able to learn something of the pasts of the Price family. Billy Briscoe and Ron Price's mother Isabella were both involved in the events surrounding the Coniston massacre. I feel obliged to discuss the event and the parts they played in this racial conflict after setting the scene of what was happening on the labour front.

---

17   Letter, HA Parkhill, Minister for Home Affairs, Canberra, CRS A659, 1939/1/996, NAA, Canberra.
18   Hill 1933.

At this time my mother was at the half-caste institution under Ida Standley's care. By now the workings of the *Aboriginal Ordinance1918* (Cth) was in full flight as pastoral capitalism expanded. The most noticeable change was that there was a shift of control from the police and 'civil society', to that of the Northern Territory administration and the Commonwealth. The 'Resident Administrator' coordinated policy and political activity although Chief Protector Cook had direct every-day control. Interest from Canberra came in the form of more visits from federal ministers mainly due to ultimate Commonwealth financial control.[19] Capitalism by this time was developing at full pace even though profits were low and labour force skills were in short supply: colonial subsidies were used to maintain European white society by providing a cheap untrained black labour workforce. The idea of training half-caste labour was becoming more prevalent.

To remind the reader, land was still totally controlled by the Commonwealth from 1911 until after the Second World War and during this time small pastoralists were prevented from expanding their leaseholds. However, pastoralists at the same time had numbers of Aborigines living on their leases for which they were supposed to provide rations collected from the Police Protector. The pastoralists believed they owned the land, not just leased it, and were angered at Aborigines hunting and moving through the properties. Because of their deep-seated racism white lease-holders saw Aborigines in an ambivalent way, on the one hand, they saw them as 'the devil incarnate' while on the other hand, they saw them as useful free labour; particularly the young women. European attitudes at the time were that if half-castes could be trained by the Commonwealth, then limited payment in kind was acceptable to European employers. Aborigines suffered because they were without leadership or political support; sometimes only having a sympathetic Church and a cynical press.

The watershed came about largely as a result of the political turmoil created by the state-based daily press reporting rumours of killings of Aborigines by white people. The white population felt they had the right to plunder lands, force Aborigines to cease using their own languages and prevent them from crossing their leased property, feeding off their stock and spooking their cattle at waterholes. This coercive action by pastoralists was no more than continuing colonial plunder and in turn caused increasing Aboriginal poverty. The Rumbalara railhead with its European, Afghan and Asian workforce was moving ever closer to Alice Springs and as such was an increasing sexual threat to young Aboriginal women. This was one problem and others were cattle spearing and conflict over Aborigines crossing pastoral leases and these two events came together at the Coniston lease that was temporarily managed by Billy Briscoe.

---

19 'Visit by Minister for Interior Perkins and Secretary, Department of Interior Brown to Alice Springs', CRS A1, 1933/243, folios 218A-219, NAA, Canberra.

So I come to the Coniston massacre in which all sides of my family were involved. The Board of Inquiry into the 1928 Coniston massacre began in late 1929 and my European relatives gave evidence. What I now know is that on the 7 August 1928, as the half-caste children were about to be relocated some distance from Alice Springs, a man called Frederick Brooks, a dingo trapper, was speared and buried in a rabbit warren at a water hole 22 kilometres west of the Coniston Station homestead.[20] In 1928 Brooks had asked Stafford if he could trap dingoes on the Coniston Station lease, some 250 kilometres from Alice Springs; Stafford agreed. At the time Brooks was cohabiting with a Warlpiri woman. Stafford warned Brooks not to disrespect the bush women and their lore because 'Myalls'[21] to the west had threatened the Aboriginal woman, Alice, for breaking kin rules.[22] Nevertheless, Brooks went to Coniston Station to kill dingos and asked a Walpiri man, Bullfrog Japanunga, if his wife Marungardi could wash his clothes in exchange for tobacco and food.[23] Brooks attempted to keep Marungardi at the station and when she returned to Japanunga without food or tobacco he attacked Brooks and killed him at what is now known as Brooks' soak. That was the Aboriginal account of events, but Stafford, like many white people in the region, believed Brooks died for nothing and that the subsequent murder of many Aborigines, 17 by the conservative official count, was justified.

In retribution a party of men, including my mother's white father Billy Briscoe, formed a punitive expedition to the site of the killing. At the time Billy Briscoe was also employed by Randall Stafford at Coniston Station lease and knew Brooks from when they both worked in the Lake Eyre region. It was not long after the retribution killings that news came to my mother, at Iwaputarka, that Billy Briscoe was implicated in Mounted Constable Murray's punitive raiding party. These events were significant to the children in the half-caste institution, including my mother as I learned much later, because many Warlpiri were 'mown down summarily' by members of the white and Aboriginal punitive party. Many of the half-caste children were direct blood relatives to those Aborigines killed and many were also blood relatives to the killers.

Documentation shows that Murray proceeded to Coniston Station on 12 August 1928. On 16 August he gathered up an illegal posse comprised of Aboriginal stockman Alick Wilson together with Randall Stafford, John Saxby, Billy Briscoe, three Aboriginal trackers, Paddy, Major and Dodger, together with two prisoners Padigay and Woolingar, who had agreed to show Murray where the nearby Aboriginal bush camp was.[24] Nearing five o'clock in the afternoon the

---

20   Wilson and O'Brien 2003: 27, 59-78.
21   Wilson and O'Brien 2003: 63. See chapter notes.
22   Spencer and Gillen 1968[1899]: 119.
23   Read and Read 1999: 35-37.
24   Wilson and O'Brien 2003: 67.

posse came across a party of 23 Aborigines and in true military style Murray moved into the camp ordering them to disarm. Other members testified to the Board that the Aboriginal men and women had no notion of what was being said. Murray attacked them and in what followed: 'four Warlpiri were killed outright, including one woman, and another was wounded and died within four hours, bringing the total killed then to five'.[25]

On 19 August Stafford stayed at the station and the posse went north towards the Tanami where a party of six young warriors were engaged and asked to disarm. Murray claims he was peppered with sticks and boomerangs to within an inch of his life, and he retaliated with his revolver, killing three men and wounding three others. By 22 August the posse had returned to Coniston where two more Warlpiri were killed, together with a young boy who was running away. On 30 August Murray again returned to Coniston where Wooligar died of wounds received around 12 August. The massacre extended into the Tanami desert when Bill Morton, a leaseholder at Broadmeadow Station, shot and killed more Warlpiri.

Briscoe claimed to be innocent of shooting anyone; nevertheless, the Aboriginal perspective has always been that Briscoe was guilty by implication. Stafford admitted shooting someone escaping the scene and discovering that one of the dead persons was a young woman. On 7 September Murray was sent to gather evidence following Morton's report to the Board.[26] The Darwin papers reported in January 1929 that 17 Aborigines had been killed over a period of time during the massacre. Of these, 15 were men and two were women. By May of the same year, the *Sydney Morning Herald* had put the total figure at 33.[27] Supporters, missionaries, protectors and researchers claimed the total deaths could be as high as possibly 300 Walpari people. This number was further substantiated by comments from the Australian Board of Mission.[28]

The Department of Home Affairs conceded that the killing of 17 Aborigines had occurred. The Report criticised Murray for failing to follow proper reporting procedures laid down by the department when reporting events to the minister. Cawood's report was equally spurious because it meant that 'Murray was on the spot, and could have been interrogated by the Government Resident [but was not]'. Similarly it was alleged that Cawood had corrupted the whole process and should have been gaoled for doing so. In addition, the Secretary's memo states that:

---

25   Wilson and O'Brien 2003: 68.
26   Letter by Morton in, 'The Findings of the Board of Inquiry into Coniston Killings', CRS A431, 1950/2768, pt 1, NAA, Canberra.
27   Attachment 'Finding of Board of Inquiry into Coniston Killings', exhibit 7, CRS A431, 1950/2768, pt 2, NAA, Canberra.
28   Article 'Aborigines, Recent Shooting', *Sydney Morning Herald*, 10 May 1929, CRS A431, 1950/2768, pt 2, NAA, Canberra.

> The reports by Constable Murray in regards to the shooting of a native by Tilmouth and in regard to the shooting of aboriginals by the police in connection with the arrest of those implicated in the attack on Morton were also merely forwarded for the Minister's information and without any comment by the Government Resident.[29]

What this implies is that Europeans applied whatever powers were necessary to protect their own interests, whether corrupt or not. It is evident that in many respects the Commonwealth Board of Enquiry was farcical because Cawood was not only the Central Australian Government Resident and a Police Commissioner Board member but also the superior officer of Mounted Constable Murray. In addition, neither followed due process because the pastoral labourers and trackers were never sworn in as 'Special Constables' by Murray.[30] Cawood too, openly expressed his prejudice against Aborigines. The Board was stacked against a fair hearing by the appointment of too many police representatives such as a Queensland police magistrate as chairperson, and a South Australian police Inspector, ensuring a predetermined outcome. Both these men were bound to find in favour of Murray. Wilson and O'Brien argued that a further set of complications affected the case: 'conflicts over land use, the effects of drought and [as already mentioned] the demise of Frederick Brooks'.[31]

Other irregularities and false accusations against Aborigines can be read in the transcripts of the inquiry.[32] It is hard to believe the level of hatred against Aborigines and half-castes by the Europeans. Impressions and some evidence of 30 witnesses were taken, but here I am only interested in the submissions by Mounted Constable WG Murray, Randall Stafford, Billy Briscoe and Isabella Violet Price. And, according to Stafford, Murray possessed a character that oozed with 'bad faith' towards Aborigines.[33] Murray was normally attached to the Alice Springs police station but at the time of Brooks' death in August 1928 was in charge of the Barrow Creek police station. Murray was an unreliable witness, who lied to Inspector Giles. In his report he said that he had 'no police experience' prior to joining the Central Australian Police, and had 'not undergone any course of instruction in Police duties'. In the same paragraph he stated that 'Sergeant Stretton gave him instruction in the art of making a police report. He was very exact and wanted everything explained'.[34]

---

29 'The Findings of the Board of Inquiry into Coniston Killings', CRS A431, 1950/2768, pt 2, folio 445, NAA, Canberra.
30 'The Findings of the Board of Inquiry into Coniston Killings', CRS A431, 1950/2768, pt 2, folio 445, NAA, Canberra.
31 Wilson and O'Brien 2003: 60.
32 'Commonwealth of Australia Gazette, no. 138, Friday 4 December 1928', CRS A431, 1950/2768, pt 2, NAA, Canberra.
33 'The Findings of the Board of Inquiry into Coniston Killings', CRS A431, 1950/2768, pt 2, folio 445, NAA, Canberra.
34 Commonwealth of Australia Gazette, no. 138, Friday 4 December 1928', CRS A431, 1950/2768, pt 2, NAA, Canberra.

In addition to police instruction, Murray's real skills were in applying military force, as Wilson and O'Brien attested. They wrote that:

> Murray was a military man, a Light Horse veteran of World War I who had also served over seven years in the Victorian Mounted Rifles militia prior to 1914 [Murray served in] the Mediterranean Expeditionary Force with B Squadron of the 4th Light Horse on 20 May 1915 [He landed] at Gallipoli on 24 May 1915 [And he was wounded] on the Western Front ... at Messines Ridge on 7 June 1917.[35]

In the same way Cawood used Isabella Price's submission to denigrate the Aboriginal perspective of the event. Mrs Isabella Violet Price (nee Hesketh) was born in England on 25 April 1877. She was the widow of Frederick Price (1867-1924) who was at one time a manager of the Alice Springs Telegraph Station.[36] On 7 January 1929 she gave evidence to the board of inquiry on the Coniston massacre. The reason I highlight Isabella Price's submission is that her younger son Ronald Price was my biological father. Although I explain about my mother's relationship with Ron Price in more detail later, I find it hard to understand why Isabella Price was asked to give a statement to the Board of Enquiry. Coniston Station was 250 kilometres north-west of the Stuart highway, whereas Woolla Downs, Isabella's property, was in the opposite direction approximately 240 kilometres east, in the Sandover, or Utopia, region. Woolla Downs was a long way from Coniston Station and I believe none of what she said had any bearing on the events covered by the inquiry. The only possible conclusion that can be drawn is that Cawood wanted to influence the other two members of the Board in demonstrating how Aboriginal employees, as well as bush people, frightened whites on the periphery of pastoral expansion. What is more, all that Price could say was that she was growing more afraid of both the Aborigines who worked for her and of those passing through her lease. As she said 'we are always having trouble with them about losing the goats and [bush people] being cheeky'.[37]

According to her transcript, Isabella Price had never shot or killed any Aborigines. However, she did recount times when her daughter Pearl[38] shot at both her Aboriginal shepherds and people in the camp a kilometre away. She added that: 'the blacks [meaning bush people] never came to my house because we keep them at a distance'. What was damning about the statements was that if the Price family used fire-arms to control the Aborigines who worked for them they were hardly the kind of people who would reveal if they shot bush people or not.

---

35 Wilson and O'Brien 2003: 66.
36 Bucknall 1990-1996: 171-173.
37 'Attacks on White men by Natives', CRS A431, 1950/2768, pt 2, NAA, Canberra.
38 Mrs Pearl Dixon was Isabella Price's daughter.

Presumably bush people passed through the area, as they did in hunting parties, and trekked to places as far away as Walmatjirri country, over the Western Australian border. From there they would either travel to Warlpiri country in the opposite direction for fire ceremonies or go further on to Urapuntja.[39] Based on Isabella Price's statement it would appear that it was Aborigines who were condemned rather than the marauding police party. It is not difficult, therefore, to understand why Price was asked to make a submission as a way of demonising Aborigines.

The terror of the Coniston killings resonated throughout Alice Springs, as well as the distant Native Institution at Jay Creek. Nor did the events and follow-up inquiry escape the notice of Reverend Davies of the Anglican Church, a representative on the Australian Board of Missions. My mother remembered the European women in town in their long black dresses asking questions about *Wati Kudaitja nga wankapie?* — which in Mardu to the young half-caste girls meant talking about Aboriginal men in ceremonial killings — and the recent massacre. The terror of the Coniston killings permeated the temporary half-caste institution at Jay Creek, and I distinctly remember my mother telling me that all the children were terrified of the *kuthi* (for the Arrernte inmates) or *kurdaitja* (for the Arrabuna and Marduntjara inmates)[40] coming in the night to 'sing' them.[41] At night the children were terrified and, by day, fell into the misery of losing their inheritance because of the influx of the European population into the Alice Springs region.[42]

The Coniston massacre was more extensive, in area and in numbers, than has ever been acknowledged in the 150 or so years of colonial occupation. It may be argued that Aborigines initiated many killings, but the Aborigines suffered more. Normally Aborigines exacted those killings due to some form of agreement that had been broken. Coniston was such a situation treated with contempt by Fred Brooks, a perspective never accepted by Australian courts. Following this incident greater legal controls were put in place controlling the movement not just of half-castes but bush people. Greater protection from the conflicts was given to colonists, but never to Aborigines no matter whether they were of full- or mixed descent. These aspects of race policies created to control people of full- and mixed descent are important in understanding the circumstances into which my mother was raised and into which I was born in November 1938.

---

39 'Attacks on White men by Natives', CRS A431, 1950/2768, pt 2, NAA, Canberra.
40 Traditional clever man.
41 The term is an English word used to put a spell on people.
42 Article 'Scandal of North', *The Adelaide Mail*, CRS A659, 1939/1/996, pt 1, NAA, Canberra.

Chapter 2
Evacuation, Mulgoa to Semaphore, 1938 to 1945

My mother like many Aboriginal women believed in the idea that the whole group cared for a child; not just the mother. However, over her lifetime things changed. This change was bought about not only of her own making, but the white society to which she gravitated. Her life on the one hand was made particularly hard by crumbling relationships and by circumstances imposed on her by government policies. My life on the other hand was influenced absolutely by her early actions and the institutions she chose for what she thought was a more superior system of care than she could provide.

Young Aboriginal women were ignorant of the western concept of parenting. Hence a young girl like my mother was unprepared for the tasks of motherhood: she only had bush, fringe camp knowledge and naivety passed on to her by other childhood confidantes and Bungalow inmates. They had been deprived of their traditional social structures of support and unable to draw on any new knowledge for a long time into the future.

For my mother there was only one option, which was to work on station properties when and where she was told to do so. The idea of family planning was beyond most Aboriginal women's thinking and my mother had only ignorance to guide her. What this meant was, close to puberty, she was only able to gain knowledge from girls close to her own age or those older Aboriginal women in the institution that had experienced traditional society. In her later years she often lamented that her life would certainly have been different had she been aware of alternatives. Many of the girls she grew up with came to grief, and I speak of some of these issues later. What made my mother's circumstances particularly difficult was the fact that she was not only sent as a domestic servant onto cattle leases but had to suffer the upheaval of the Japanese threat.

I was born at the Old Telegraph Station Native Institution in November of 1938. My birth certificates states that my father was 'unknown' and my place of birth a 'half-caste institution'! My mother left me there soon after recovering from my birth. She was sent to Granite Downs Station where she worked as a cook and later to stations north of Alice where she worked possibly as a domestic help. Two women of significance, or I should say, two young girls looked after me while my mother went to work on cattle leases north and south of Alice Springs. Millie Glenn and Nora Carew accepted responsibility for both me and another boy born under almost the same circumstances as me, an infant called Gerry Hill. Millie was born at Glen Helen Station and Nora was born at Titjikala. These two girls had been cared for by my mother when they were taken from the camps in their own country as young children and placed in the half-caste ration depot in Alice Springs, Jay Creek and the Old Telegraph Station.

All this was to change, however, when on the 19 February 1942 a large force of Japanese aircraft attacked Darwin killing 243 people and injuring another 300. Another 62 Japanese raids occurred across the north from Broome, Darwin, Port Hedland and Wyndham to Townsville. In the Territory this triggered a response of a military take-over. So far as Aboriginal people were concerned Native Institutions were closed as well as leprosariums, native hospitals, government ration depots and many religious missions across northern Australia. The Australian government feared that Aboriginal people of both full- and mixed descent would collude with the invading Japanese forces as they advanced down the archipelago.

The military ordered civilians out of the Territory in 1942. And although I was very young I am still able to recall the closeness of the water hole in the Todd River to the dormitories and the way many of the younger children were happily playing while the adults panicked at the thought of the invasion. I recall drinking the water from the river, and eating the mud, as we were rushed to the army trucks. The panic heightened our senses; smells and tastes of that day have lasted with me throughout my life. Tensions still within me, I believe, relate to the events of the 1942 evacuation when most of the institution's residents were suddenly moved interstate. Those who remained either worked for the government or the combined American and Australian military force.

While travelling, new types of rations were fed to us on the long truck and train journey from Alice Springs to Oodnadatta, again these tastes and flavours still remain with me. Food in the half-caste institution, just before we left, all tasted like tomato soup. I talked to my mother later about why everything tasted like that. She told me that there was no way most foods could keep fresh for any length of time in the outback. The flour for damper always seemed as though there was something wrong with it or it tasted mouldy. Beef, goat or sheep meat only lasted a couple of days and they would be fly-blown. Vegetables would perish after only a day or so. Water storage was not good and when the army moved in during the early part of the Second World War food became even scarcer. Tinned food was brought in to Alice Springs by the army and the cooks at the Bungalow had to supplement every meal in the last few months with salt beef and tomato soup. Many things were short and even being evacuated south by train and truck was difficult. Troop trains coming north prevented southbound trains from having a clear run. Military trucks carried us to Oodnadatta, and from there we went by train on to Adelaide via the Flinders Ranges. Our journey continued by train to Melbourne and onwards to the refugee camp at Mulgoa west of Sydney.

I recall the day we were evacuated because it was very hot and the dust and smells coming from the unfamiliar military trucks was strong in my nostrils. One of my strongest recollections was being lifted, for the first time, onto the back of an army vehicle. I could feel the dark green canvas rubbing across my face as I was lifted into the truck. The smell of petrol was strong along with the smell of oil on the floor. I recall being with my mother and her two young sisters, Millie Glenn and Nora Carew. We left Alice Springs during the mid-morning and travelled south by military convoy to Oodnadatta arriving early the next day. The military vehicles drove through the town and we were then loaded onto cattle trucks and sent south to Quorn.

My memory of Oodnadatta is of seeing more soldiers, Afghans, bush Aborigines and Chinese workers than I had ever seen before. The Afghans came into the marshalling yards with their laden camels. I also remember my mother speaking in Marduntjara to the Aboriginal shepherds who worked with the cameleers. She later told me she knew them as relatives from Lilla Creek, the place of her birth. Oodnadatta was the largest town I had ever seen, with two-storey buildings and a very large railway yard full of soldiers and cattle trucks. It was on this stretch of the journey that I distinctly remember sleeping on the floor of the cattle truck, which was rather like being on a barbecue griddle. The floor was criss-crossed with raised timber to allow stock to travel without losing their footing. The smell of cow dung was very strong in my nostrils and the taste of military rations such as tinned fish, tinned sausages and vegetables lingered for years. What they called 'army biscuits' was a new food item and the taste left a lasting flavour in my mouth, a taste I now realise similar to milk arrowroot biscuits and one I have not forgotten.

The journey from Oodnadatta to Quorn was unforgettable, not simply for the impact of the food, smells and sleeping arrangements, but also because of the noise, smoke and smell of steam engines. Steam trains have an unforgettable smell of coal fire smoke. Then of course there was the smell of steam mixed with dust from the desert and the overpowering noise of the engine as it passed the cattle trucks. As the train left Oodnadatta I remember how far you could see from the train. The countryside was very flat and travelling south it was possible to see a distant creek on the left and right of the train; and then a distant hill where there were a great many tin shacks and what seemed to be hundreds of camels. The terrain shifted and changed from open plains where hills could be seen in the distance to low flat topped hills streaked with yellow, red, brown and white clay.

We stopped quite often as other trains full of rowdy soldiers passed, travelling north. This happened throughout the first night and into the dusk of the next day. As the sun fell to the west we kept rising higher into the Flinders Ranges and the mountains and trees became more numerous until we reached Quorn at dusk. The trees changed from river gums to wattles, and then other trees that looked like tall thin pine trees. It was dark when the train came to a stop and as we moved slowly towards the lights I could tell that there were many uniformed men holding plates speaking loudly, and in a language I could barely understand. The women behind the tables handed us soup in tin cups and plates of potatoes and big fat beef sausages. Quorn appeared to be quite a big place with many street and shop lights. At Quorn the convoy of half-castes were shifted from the cattle trucks into carriages with long corridors and seats that stretched lengthwise along the carriages. While there I recall these rows of men and women being fed curried sausages and boiled potatoes.

Our train left early the next day with a very big jolt, waking most of the children, I remember, as the train shunted forward and many babies began crying. Instead of going directly to Port Augusta, the train headed for Terowie to leave open the north-bound line for troop carriers. This meant taking the narrow gauge route via Terowie and Balaklava to Adelaide. There was a perceptible difference in motion changing from the army truck to the cattle trucks hauled by steam engine and from narrow to broad gauge.

As the train came into the Balaklava Station there was a lot of noise from the carriage we were in. The half-caste contingent was made up mostly of women, young girls and boys and a considerable number of babies. I remember the commotion as those leaving the train grabbed and hugged each other and I distinctly recall Elsie Minchin, a close friend of my mother, leaving together with some of the Hampton boys and their mother. Looking out of the carriage window I could see the Aboriginal people being pushed, with their babies, to one end of the station by soldiers in heavy coats and funny looking hats with badges that glittered on one side of their heads. Other Australians would have recognised these as slouch hats. Then looking out of the carriage window I could see right down to the ground as the Aboriginal contingent began crying and yelling.

I learned much later that the half-caste group was divided along religious lines. For example, some Aborigines had never been baptised because they came from pastoral leases directly to the evacuation point and were kept in aliens' camps by the military. This was a convenient way for land owners and lease managers to cull their surplus bush populations – they simply put them on army trucks and shipped them south or to nearby missions. Those who were baptised were kept together as a denomination and were sent to various state religious centres around Australia. Lutheran priests and inmates of their missions were either 'gated' or sent inter-state to be monitored by the military. Blood relatives, therefore, were split into Catholics, Protestants and 'heathens'. The ghastly thing was that the different religious bodies took their converts; those left went straight into the aliens' compound and kept there for the duration of the European and Japanese Wars.

That night, at the Balaklava rail station, it was impossible for anyone to know what would happen to the travelling half-caste population. The aliens' camp, as I would later experience, was a compound governed by the military, located on the Balaklava race course and surrounded by a four metre high fence patrolled by soldiers with rifles. My small family would return to this aliens' camp later in the war. On that night, however, peering out of the train I could see the steam coming from the engine as it passed the women on the station below, one or two of the older women could be seen as the steam surrounded them, and then disappeared in an instant; it seemed to me, in hindsight, that they may well have known what was in store for them.

Our group left the station and the wailing subsided some distance down the track; the next stop was Adelaide. The Reverend Percy Smith was there in an Army uniform to meet us, and from the station we were taken to a Church Mission Society tea room opposite the Adelaide railway station. This railway station was the largest building I had ever been in, with the longest staircase and the noise, once more, was greater than I had ever experienced. Steam trains were coming and going with whistles blowing. Hundreds of people spewed out of trains, rushing up stairs, hurrying past us as we left the Adelaide railway station. From the station we crossed North Terrace and walked up an alley to the travellers' refuge. Our group filled the tearoom and many of the new faces that joined us there would become very familiar over the coming weeks and years. There in the tea room, however, all I could do was eat and sleep most of the day. The trip from Alice Springs had been traumatic but in Adelaide things began to settle down.

By the evening, refreshed from our trek, we were back on the Adelaide railway station, boarding a train for Sydney via Melbourne. The Melbourne section included refreshments and the Sydney leg of the journey was unremarkable, except for one big event. In hindsight I believe I must have been exhausted by the earlier travelling. The first real memory I had after leaving Melbourne was crossing the River Murray as the train made its way to Albury. I saw a gigantic river that must have taken minutes to cross. The incessant movement of the steel girders criss-crossed my line of sight as I looked down through the carriage window to the biggest stretch of water I had ever seen, an indelible image I have been unable to forget. Night fell quickly as the trains now travelled much faster than the earlier goods trains but all that I recall was stopping for meals and the pungent smell of coffee, another smell new to me. Ours was now a cohesive group, some of whom I recognised from the Alice, others as arriving at the Bungalow from the north, days before.

The railway journey in from the outskirts of Sydney was most memorable, with open green fields, yet another sight I'd never seen before. The hills seemed so close I could touch them; the fear of tunnels and bridges was very clear in my mind together with the train's movement from side to side. The tension increased too as from the train's window I could momentarily see the Sydney Harbour Bridge. Closer to Central station the number of lines increased and for the first time I saw many trains going in the same direction. Passing the stations en route to Central was strange and although my mind was alert it took years for me to understand what they meant. As we approached Central station the noise intensified as we flashed past signs and houses, then silence punctuated only by the rhythm of the line on the steel wheels and the shift of the carriages as we went from one side of the rail yards to the other.

At Central itself we slowed to almost a walk, the larger buildings came into sight as we pulled into the main platform and life seemed to stop. Central station was even more astonishing than Adelaide railway station and it left a lasting impression on me as we were spirited off to a hostel at Burwood called Mulleewa. Years later my mother filled in the details as confusion around me intensified. Mulleewa, we were told later, was a local Aboriginal word and so was Mulgoa, the refuge which would be our home for the rest of the war. But at Mulleewa the group was further divided. Some of the older women, with two or more children, like Alice Roberts and Marree Bourke, were to stay with the babies. The younger girls such as Millie Glenn, Rose Foster, Amy Tennant, Nora Carew and Heather Wesley all stayed with the group at Mulgoa; some either went back to primary school or were sent out as domestics on the nearby farm properties. My mother, together with other young women, was farmed out as military hospital labour, domestic labour, carers for children of working white women and, finally, cooks for American military 'top brass'.

There are many clear images embedded in my mind of this time, together with memories of close Aboriginal people that have come and gone throughout my life. Once leaving Mulleewa it must have been some months before I saw my mother again, but I felt safe with my mother's sisters. First, I remember going to the St Thomas's manse at Mulgoa with Millie Glenn, Nora Carew and Rose Foster, who all took care of me and my relative Gerry Hill. Other Mulgoa boys I became acquainted with, around my age were John Moriarty, Wilfred and Robert Huddleston, Timothy Campbell and Ken Hampton. As a four year old I was not fully conscious of them all then but I talk more about them later. At this particular time at Mulgoa, when the girls — and they were only girls — made their palliasses up in an upstairs room facing the front entrance to the manse, one palliasse was made up for me.

The manse was a three-storey 15-room mansion located about 20 kilometres south of Blacktown. The structure was built around the 1830s by convicts, in the halcyon days of pastoral development after Governor Macquarie's time, and was a gift to the Church by a wealthy colonial pastoralist. The Anglicans also owned the attached 20-acre property. We half-castes had our meals in the lower rooms close to the kitchen. Then there were living rooms on the entry floor, which had wide verandas circling the whole building with a third floor mostly used as bedrooms. The layout of these rooms became clearer when the missionaries came to take charge of us. I do not recall all of the missionaries but a woman called Sister Dove was in charge. I learned much later that she was an ex-missionary from Millingimbi.

I remember a number of things about Sister Dove. She was a short stout white woman with greying hair and was, I recall, a kindly woman. I remember seeing her every Saturday without fail because this was the day our hair was shorn off and we were deloused for nits by covering our bald heads with a white powder. That was not the end of these rituals because this was also the day we were lined up outside the breakfast dining room and were compulsorily dosed with Epsom salts, malt molasses (that is malt with a sulphur mixture) and sometimes milk emulsion. These were all new forms of medication for us; we were told it was all good for us. Another set of rituals began on Sundays of each week when after Church Miss Dove conducted the Sunday school where she taught us all three classic Christian hymns that I will never forget. They were: 'Bringing in the sheaves', 'Rolling over, rolling over, my heart is full and running over, when the Lord sees me I'm as happy as a bee' and so on, and, finally, 'Jesus wants me for a sunbeam'. Church services and the singing of hymns were a big part of life and I had occasion to attend funerals either for the deaths of white parishioners or for members of our own group.

Sometimes, with other children near my own age, I would be attracted by the music or the crowds at the church a couple of hundred metres away. We would walk up to the Church and listen to the singing. Sometimes we would sit on the gravestones mesmerised by the sad hymns echoing through the bush. The church was called St Thomas and had a big pipe organ that could be heard from miles away. Some of the older boys would have to pump the handle at the rear of the contraption to blow air through the pipes. Alternately, sometimes the organ pumper would fall asleep and the choir master would have to go behind the choir stalls to wake him, always him. Yes, it was always a male because the pump was not only difficult to push up and down but also the pumping had to be maintained for a very long time.

Some weeks after arriving many of the children contracted pneumonia and I was one of these; I nearly died from the infection. What made matters worse was the fact that this group of 100 or so mothers, young children and babies was crowded into ten bedrooms in the manse. While seriously ill I was bedded down on the outside veranda at the rear of the manse and it was there that my mother came to see me, and I felt special with this visit. These conditions remained in place until a large military styled wooden hut was built about 100 metres away from the main manse. The missionaries moved in immediately, the old house was scrubbed after our illness and our general use. Once the dormitories were built a wave of influenza, mumps and measles swept through our population. I recall being inside and having doctors pawing over us while these infections persisted. One procedure remains vivid and that was the 'old pump treatment' which meant a rubber hose pushed up the rectum and the fluid drained off. I cannot recall my mother coming back on that occasion but I certainly remember the procedure and recall being confined with the many other children affected with these illnesses.

On a number of occasions I went to Sydney to have short stays with my mother, and, there were times when she came to Mulgoa. On some of these visits the whole group would walk into the Blue Mountains as far as a location called Norton Basin, a beautiful location on the Warragamba River some short distance from where the dam wall was eventually built. We would catch fish, locate platypus, *perentie* (a black tree goanna), witchetty grubs (*tjapa* in Mardu) as well as rabbits that were cooked on an open fire and eaten. The rabbits we would catch while walking through to the Mulgoa village, on into the mountains where we would camp in the bush, cook and eat the game on the spot and return the following day. Wallabies and grey kangaroos were something of a treat. These animals would either be caught by hand or, if we were lucky, be picked up as 'road-kill'.

The whole region during the Second World War was either made up of farms, open fields or bush. Occasionally the older women would find a bullock which we would run over a cliff, climb down, skin the bullock for meat and consume as needed. Since we numbered in the twenties the carcass would feed us for a couple of days. Millie Glenn was a great hunter and could find bush honey very quickly. She also caught perenties by climbing a tree, grabbing the lizard by the tail and cracking it like a stock whip for the kill. We would also supplement our food with rabbits, caught at will after hunting them with sticks or killing them in the squat. Once, when returning after a few hours looking for bush honey and rabbits my mother came to see me and as always she was a welcome sight.

Meanwhile, one of my mother's first jobs was as a domestic servant and cook for an American naval officer called Commander Dodge. The Dodge family lived at Kirribilli, about four or five doors from Kirribilli House and Admiralty House.

Eileen never knew quite what the high-ranking American Naval Officer did but it was obviously war related. She lived in the same building as the Dodge family in an attic high in the roof with enough space for a bed, a small cupboard and chair. When I stayed with her we slept in the same bed, me at one end, and my mother at the other end, I clearly recall being woken up each morning to the sound of doves and topknot pigeons. The other thing I also remember was seeing my mother from the attic window with a soldier who left her at the front gate. Mrs Dodge sometimes let me stay for the weekend and that often meant trips around the harbour to various parts of Sydney. Sometime we would visit other Aboriginal women who had come from Alice Springs such as May Hill, Sporty, Netty and Daisy Pearce. May and Sporty were Eileen's favourites. After the war Sporty married Stumpy Thomas in Alice Springs and became the mother of Harold Thomas, the designer of the Aboriginal flag. The two sisters had a flat at Taronga Park and I remember going by ferry, then by tram, and walking up what seemed a very steep hill to their third storey flat. Sometimes they came to meet us as they could see our arrival from the flat when they looked out over the harbour.

Although I never spoke to my mother about much of her time in Sydney there were two specific health related events that I clearly remember. One was leprosy. This was a disease people can be infected by and harbour for years before it breaks out. Some of the mothers from tropical areas like Arnhem Land were diagnosed with the infection (caught some time earlier in their lives) and were sent to infectious disease hospitals in Sydney. I think this disease was mainly confined to one or two families who came down from the tropical north and joined our group during the evacuation. Leprosy takes a long time to reveal itself and Sydney was a place where you could easily catch that disease.

The other health problem was tuberculosis, an illness that many central Australian Aborigines either carried or went on to develop and often ultimately died. It was a problem for May, Gerry Hill's mother who was a full sister to Tilley Tilmouth. May had come from Arltunga an old gold mining town north-east of Alice Springs, where her father was a Chinese market gardener with a lot of children and many Aboriginal wives. The living conditions in the small hut where she lived until she was about nine or ten were cramped. I was told that she had contracted tuberculosis through this overcrowding. Sometimes the disease lingers in the body and if not treated it becomes life-threatening, which is what happened to May. She died in a Sydney infectious diseases hospital some time in 1944. This I know was a very sad time for my mother and her close sisters who visited her often; and I recall vividly the grief they felt when May died. The saddest part about this event was that Gerry was never told about his mother's predicament. I know this because I was later to spend many years in the boys' home with Gerry who knew almost nothing of his past.

I first started school at Kirribilli Primary during one of the short periods I was living with my mother. One lasting memory at Kirribilli was the strange trough at this school, with many taps and a dividing wire wall. Each time I recall Kirribilli school I can see that wire wall with hundreds of children yelling and screaming at me through it from the other side. Other memories of Kirribilli school are vague but I have vivid recollections of the Mulgoa school I later attended; a one-teacher school with the desks lined up in a regimental style that signified each grade. I sat in grade one but the most significant task for me was catching flies and tearing off their wings. A better image of the time was that I recall playing rounders with white children and those from our group. The bat was always made from a dry gum branch collected on our bush trek to school. I can clearly remember the girls would tuck their cotton dresses up their pants when they were batting and scampering around the bases. Everyone played and even us smaller children were always given a go, or made to be in one of the teams. Certainly the half-castes had no shoes to wear and this made us run faster. But this had its problems too as the winter frosts stung our feet on our way to school. On arrival the one-room school was always hot enough to warm our feet because the teacher had attended the fire. But my early schooling was fragmented. Neither at this time nor later could I fathom what was happening to me. Unfortunately, it took many years before I could find a satisfactory answer to the question of why I was such an unresponsive and erratic young student.

Another vivid memory was the day that a member of our group, Wally Macarthur, suffered a psychotic episode. Nobody has ever been able to really explain his actions. For some reason or another he had a confrontation with the teacher; the local police came and placed him in a shed at the side of the school building. Wally was a very strong young boy and was later dragged out into the yard with some difficulty by the two policemen. This event occurred at recess time in sight of all the other students. Somehow, Wally took hold of an axe or small tomahawk and chopped the leg off one of the tables. Soon after this an ambulance arrived and the police took the cutting implement and held Wally to the floor while two ambulance men appeared to poke a needle into his behind. That was the end of the struggle and Wally left with the ambulance via the mission. I never saw Wally again until 1949. (I will pick up on his story in a later chapter.)

Soon after this event my mother came back to Mulgoa expecting my brother Bill. Much later I tried to find out from my mother who Bill's father was but failed to do so. Records do not indicate who it was but it is quite likely that a soldier was 'responsible'.[1] I can recall in Sydney being with soldiers who had strange accents: it could very well have been the American soldier who I saw from the attic window at the Dodges' Kirribilli house. I suspect my mother gave

---

1 'Transfer of Half-Castes, NT to Racecourse', 4 June 1942, CRS A659, 1945/1/2493, folio 9, NAA, Canberra.

very little thought either to how pregnancy would affect her life in Sydney or how she would cope during and following her confinement. I have already discussed how Aboriginal women think about child conception as a process: first, it had to do directly with metaphysical or ideal life and, second, to do with material life such as the child's relationships to others. Family planning had no place in my mother's thinking as life began crowding in on her and confinement followed. Wartime in Sydney, as well as her gullibility, meant she had to rely on her close friends and the missionaries at Mulgoa.

My mother stayed in the Dodges' employment until the department made arrangements for her confinement at the Crown Street Women's Hospital, where my brother Bill was born in November 1944. She returned to Mulgoa for a short period after Bill was born and was subsequently placed in employment with a Mrs Moody of Lindfield. I was left at Mulgoa because Mrs Moody could not cope with a woman and two children.[2]

In January of 1945 the Under Secretary of the Department of Labour and Industry and Social Welfare in New South Wales wrote to the Director of the Department of Native Affairs stating that a number of half-caste women, including my mother, had become 'a problem' especially in regard to employment, their character in general, and their pregnancies. One problem was that the girls in most cases had more than one child, which made them difficult to place in domestic roles as they had no time to attend to their domestic duties while looking after their own children. Further problems were that the girls were leaving their children unattended at night to go out and form associations with either servicemen or civilians. It was also noted that because they were half-caste coloured girls they were unable to mix in 'better circles'. In summary, the Under Secretary was of the opinion that the girls would be happier if they lived at a compound where they could have a certain amount of social life and at the same time their children could be cared for. The recommendation was that the girls be returned to Balaklava in South Australia. An attachment to the letter outlined the history of each of the half-caste women involved.[3]

My mother later told me that she was given her wages, a rail-pass for herself, me age six years and my brother Bill age six months. My recollections of leaving Sydney by train, in late January 1945, with my mother and her new baby, are vague but what I do remember clearly is arriving in Adelaide on the Melbourne Express sometime early in the morning. Soldiers were everywhere and Eileen intended to sit on the station until the surge of soldiers, other passengers and luggage trolleys were cleared. She had no inkling of what was to happen next.

---

2   Letter from Department of Labour and Industry to Mr Chinnery, 24 January 1945, CRS A659/1, 1945, folios 14-15, NAA, Canberra.
3   'Transfer of Half-Castes, NT to Racecourse', CRS A659, 1945/1/2493, NAA, Canberra.

However, the Department of the Interior determined that we go to Balaklava rather than back to Alice Springs where she wanted to go. At the time we were unaware that the allies were still at war with Japan and the military in Adelaide refused to allow us to travel north. My mother, my brother Bill and I were non-citizens and remained that way until late in the 1960s.

As we moved towards the station barrier with Bill strapped in a shoulder holder my mother produced her railway pass, the station guard called a soldier and policeman, beckoning that this woman had no identity papers. After some minutes they decided that the military would take us into custody. We were ushered into a military office and some-time later moved to a waiting truck. Later that evening we arrived at the aliens' camp at Balaklava racecourse where we stayed for the duration of the war.

After experiencing once more the familiar smells of petrol, together with the jolting journey to the racecourse at Balaklava, we were given three palliasses and a bale of straw. The straw was used to fill the palliasses in the horse stables, a short distance from the rear of the grandstand. At first I was unaware that we were living in horse stables, however, I gradually realised where we were when I saw that the floors sloped towards a metal drain running down the middle of the stalls that flushed the horse dung out of the stables.

Meals were served in a large area beneath the grandstand and after preparing our beds we ate a meal in the communal dining area. It was precisely at this point that I realised that there were many white people living and mixing very close to us. This was strange because not only were there white people but there were also other strangers such as Chinese, Italian and German people among us. I distinctly recall the smell of caustic carbolic soap. The soap had no other aroma than the caustic from which it was produced; the tables were scrubbed with this soap as was everyone's bodies and clothes. The overwhelming feeling each morning as we came to eat breakfast was of nausea. I still feel like vomiting whenever I encounter that rancid smell that penetrated everything. Ultimately, however, hunger gave way to melancholia.

I recall sitting eating my meals close to German monks, Italian prisoners and Chinese market gardeners. Later I learned that these people like us were aliens; arrested and detained in these alien compounds for the duration of the war against Japan. The German monks wore black cassocks with a bright red waistband and a metal cross that swung when they walked. Some prisoners were Italian, that is what we surmised, and wore a blanket-grey uniform with a little grey hat; much later I was to recognise the Italian language. An old Chinese man normally sat opposite us at meals and wore a whitish cotton top with similar types of trousers and sandals. He was a small man with a very long pointed grey beard. The beard was most recognisable because at every meal he would spill the food down it. I would mention this to my mother as the food ran down and she would scold me for pointing it out.

During mid-year in South Australia I remember it rained a lot. When this happened the children would go out around the racecourse, collect mushrooms and catch rabbits. We would take them back to the laundry and cook them up in the copper. This tended to supplement the tinned food, dog biscuits and fatty sausages served in various forms for meals.

Some time at the end of winter the Reverend Percy Smith came to the aliens' camp, spoke to my mother and produced a release form signed by a Mr McCoy. I recall this name for two reasons. The first was that Billy McCoy was the manager of the half-caste institution at the Old Telegraph Station Bungalow. The other reason was that my mother remembered him as the man who adopted a child called Ronny Tilmouth and renamed him Ronny McCoy. The upshot of all of this was that we were allowed to leave the compound. I remember pushing my brother Bill in a stroller to a house in Kensington Gardens. This was the last time that I lived with my mother: my mother left me with the Reverend Percy Smith when she went to work in the laundry of the Repatriation Hospital at Victor Harbour. I spent the next 11 years in an Anglican institution for boys of mixed Aboriginal and other descent.

Chapter 3
Racial theory and a religious solution, 1920s to 1945

Between the two world wars racial theories abounded as to what to do in relation to the 'half-caste Aboriginal problem'. The white frontier attitude was that bush Aborigines were devils, but as time went by they and their off-spring became a useful economic asset in the face of the absence of a white labour force, and finally there was the Baldwin Spencer and JW Bleakley idea of removing half-castes from the bush people and institutionalising them as educated labour. For my mother, racial theories meant little because in Adelaide in the post war era it just meant more difficulties looking after two children with few resources. However, a solution was provided for her that she could not refuse! As a six year old, I would have had little understanding of the implications of my mother's relief but this alienation most certainly influenced my attitudes to others. This feeling of loneliness that affected me in growing up in an institution, away from a mother's affection, would have, no doubt, echoed among the other children with whom I identified.

The solution for my mother came from Father Percy Smith's decade-long observation of half-castes; combined with his strong religious beliefs. In 1945, Father Smith was demobbed from his role as a military chaplain, and as the superintendent of a new institution in Adelaide contemplated the idea that, if educated, boys of mixed racial descent could be equal to other Australians. Throughout my adolescence I often wondered whether Father Smith did what he did for the military, the church or for government. But for what ever reason, Father Smith put forward the theory that if you took half-caste children out of their dependent, poverty stricken decrepit circumstances, put them in urban society backed by religion and public education, then you could transform them into citizens of equal worth. With this strategy he, like those who supported him, thought that that would be an end to the half-caste problem. In this simple religious view he was wrong – it was only the beginning!

Whatever other people's religious faith was about, overcoming class and racial prejudices was a romantic approach embedded in Father Smith's unyielding Christian beliefs. But of course, faith is not limited to religion alone! Father Smith believed that, if provided with the same prospects as working-class people, half-castes would triumph. Like other well-meaning priests, scientists and bureaucrats such as Baldwin Spencer, and like Father Smith's friend and colleague Charles Duguid, Father Smith believed his plan would solve the half-caste 'problem'. This was an explicitly bold perspective, but put simplistically it was both a class and racial minefield, with no tested social evidence of its outcome. For me and others who were the subjects of his experiment in social engineering, this was the beginning of a long period as 'wards of the Commonwealth and the states'. Initially it covered the period from 1945 under Father Smith's care, right up until the second term of the Menzies Liberal-Country Party's rule and beyond. Father Smith's ideas need some discussion in this chapter as well as some idea of my own feelings about the impact of these religious and political policies.

To appreciate Father Smith's predicament some historical understanding of the causes of his actions need appraisal, other than simply my own family connections and what happened to me. There were a number of forces at work. The 1927 Coniston massacre inquiry left the minds of the white people in the Northern Territory at ease but stuck fast in Aborigines' minds. The pastoralists, on the other hand, shaped up for a confrontation over wages for half-castes for the quality of work they did; and whether government would train staff for them to continue exploiting the delicate desert lands for profit. Lastly, Aborigines were banished from the Alice Springs town areas only to return as day labour.

The Commonwealth had ruled the Territory for nearly 20 years up until 1930, and little had gone smoothly so far as the 'race' question was concerned. Half-caste children had been shifted to Jay Creek with Ida Standley as Matron,[1] and the national economic depression constrained building there which meant children were forced to live, once more, in hovels. The issue of sending girls to Adelaide as domestics was an administrative nightmare not only because those girls who went were all 'wards of the Commonwealth' but also because they became stranded in Adelaide, as if jailed; female inmates at Jay Creek feared that the older girls would be next. More problems arose as pastoralists in the Alice Springs area employed young girls, as young as ten and eleven as domestics in the 1920s; one of these girls could well have been my mother. The government and pastoralists were at loggerheads over unresolved payment issues and many of the half-caste girls had no knowledge of their predicament and were shifted around ignorant of their rights, without payment, well into their twenties.[2]

Tuition, and 'master-and-servant', theories abounded while, at the same time pastoralists, trade unions, the Protector of Aborigines and Northern Territory administrators met periodically without success. Gradually these interest groups moved to make changes to the *Aboriginals Ordinance 1918* (Cth), setting out amendments to the 'Apprentices (half-castes) Regulations'. The protectors,

---

1 Letter from Deane to Secretary Commonwealth Treasury, February 1929, CRS A659, 1939/1/996, NAA, Canberra.
2 Letter Bleakley to Commonwealth, 1929, CRS A659, 1939/1/996, NAA, Canberra. See also 'Half Castes Employed outside NT', CRS A1, 1936/7846, NAA, Canberra.

on the one hand, wanted action to relieve themselves of the pain of getting Aborigines employed, while others such as the stock and station agents and the Territory lessees' association wanted all labour subsidised.[3] The system worked against Aboriginal society at all levels. What did this have to do with Father Percy Smith and how did this happen?

Pastoralists were represented not just in the Northern Territory but in the large pastoral markets throughout Australia by stock and station agents like Elder Smith, Goldsborough Mort and the British cattle company, Vesty Investment Agency. These agents played politics to ensure that pastoralists got land leases 'dirt cheap', and were provided with free stock routes to railheads, windmills for travelling stock, dog and buffalo control subsidies, cheap 'black labour', cheap transport for travel to fatten stock for ultimate sale and attractive taxation benefits. Half-caste institutions were created to satisfy European women who thought Aboriginal women caused their husbands' sexual appetites to boil over and to educate labour for domestic and pastoral employment. By contrast Aborigines were bereft of almost all economic or political representation. The Bishop of Carpentaria sent Father Percy Smith to service baptised Aboriginal Anglicans and to care for their moral safety, and he was appalled at what he saw.[4]

The question was, then, whether Father Percy Smith would be part of the solution or part of the problem? Government agents segregated the half-castes from their bush relatives, and concentrated them in hovels for police and patrol officers' convenience. They placed them in institutions, took away their liberties, and, those males in charge of female employees either made them pregnant or sent them to remote pastoralists to do likewise. In short, stock and station agents and their clients acted as agents of profit. In addition, these privateers themselves became barriers against any humanitarian changes to Aboriginal male and female workers' emancipation.[5] The Bleakley report of 1927 looked at both half-caste and 'full-blood' labour conditions; whereupon the Native Welfare Department through Dr Cook began preparing changes that would appease pastoralists and their agents.

Protector Cook was a medical doctor with expertise in the management of leprosy. In this period, however, Cook was head of Commonwealth health with a significant role in controlling Aborigines; he fought for his ideas on managing race on two fronts. On the one hand, there was the question of wages and employment for Aborigines of full- and mixed descent. The issue of Aboriginal labour was emerging as early as 1911 with half-castes as the focus but by 1935

---

3   'Half-Caste Apprentice Regulations', CRS A1, 1933/479, folios 1-10, NAA, Canberra.
4   Smith J 1999: 13-74.
5   'Half-Caste Apprentice Regulations', CRS A1, 1933/479, folios 1-10, NAA, Canberra.

the issue began to be understood as a racial question. The management of Aborigines, and in particular the children, was proving difficult to organise as quickly as government wanted. On the other hand, Cook practised melding ideas of managing 'race' by laying the groundwork for 'assimilation'. What this meant was that Aborigines, either full- or mixed blood, had neither claims of heritage nor legal, civil or political rights. Christians wanted only two things: first a monopoly over any moral charges they may gain control of; and, second, to Christianise as they pleased. Equally, pastoralists wanted free or subsidised labour. Profit demanded the workers be ready and it mattered little about labour laws or Aboriginal social organisation! After reading the Bleakley report Dr Cook questioned the views espoused by Baldwin Spencer's two reports, one in 1911-1912 and the other in 1923-1924, in which Baldwin Spencer claimed that half-castes were the ruin of full-bloods.[6] Cook wrote that although half-castes were considered to be Aborigines, they were regarded as whites for the purposes of government policy and were useful labour. Cook faced ignorance on both sides: his superiors in Canberra were blocked by their racial prejudice while pastoralists wanted free or heavily subsidised labour.[7]

> Dr Cook argued that if half-castes were treated as whites it meant that assimilation policies were one step away from adoption by Australian society. He wrote that:if the half-caste is to be admitted to full citizenship as a white, that those influences which press him towards the blacks' camp should be as far as possible removed. To this end it is desirable that he should marry young and marry a girl of his own stock. A number of eligible half-caste girls are being and will be maintained at Government expense in Darwin and should be available to marry these boys.[8]

Dr Cook convinced the union movement that government was on its side as the matter went before the Arbitration Court. The Court ruled that Aborigines were a part of organised labour, but were covered by the *Aboriginals Ordinance 1918-1930*. This Act stipulated what wages and conditions Aborigines could be paid under.[9] This left open the payment of apprentices or female labour and in turn allowed employers to continue to exploit Aborigines, in general, outside organised labour. This included inmates in the half-caste institutions of Alice Springs who did not need to be paid; so for half-caste child labour it was business as usual. Like the religious representatives, Dr Cook went on refining his perspective on how he was going to manage the 'half-caste problem'. Part

---

6 'Report on Hermannsburg', CRS A431/1, 1947/2348, NAA, Canberra.
7 'Half-Caste Apprentice Regulations', CRS A1, 1933/479, folios 53-55, NAA, Canberra.
8 'Half-Caste Apprentice Regulations', CRS A1, 1933/479, folios 53-55, NAA, Canberra.
9 'Half-Caste Apprentice Regulations', CRS A1, 1933/479, folio 291, NAA, Canberra.

of the plan was first to prevent half-caste women walking the streets, thereby offending the sensitivities of the few whites in towns en route to Darwin, and second, to examine them for diseases before confining them in institutions.[10]

A storm of criticism continued around ideas of managing 'race' in general and, more specifically, laying the groundwork for future ideas of 'assimilation'. This process was typified by colonial practices across Australia against Aborigines and their descendents and played itself out in the hands of the 'intelligentsia'. Anthropologists, who feared reprisals against their ideas, their self-interests and their advocacy, practised professional silence. Historians vacated the field as the province of anthropology and archaeology. The city newspapers haunted the managers of 'race': governments, pastoralists, the church, the scribes of the humanities and native administrations. The journalist and author Ernestine Hill told readers across Australia in the 1930s that libertarianism – sexual licence – had become an 'art form' in the hands of 'white male trash' that were imperialising the Territory under Commonwealth control.[11] Trade unions and left wing pastoral workers together with writers like Hill, Xavier Herbert and very much later John Mulvaney, explained the nature of the Australian peripheral culture 'of the white barbarians', including those representing government bureaucracies.[12] Exercising less constraint than most were the likes of Cecil Cook and his regional protectors, in dealing with natives and the 'half-caste problem'. Dr Cook was a strong supporter of close management of 'The Territory Government's half-caste problem'.

> Cook's ideology on race resembles race theories where:a study of human improvement, in all aspects [was to be] by genetic means. Its goal is to increase the proportion of persons with better than average genetic endowment. It draws from psychology for analysis of the part played by differences in heredity and environment in the development of personality, intelligence and character; from medicine and medical genetics for information on hereditary defects and susceptibility to diseases; and from demography, for rates of births and deaths, the mating habits, and the social and physical factors that determine the relative increase or decline of persons with different characteristics.[13]

Central to these ideas was the notion that the medical profession, to which Dr Cecil Cook belonged, was highly influenced by the point of view of deterministic perfection that could be achieved through social engineering as well as

---

10 'List of inmates; including Eileen Briscoe', CRS A659, 1939/1/996, folios 403-405, NAA, Canberra.
11 Markus 1990: 37-49.
12 '…Reported Murder of in NT', CRS A1, 1936/2763, NAA, Canberra. See also 'A.X. Herbert, Appt Dispenser Dresser NA'CRS A1, 1937/1718, NAA, Canberra. Herbert worked for Cook but was a chronicler of what went on both in and out of Darwin. See also Mulvaney and Calaby 1985: 169-380.
13 The New Encyclopaedia Britannica 1976: 1023-1026.

economically managed control. These ideologies, theories and practices contained all the underpinnings of 'eugenics'. Bleakley wrote, long after he retired, that a plan was devised to launch a great public movement in Queensland, 'for the purpose of arousing wider interest in the welfare of Aborigines'.[14] A meeting at the Queensland University, opened by the Governor of Queensland, proposed a set of political demands built on 'segregation, religion, uniform policy, social tuition for industrial training' and 'self-dependence'. Laws were to be based on 'native' culture, psychology, health, discipline and protection from social vices. Equally, there were suggested laws to control marriage, morals, property and succession of any possessions. These proposals went much deeper than focusing only on gaining the approval of the upper classes; agreement too was sought from the Protestant church and government alike. It was argued that the moral force was not 'racially-based' but focused on post-war labour demands. The union movement argued for inclusion of Aborigines into general wage fixing arrangements, but pastoralists wanted slave labour, rejecting outright notions of paid Aboriginal labour, knowing the *Aboriginal Protection and Restriction of the Sale of Opium Act 1897* (Qld) already provided subsidies for 'black segregated labour'.

Supervisors of the half-caste institutions were actively involved in implementing these policies. Ida Standley was the first teacher supervisor at the Jay Creek Bungalow, followed by Mr and Mrs Thorne as a temporary husband and wife team. They soon left and were followed by a Mr and Mrs Freeman.[15] When Freeman arrived my mother was 14 and undergoing medical treatment for an un-stated ailment. Later in life she related a story to me about when she had finished her training and was first employed as a day labour domestic for white women in Alice Springs. A bus would pick up the young girls in the morning and return them at the end of a day's work. They sometime went to the film shows in town but were forced to sit in the front of the open air theatre for fear they might copulate with white men while the lights were turned off! Sometimes the bus driver would fraternise with one or two of the young women and delay returning them to the Jay.[16] She said that all the white people, including those passing through Alice en route to Darwin, believed the Aboriginal women and girls were consorting and accused the half-caste girls, in particular, of being prostitutes.

Most supervisors were judged for the positions on their attachments to Christian institutions or on the community standing from which they came. No training at this time was required nor asked for. Mr Freeman fitted this pattern well

---

14   Bleakley 1961.
15   Smith J 1999.
16   Pers comm with Eileen Briscoe 1972 about her memories of Jay Creek and Freeman's tenure.

because he had no personal or professional knowledge of Aborigines; yet he set himself up as an expert. His reports reveal his own assumptions on Aborigines. He wrote that the:

> half-caste Aboriginal problem of Central Australia [is different to other places]. Aborigines differ in customs, physique and mentality from … other parts [of Australia]. The girls under the care and guidance of the matron [received] a thorough training in all domestic duties, and when they leave the Institution are competent in all branches of house work, cooking, (plain) bread making etc., besides being able to make their own clothing, knitting and fancy work. The boys are in addition to schooling being trained, as far as possible to fit them for work on stations.[17]

Freeman, therefore, knew exactly in what direction assimilation was heading, as if Dr Cook had spoken directly to him. Neither he nor Dr Cook were able to satisfy the baying press while Ernestine Hill, however, was directing her attention at the latter.

Hill sensed what managing race fertility involved and was also aware of 'white Australia's fear-mongering', directing questions at Dr Cook in order to tell readers that there would be no 'American Negroid' problem in Australia. Politics, capital and democracy would never be put in the hands of 'throw-backs', half-castes, quadroons, octoroons and possessors of 'atavistic tendencies'. The Australian native would disappear after six generations, thus obliterating the 'half-caste problem'. There would be managed breeding between white men and half-caste women, under strict supervision, as she put it, by selecting girls from 'the Darwin Compound and mission stations provided that they are in a position to adequately maintain themselves and their children'.[18]

Deep down this economic thinking provided a rationale for capitalism, but not a justification for free or taxpayer-funded support to groups or individuals. If people could not pay for the 'services' they took from the state, then somebody else would! Critics such as Hill painted a picture of incest, miscegenation, prostitution, over-population and Mendelian race theory where the 'Australian native [was] the most easily assimilated race on earth, physically [and] mentally'. But breeding with Asiatics was 'not desirable [and the] quickest way out' was 'to breed [them] white'. This practice and debate went on into the late 1920s, both within white society and inside the political arena as a renovated 'Old Telegraph Station' was about to be populated by the inmates from Jay Creek.[19]

---

17 'Freeman's Report, 26 March 1932', CRS A659, 1939/1/996, folios 417-424, NAA, Canberra.
18 Hill 1933.
19 Hill 1933 (Hill described 'The Old Telegraph Station' as a 'Half-caste Institutional Compound' 15 kilometres out of town to the west).

These were the conditions faced by Aborigines of mixed descent when Father Percy Smith arrived on the scene. Different creeds had been arguing the right to give religious instruction to inmates of the 'Native Institutions' since the early 1920s. But nothing happened until Reverend Davies sent his report to the Adelaide Advertiser in July of 1929. Following this the Presbyterian as well as the Baptist Churches began baptising half-caste children in the camps around Alice Springs, at the same time raising the half-caste question with the Australian Board of Missions. The Church of England Bishop of Willochra, the Right Reverend Dr R Thomas wrote to Parliament following Davies' letter and soon after a cleric was despatched. By 1932 all except Roman Catholics, who had a mission at Arltunga and one between what was later called Anzac Hill and Middle Park, attended religious instruction according to Freeman's report of May 1932. The Reverend Percival McDonald Smith (Father or Percy Smith as he became known to Aboriginal people) arrived as the permanent curate whose role was to service and baptise children and their siblings.[20]

Records reveal that Cook wanted secular 'Native Institutions' but from the late 1920s the Church and the media forced the issue. John Smith, Father Smith's son, wrote that when his father arrived in 1933:

> There were over one hundred children at the 'Bungalow', of whom eighty were Anglicans, so he had a pastoral responsibility to them. Father [Smith] wasn't impressed with the conditions of the Old Telegraph station site.[21]

Father Smith had one focus and that was the proselytisation of half-castes. In this way he differed from the wider Australian missionary policies, characterised by the historian Markus in this way:

> The direct involvement of the Churches with Aborigines can be said to have changed from next to nothing at the turn of the century to a little by the 1930s. Of funds collected for missionary work, only a small percentage was spent in Australia: the heathen in Asia and other parts of the world were accorded a higher priority. While there was an expansion of missionary activities in the [Northern Territory], there was no major commitment by any religious denomination, and the few missionaries were starved of funds.[22]

---

20 Fraser 1993. See 'Half-Caste Institution', CRS A1, 1936/9959, NAA, Canberra; Smith J 1999.
21 Smith J 1999: 31-51.
22 Markus 1990: 68.

This theme of the parsimonious nature of governments and religion is one that drove the history of the politics of European prejudice, and into which Father Smith was engulfed.[23]

Nevertheless, Father Smith persisted and formed his own ideas about Aboriginal affairs, like most white people who came to the Territory. He was born in Woolloongabba, Brisbane, on 29 March 1903 to an English-Irish migrant family. He came to the Church of England priesthood through the Brotherhood of St Paul and the 'the Bush Brotherhood', when he became a deacon stationed in Charleville, western Queensland in 1926. However, his health was weakened by a chest infection, possibly tuberculosis, and he was not ordained until 1927. His colleagues criticised the proposed ordination because they maintained that Father Smith was not a scholar and did not have a complex theological degree. Instead Father Smith was privately ordained for his other qualities such as devotion, humility, undemonstrativeness and a shunning of 'grand occasions, preferring working quietly and resolutely'.[24] Sometimes, as history shows, working in this way can leave the individual unexamined. Father Smith could also be thought of as a 'convert' with an understanding of existential thought, and being a 'people's person' with a stress on mending people's character and concreteness of life. However, he lacked a deeper knowledge of Biblical scholarship, Latin, Greek and Hebrew; the roots of the Christian text.

His great strength was that he was able to listen to people's woes and relate them to Paul's conversion on 'the road to Damascus' which could be seen in the everyday lives of people. In outback Australia these assumptions became real life, as other writers have shown where people had to cope with isolation, marriage break-up, the effects of drought and flooding rains, cyclones and social dislocation. John Smith later revealed that his father was an understanding man who related to those with whom he came in contact. The sociologist Berger's comments are appropriate to Father Smith:

> Most of us do not set out deliberately to paint a grand portrait of ourselves. Rather we stumble like drunkards over the sprawling canvas of our self-conception, throwing a little paint here, erasing some lines there, and never really stopping to obtain a view of the likeness we have produced. In other words, we might accept the existentialist notion that we create ourselves if we add the observation that most of this creation occurs haphazardly and at best in half-awareness.[25]

Father Smith sensed the 'bad faith' propagated by government as soon as he set eyes on the institutionalised half-caste children at both Jay Creek and later as

---

23 Rowley 1971b: 109-113.
24 Smith J 1999: 9.
25 Berger 1963: 75.

their numbers grew at 'The Bungalow Telegraph Station'. He would have heard the words of Jesus saying: 'Come unto me all you that travail and are heavy laden and I will refresh you' in his mind's eye, and saw both the idea of 'freeing' the children from the shackles of the government as well as putting them through baptism and then onto 'confirmation'. He wrote to Cook saying that some half-castes were baptised and he wanted contact with them. My mother told me that she was baptised at the rear of the Stuart Arms Hotel by his predecessor. She first met Father Smith in 1933.

Father Smith arrived in 1933 at the half-caste institution and by 1938 had baptised and confirmed a considerable number of the children; and had a concrete plan forming in his mind. Three things weighed heavily on him. One was the recent charging of the superintendent for sexual harassment of Aboriginal females.[26] Another was the racist language used by white people in Alice Springs when they were speaking about Aborigines – as Smith indicated to his son John.[27] And, finally, education as understood by government he thought farcical.[28]

Policy formation under Dr Cook was a high priority. Policy practice was lax, however, because bureaucrats could not articulate what they wanted and were unable to direct parliament toward a firm solution. One big drawback was that administrative staff from South Australia, such as teachers, found that living and class room conditions affected their health and were not helped by the racism of townsfolk of Alice Springs. Local white people along with transport and rail travellers looked on Aborigines and half-caste children with contempt, undermining the confidence of southern teachers working with the children. Attitudes ranged from, 'that they should be sent back out bush' to the idea that 'the government should not be spending money on educating them'.[29]

This upset Father Smith, the existentialist Christian. What looked like an oxymoron was that somewhere Father Smith had read, not just about how 'faith' in God works, but that there was another side to those ideas and that was 'bad faith'. To him this idea of 'bad faith' permeated everything about what was happening in Alice Springs. Governments oppressed half-castes and deprived them of the best circumstances that humanism could muster including the prospect of 'freedom'. Through his Christian theology Father Smith believed that he understood the dilemma and difficult decisions that had to be made about these children. Involved in this process was the choice of whether to remove them from familiar surroundings to live in alienating church homes, or leaving them to run wild and free in the township of Alice Springs and more than likely, in wartime, to be arrested by police or soldiers. To Father Smith, the

---

26   Smith J 1999: 50.
27   Smith J 1999: 51.
28   Smith J 1999: 50.
29   Smith J 1999: 51.

children appeared most free when they were taken away from the institution and demonstrated their capacity to hunt animals and gather other food they knew about and enjoyed. Father Smith sensed when he first saw them at Jay Creek that they were desperately unhappy, but he felt a change would occur when his brand of Christianity was applied.[30]

Of course, it was difficult for Father Smith to see or accept that he was replacing one form of constraint with another. Father Smith could not see that these children's escape was in fact an escape from an identity of which government wanted conformity. He recognised the oppressiveness but had no nature to bring it down. Father Smith, according to his son John, read and understood theories of religion and existentialism, and what became an anthropological theory of the early twentieth century — freedom was something that only God could bestow, and 'bad faith' was something that had to be endured.[31]

In the years between 1938 and 1942 Father Smith experienced successes and failures as his personal solutions of the half-caste problem matured. Early on in this period one of the older boys, Joe Croft, was sent down from the Anglican depot at Borroloola to Alice Springs where the half-caste institution now offered up to grade three primary school classes. Joe had already received a very basic education in Borroloola, and had shown some aptitude for studying at higher grades when transferred to Alice Springs. Because of this success a school teacher, Walter Boehm, along with Father Smith, tutored and encouraged Joe to sit for the South Australian Junior Certificate.[32] If Joe passed this test he could attend secondary school: but where? Through this philosophical crack Father Smith crawled as his ideas fermented into obliterating 'the half-caste problem'.

Joe Croft's background is interesting and relevant. His mother Nancy Croft contracted leprosy and was quarantined at the Borroloola ration depot. When Joe's mother was transported to the leprosarium at Mud Island he was cared for at the small but over crowded Anglican ration depot. Leprosy between the wars had become endemic and grew out of the nineteenth century labour shortage. A panicking colonial government imported a large Chinese labour workforce which was later attributed with introducing the disease into Aboriginal communities. Again, one of the reasons leprosy spread so quickly was that the Chinese who came to work in the Territory mining industry came without their womenfolk. This caused a glut of males who either developed casual sexual relations with Aboriginal females or took them as sexual partners. The Territory administration forced the Church to take its lepers back to Borroloola when the leprosy epidemics occurred in the late-1920s and 1930s. In a chaotic

---

30   Smith J 1999: 54.
31   Jaspers 1932: vols 1-2. See also Kierkegaard 1976[1936]: 73-79; Berger 1963: 163-164.
32   Smith J 1999: 54-56.

situation good people, driven by religious text, chose solutions outside the rule of law. But the priests had one priority, and that was to lessen the chance of the children being infected; most of the children were moved to Queensland. Joe, however, was one child who was sent south to the Bungalow in Alice Springs by the Anglicans; possibly because he had reached grade three at Borroloola. Administrator Cook complimented these strategies allowing Joe to move to the Old Telegraph Station. Cook was aware that with the aid of special tutoring, as mentioned above, Joe could and did successfully complete his junior certificate examination. As a mentor, Father Smith used the opportunity to then have Joe admitted to the prestigious College of All Souls Anglican boarding school at Charters Towers. Following this Joe entered the Queensland University to begin a degree in engineering in 1942. Joe's success validated Father Smith's idea that if you removed half-castes from their circumstance of poverty and degradation they would prosper. This success gave Father Smith sufficient evidence to convince both the Anglican Church and the Department of Native Affairs in Darwin that it was fulfilment of the idea that the half-caste problem could be solved.[33] Altruism comes in various forms and in Father Smith his was a genuine philanthropy, but Christianity can impose a life-long commitment and obligation if wrongly taking peoples trust in hand. This was Father Smith's problem but again he assumed that he had an answer where none previously existed.

But as the war gathered pace Father Smith's patience with government wore thin as bureaucracy overburdened theology. Authority and wartime chaos decided the fate of a number of half-caste boys, and briefly the half-caste 'problem' appeared to have a solution. Digressing slightly, by 1944-45 a number of things spurred Father Smith on to rethink his earlier ideas. First of all the war forced all Native Institutions in the Northern Territory to be closed except perhaps those run by zealots such as the Roman Catholic, the Lutheran and the Presbyterian Churches. The Catholics had two missions in Alice Springs: one was at Charles Creek; the other was at Arltunga, a town resulting from the gold rush late in the previous century. The Presbyterians created a hostel in Alice Springs where, in their view, the half-caste 'waifs' and 'strays' could be collected up in the style of Ida Standley's and Sergeant Stott's practice, thereby creating another 'Bungalow'. In an act of near-lunacy following the threat of Japanese invasion, the Presbyterians gathered up their camp children and took them to Croker Island, closer to the enemy lines. When the Department of Native Affairs evacuated many of the half-castes southwards, the Roman Catholic nuns moved their flock into the vacant buildings of the Old Telegraph Station. Bureaucracy had provided a barrier to Christian work but they soon adopted 'direct action'; pushing aside 'the rule of Law' that was replaced by 'martial

---

33 Smith J 1999: 53-56.

law'. This move benefited the townsfolk of Alice Springs because labour was scarce and Australian and American soldiers were arriving in growing numbers. In order not to offend white American sensibilities townsfolk surmised that 'full-bloods' could be kept out of town. However, there was still the 'night-soil' to attend to and the menial jobs like cleaning and domestic work where labour was needed; military planning allocated these tasks to those of full descent. On the other hand, many of the half-castes filled the jobs close to white townsfolk and military personnel. The more sought-after tasks were in the military kitchens where waste foods and offal were prized. In the middle of this chaos were the children of a number of women of mixed Aboriginal and other descent. Among these women were Hetti Perkins and her sister Mary Bray, then living at Deep Well Station south of Alice Springs with her husband Billy Bray and a number of their children. Among those who remained in town were Melba Palmer, Edie Espie and Maggie Smith and many more working girls. There were also a number of women from the Tilmouth family, and descendants of Afghan and other Asian cameleers, and mine workers. Some of these people were attached to the Nayda, Satour, Sultan, Furber, Ah Chee, Ah Fat, Ah Kit, Hong and Ah Mat families. These chaotic circumstances created situations in which many of the younger and older women were swept up in employment for the American and Australian armies while the children were left to their own devices. These events worked against Aboriginal families and favoured Father Smith's ideas.

Although the military began conscripting Aborigines[34] to some extent in work gangs there was in general only one form of employment; that was in the pastoral industry for men and domestic duties for women. And the *Aboriginals Ordinance1918* (Cth) appeared to fall into limbo. Coming from a world of drastic economic deprivation to one of total freedom was traumatic for Aborigines. It created too much freedom, too much money, too much food, which resulted in many of the children of half-caste families being left without adult care. Their mothers were working for higher wages and living in total freedom in military huts which were used as billets or tin shacks in 'Rainbow Town'. They worked unrestricted hours with little or no supervision. This work regime resulted in the women's lives being turned upside down and out of control. The younger children were left to run rampant around the township of Alice Springs, while their adolescent sons were taken north to work in military gangs and their daughters removed to work in gangs in military kitchens or as domestics.

Many of the boys who stayed were dragooned into military work camps, dressed as soldiers, fed by the military, billeted in army tents, looking to the entire world like soldiers. Martial law allowed the military to treat them as unskilled labour; on low pay and to be shifted anywhere between Darwin and Adelaide. Then of course there was stock work for the very young. Sometimes they

---

34   Berndt and Berndt 1987.

worked for their Aboriginal fathers as contract musterers or for nothing with white pastoralists. This was a time when there were no regulations and nobody to monitor what was going on. If stock work was unavailable fettling on the rail-lines helped provide local employment. Afghan camel trains by this time had been partly superseded by the railway that required skilled labour. Camels, however, remained the beast of burden in out of the way places and transport routes not serviced by rail.

For the young, in town, petty larceny and trafficking of sorts, such as fetching and carrying kept them busy. This is where Aboriginal children often began to turn to crime and they now had two types of police to evade. The police force was increased 300 per cent by the military police, who had in turn little appreciation of the children's circumstances and had limited scope to help. In their defence the job was made more complex because troop trains now passed through Alice Springs, trebling the population. Under these conditions Aboriginal children, military drunks and prostitutes filled the lock-ups. The children were often left to run wild while their mothers were working long hours. In addition to this added freedom there was the problem of tougher bush kids, such as John Palmer from Bond Springs and Malcolm Cooper from the Hermannsburg Malbunka family, coming into town and picking fights with the locals. Kids from Tin Town, or Rainbow Town in Alice Springs would attack the likes of Charlie Perkins as a Bungalow depot boy. Charlie was bullied by these bigger, tougher and better fighters and this was to have a lasting effect on him. Father Smith was concerned that some of the younger boys were getting detained by the military and local police, and as a way of combating this unruly behaviour, he started up a home for boys called St John's Hostel. It was from this establishment that Father Smith later arranged to take the boys to Adelaide, if their mothers agreed, because there were too many children to be accommodated at the public school.

These were admirable ideas but lacked much thought for the future. Some years earlier Father Smith had met a like-minded person in Dr Charles Duguid. Duguid, a Scottish migrant and the creator of the Ernabella Mission, was then in medical practice in North Terrace, Adelaide. Drawing on his experience of Christianising bush people, Duguid had carried out a number of surveys in the Pitjantjatjara lands in the south and south-west of the Territory during the 1920s and 1930s. He had already created an orphanage at Oodnadatta where white pastoralists could dispose of their unwanted mixed blood children or be taken directly from their camp mothers. Praise for Father Smith's Christian ministry came very easy to Duguid: they were both unable to see any hope in the way white people and government were treating half-caste children; besides they had the newspapers on their side to condemn current adolescent control practices. But changing laws was not the business of the Church.

These two men channelled their criticism mostly through Christian publications that only the faithful read.[35] Both Smith and Duguid focused their attention on pointing out the appalling outcomes of government actions.[36] They agreed that Christian care and teaching appeared to be better than the plans and programs provided by white Alice Springs townsfolk of earlier times such as Sergeant Stott, Ida Standley and more recently, Dr Cook. Smith and Duguid believed that the children were in the hands of unscrupulous white people, but that they 'could be trained to be useful and respectable citizens, if given a chance'.[37]

Father Smith's son John wrote later that he believed his father was a man of action and word.[38] In 1941 Father Smith utilised St John's Hostel on land attached to his rectory, to further develop his plans for half-caste children. With martial law and the Ordinances suspended he put into practice his actions and his word. The first intake of Aboriginal boys – Noel Hampton, John Palmer, William Espie, Malcolm Cooper and Charles Perkins lived in Father Smith's rectory. These boys will feature throughout this memoir. John Smith wrote the following:

> At various times during the period 1942 to 1944 the mothers of the … boys talked to [him] about the possibility of their respective sons having the opportunity to reside at St John's Hostel. With the result being that in each case they were accepted and appropriate financial and settling in arrangements were made. It was an arrangement based on trust and respect that would lead to better education chances being made available to Aboriginal children.[39]

These were fine words but it has to be remembered that this process began with an offer that was made on trust and where no records were kept. In hindsight assimilation was one aspect of the new idea and the other was Christianisation in the false hope that the 'half-caste problem' would disappear. The hope may have been that most of the boys would be spirited off to Adelaide before the end of the European War, and that many would never return.

Doubt in the minds of governments, Australian society and the churches over 'racial theory' and the success of religious moral action left the whole policy in a vacuum. The government was never sure whether their protection policies referred to bush people or half-castes. Bureaucrats and society in general were unsure whether to apply 'the rule of Law' or change the policy from general protection for either an undefinable Aboriginal population or create a new

---

35 Duguid 1963.
36 Smith J 1999: 62-63.
37 Smith J 1999: 63-64.
38 Smith J 1999: 65.
39 Smith J 1999: 65.

policy dubbed 'assimilation'. Australians, through the eyes of the press and a confused government, opted for a 'head in the sand' approach and left welfare to anyone who showed a modicum of moral action. Father Smith, operating on behalf of the Church did so in the belief his moral action was in good faith but history may not validate that perspective. Some believe that he took on a thankless task. I will leave others to ponder the question as to whether the boys who were taken to St Francis House were better off than those left behind in Alice Springs. But to answer this question there is much more to this, my story!

Chapter 4
Pembroke Street to St Francis House, 1946 to 1949

My mother, brother Bill and I left Balaklava sometime around late October of 1945. She took me to Father Smith's home for boys of mixed Aboriginal descent at Pembroke Street Kensington Gardens, Adelaide. My mother did this in the belief that education in a white urban setting would give me far better opportunities in life than she could offer me in Victor Harbour or Alice Springs. Hope existed in abundance on many fronts as the wars around the world were coming to an end. Father Smith had moved six boys from St John's Hostel in Alice Springs to Kensington Gardens and requested financial support to care for them from governments and the Anglican Church. This hope of financial support was some years in the making, and so the dream became more and more difficult to realise. I recall the tensions later at St Francis House. As time went by Father Smith was forced to fall back on charity to support the home; the practical side of theory now faced failure. On the other side of town in Kensington Gardens, St Peter's College stood as one model of education while Ethelton School in the working class suburb of Port Adelaide loomed as the alternative prospect.

Our mothers were never involved in the process of choosing what quality of education Father Smith would provide for us. In the end a public school was chosen because of the level of charity that Father Smith was able to muster. Although the Adelaide Anglican parishioners rallied, the amounts raised were still insufficient to realise Father Smith's hopes. In the short term accommodation was found, but the dreams of long term upkeep and an excellent education were already beginning to fade.

A Miss Murphy owned two houses in Pembroke Street; one was her home and the other was a disused private hospital. Miss Murphy was a nurse who had in earlier times worked with local general practitioners in the private hospital but after the practice failed she was left with an empty house. Miss Murphy was a charitable woman and loaned the property rent free to the Church. Father Smith looked forward to the boys being educated and socialised successfully at nearby Marryatville School but even in the early days that vision was beginning to falter. Father Smith's health was not robust and he was also anxious as to whether his wife could cope as a house mother to the growing number of children he now cared for. Mrs Isabel Smith, his new wife, was a refined lady who taught piano with methods more appropriate to upper class rather than working class students. But nevertheless, Father Smith went ahead and was soon in discussions with both state and federal governments for financial support while at the same time searching for a permanent home for the now seven boys in his care, and prospects for an increase. In 1946 he found a large unused mansion called Glanville Hall in an isolated location close to Semaphore beach, with a large attachment of land that would be perfect for the new hostel. However, this was all in front of him as I settled into Kensington Gardens and Marryatville School with the other boys.

I remember leaving the aliens' camp and being left by my mother to make up the seventh child at Father Smith's boys' home. I also remember being very upset, crying and being consoled by Mrs Smith. There were two women in the house, Mrs Smith and her mother Mrs Almond. I suppose I warmed to the women but was never greatly attached to them as they drifted in and out of my life. The other boys were a different matter. I remember some from the Bungalow such as Charlie, David Woodford and Peter Tilmouth but I had no memory of John Palmer, Bill Espie or Malcolm Cooper. Nevertheless I soon familiarised myself with them over the next day or so. They were in order of age, John Palmer, Bill Espie, Malcolm Cooper, Charlie Perkins, Peter Tilmouth and David Woodford. Because these boys knew me as a baby at the Bungalow they immediately called me 'Nicky' the name my mother had always called me. As soon as Father Smith heard the boys calling me this name he scolded them and ordered that I was to be called Gordon, the name on my birth certificate but one that I was totally unfamiliar with. Later, however, belligerent boys changed my name first to Brugget, and then to Biggo as we grew older. A nickname many still use.

I only saw my mother a couple of times in those first few years from 1945 to 1948. In my new home in Kensington Gardens and with my new name I walked to the Marryatville kindergarten and public school. I did this with the other boys and soon got used to the routine of going to school, but learnt little. The bad start I had at Kirribilli and Mulgoa continued at the Marryatville School. One problem was that I had never really been used to wearing shoes and I was always getting scolded for tossing them in the canals I passed on the way to and from home. Kensington Gardens is in the Adelaide foothills and had the many run-off streams that came from the higher ground. The canals were used by us to play in during the dry weather and provided short cuts to school – a shorter way to and from Pembroke Street – where I learned to play with, and kick, a football.

On the first Sunday at Kensington Gardens I began going to church and Sunday school. This custom turned into a weekly ritual that was immutable. The weekly kindergarten classes became a problem because I could not read well. I preferred to be distracted by the girls of my own age at school rather than learning to read, write and count. I had great difficulty in moving up from grade one to two. It must have taken me from 1944 to 1948 to complete grade one. I don't think I ever graduated from kindergarten at Kirribilli or grade one at Marryatville because Christmas always came upon me before I had mastered grade one lessons.

My eyesight was very good and I was reasonably articulate. I could, I remember, tell the class about walking up the foothills of the Mount Lofty Ranges with the other older boys from the home. I would tell my class stories about walking up the drains to Waterfall Gulley, carrying our galvanised iron sheets as toboggans to slide down the steep hill-sides on Saturday afternoons. I was careful in the grape season not to tell them about stealing grapes from Hardies' wineries on our way to and from the gully. Drawing was another of my preoccupations. I would draw gum trees, desert and acacia trees (*Kalka* in my mother's language). Other boys from the home such as John Palmer could reproduce Albert Namatjira style paintings and he would tell me about the *Kalka*. He would tell me about the *Kalka* nuts that his mother would make into necklaces for her many sisters. John's mother was a sister to my mother and we were very close to each other in the half-caste institution. John drew me to him in two ways. First he and Malcolm Cooper were good boxers and, second, both were really good footballers. Soon after settling down they taught me how to box and kick the footy.

There was no real call for me to learn how to box. I cannot recall being threatened, bullied or discriminated against by white people during my time in kindergarten at Marryatville, but the strains of living with the new boys prompted some self-protection. I think the reason behind learning to box was that I was just fascinated by John Palmer and because I was the youngest I was sometimes bullied by boys in the house. I know I was never protected in these public confrontations by either Mrs or Father Smith. The oldest boys, I thought, often took advantage of me by giving me jobs like collecting the hens' eggs, washing the bath tub and because I often threw my shoes away or wet the bed, they took every opportunity to tell tales on me, which made me angry. I did get some relief by befriending John Palmer, whom I thought of as a protector.

Nevertheless, I can recall fighting at Mulgoa and I carried the fascination forward. The older boys rigged up a punching bag in the back yard where they taught me how to punch, evade a blow and learn to skip. All this came in handy when Brian Butler was added to our numbers because we were made to fight each other. I cannot recall any malice, or intent, about fighting each other; it was mostly because we were the same age. Most of the boys were much older than me; their ages ranged from about ten and 11 to 14. I was seven going on eight and the only relief I got from the taunts of the older boys was when Brian Butler came or I went to stay next door with Miss Murphy. Brian Butler was the oldest son of a white contractor from Alice Springs. Brian's Aboriginal mother became very sick and was unable to care for him until she was cured, possibly of tuberculosis. With the arrival of Brian I occasionally stayed elsewhere – usually next door with Miss Murphy. I enjoyed this because she kindly allowed me to have toast with honey and fresh cream on top for breakfast, a rare treat. As time passed I became much more settled and happier; at the same time becoming closer to the older boys.

It was during this period of stagnated learning at school that I developed a passion for Australian Rules football. I learnt my skills in Kensington Park; it took a lot of practice but it provided me with some relief from the madness of continually doing what I was told. On most winter weekends the older boys and I would head up to Kensington Park to kick the footy and during the summer we would take the cricket bat and ball to the same park. Cricket was Father Smith's favourite sport and he had the skills to go with it. Being a Freemason, I realised much later, he had friends in high places; some were members of the South Australian Cricket Club, which meant that we were often taken to see Test matches from the members stand.

While at Pembroke Street we would often go via the back streets past the Kensington Oval to where Don Bradman lived while he played cricket for Norwood. We had to pass Bradman's house and Father Smith would tell us about how Bradman played for Australia and he himself played cricket in Brisbane for his church school. Father Smith's keenness on cricket spilled over into teaching, and it was he who coached us on the finer points of batting and bowling. These skills meant that as we got older we were always picked to play for the school as well as making up our own teams.

Although Brian Butler was not a cricket star his presence enabled me to have a reprieve from the stress of coping with the older boys because I had an ally. But the reprieve was short lived as his mother's health improved and the family moved to Port Augusta so I was again left to contend with the older boys. By this time the Japanese War had ended and we attended the celebrations in Hindley Street. The rejoicings began with dancing in the streets followed by fireworks displays. Everybody got dressed up and I was decked out in a brand new grey woollen suit, long woollen socks, and a brand new pair of black shoes. Then, on the day of revelry, we went by tram from Marryatville shops into the City where thousands of people headed towards Hindley and Rundle Streets. All the buses were packed with people. In the City we saw, and joined, large crowds singing and dancing the whole day through. We then went on to King William Street, after watching the football at Adelaide Oval, and sat in the gardens surrounding Government House as night fell, overlooking the River Torrens. All this was new to me, but the euphoria came and went and so did the big boys.

Father Smith earned extra money by taking on relieving jobs in other parishes as one way to keep his family and to pay urgent bills. I would travel with him in a borrowed car, normally the Bath's Chevrolet, to country towns as far north as Clare in the Barossa Valley, east to Mannum and Kan-Man-Too, near Murray Bridge and south to Narellan and Blackwood. Father would teach me how to serve communion and treated me like the son he did not yet have. In his relieving jobs in Adelaide I would both serve and sing in the choir. When I was as young as seven or eight he would dress me up in either a red or black cassock well before I could read either the common prayer or hymn books. We would go with the other boys to Unley Church, where we would attend the harvest festivals and then collect boxes and boxes of food gifts. We would all go to the church at Kensington Gardens and other places of worship in Adelaide itself. Father Smith would often go and assist with the communion services at the Goodwood church and it attracted me for two reasons. After church they had no Sunday school but had a great breakfast of scrambled eggs, a breakfast I always liked.

Father Smith allowed the boys to attend a nearby gymnasium every Friday evening during our time at Pembroke Street. There we were taught to use the monkey bars, roll on the mats, and swing from the parallel bars, together with more boxing and an exercise regime. The gym was about two kilometres from our home in Pembroke Street and we had two regular customs while going back and forth. One was to steal fruit in season from people's back yards and the other was to run along the tops of the highly manicured and closely-knit cypress hedges. These hedges were strange to us; we had never seen their like before. Most of the boys would run along the tops of these hedges, but occasionally a boy would disappear! We could never work it out until we were much older, how we could walk on top of them and why nobody was ever seriously injured.

Sunday school at the Kensington Gardens Anglican Church, however, was something of an event for there was nothing more significant in our lives than people telling us how different we were. These Sunday school gatherings were where we sang the same old Mulgoa hymns. From memory they were 'Bringing in the sheaves' and 'Jesus wants me for a sunbeam'. The hymns were played and the stories reinvented, punctuated by games such as 'put the match box on peoples' noses. For the white children with their sharp pointy noses it was an easy task but for us half-castes with our broader noses it was impossible. I remember the first time the white children and the Sunday school teachers yelled out 'you've got no nose'. We never forgot the embarrassment of being singled out.

As Christmas approached the bigger boys started to get excited about the long trip to Alice Spring. It was time too to acknowledge that at seven years of age the idea of Alice Springs being my home meant little to me. At the time my mother was still working at the Victor Harbour repatriation hospital and so it was seen as unnecessary for me to return to the Northern Territory. I was now the only boy left at the home. This first Christmas with the Smiths was a memorable one. Not just because it was the first one that I was conscious of but because I met the Bath family who really touched me. The Baths were a Christian family who attended the Goodwood Anglican Church and had befriended Father and Mrs Smith. The Baths had grown-up children and were, I guess, in their late 50s or early 60s. Mr Bath, I think, was a lawyer-banker and Mrs Bath was a housewife. Looking back, they were either wealthy or socially comfortable as the saying goes.

Father Smith would sometimes leave me with the Baths, and I liked that. There was nothing that I can in hindsight put my finger on but I liked them and I always felt safe with them. I don't think I was fully comfortable with Mrs Smith or her mother, probably because my manners were rough and ready. Besides I was not their child and came to them too late for them to change some of the 'bad' habits together with strange things my mother and Mulgoa had taught me. The tension was always high between me and the two women. Nevertheless, I recall I did take to Father Smith and the looming Christmas of 1946 eased some of the tensions.

At Christmas time I listened to stories about how Santa Claus would come down the chimney and fill my pillowcase full of toys, fruit and presents. I imagined I saw him in the dark as he moved across the room to attend to my stocking. Christmas Day turned out to be an exciting day and I received a big toy top, the first one I had ever had. True to the Smith's stories Santa left quite a lot of presents and other nice things. Soon after New Year, because I was the only boy left, I went to stay at Mrs Smith's brother's house on Semaphore Road, Semaphore. This was only the second time I remember going to the beach. The first time was at Collaroy, a northern Sydney beach in about 1943. There I recall the large expanse of water and being swamped by a big wave, nearly getting drowned in the process. Later I learned to swim at Mulgoa and because Semaphore was a very calm beach, I took to the water with gusto. The Almonds, Jean and Jack had a daughter Judith who was about two years older than I was. Judith along with a friend looked after me for the Christmas holidays. We swam most days from early morning until dusk and later returned after our evening meal to attend the sideshow and revolving swings in the fun fair on the foreshore.

This location was significant because it was close to where I would be living for the next ten or 11 years. One day Father Smith called and collected the whole family and me from the Semaphore address. We travelled about five kilometres south along Military Road to a big old mansion called Glanville Hall. The house looked like an English castle with a big tower on the southern end. I learned much later that the tower was built and designed by a Captain Hart, the original owner, so that he could peer across the sand hills to check if his cargo vessels had arrived from other parts of the world, particularly England.[1] The place had 15 rooms including a large lounge and dining room, a very big study and a ballroom attached to a common room or library. There was an annex which stood as a kitchen and serving room and a large courtyard complete with stables, with workshops as well as gardens at the rear. To Father Smith the place was perfect but in need of some repairs. The Australian Board of Missions and the Territory Native Welfare had to approve the project as well as put up some of the money for the repairs.

While this searching and purchasing was in full flight the issue of post-war development was talked about around meals at Pembroke Street. One point that caught my ear that I have never forgotten was the British testing on the rocket range, cutting through Pitcha Pitcha Lands. Early in 1947 Dr Charles Duguid, a friend of Father Smith's, spoke to him about the Australian Board of Missions getting involved in protests that were soon to take place in Melbourne, Adelaide and other places. Duguid asked Father Smith if he would help to organise the Adelaide protest at the Willard Hall in the City on 31 March 1947 and at a later date at the Adelaide Town Hall. That day sticks in my mind because Father Smith rounded up all the boys to attend the protest meeting. I heard Father Smith talking about the tests when Prime Minister Chifley announced the British-Australian compact in 1946. The project angered Father Smith and Dr Duguid and I overheard other prominent persons' names mentioned, such as Elkin, Thomson and Strehlow.

The newspapers were full of how Elkin (Professor of Anthropology at the University of Sydney) had betrayed Aborigines by helping government to steal Aboriginal lands. I think I wrote to my mother who was in Victor Harbour asking her if her mother was affected and I asked Father Smith if my grandmother could stay with us. Later it came to me that following Chifley's statement, an Aboriginal man called Bill Ferguson could be heard on the wireless protesting about the infringement by the British and Australian governments in taking Aboriginal land for rocket testing. Again I thought of my grandmother but Father talked not about poor Aborigines but the poor Church and nothing more happened as the purchase of Glanville Hall at Semaphore took-over the table-talk.

In mid-1947 Father Smith put the proposition to the Church and the Commonwealth government that they buy the property. This project could only be realised, Father said, if the Commonwealth broadened the welfare program it had adopted to include half-castes. Failure was not something that Father accepted and he was bullish even in the face of difficulty which at the time I thought was worrying. In any event, eventual agreement between the South

---

1   Dunn 2004.

Australian Education Department and the Australian Board of Missions allowed Father Smith to commence his project. So, late in 1947 plans for funds to run the project went forward and during the Christmas break of 1947-48, the Smith family moved into Glanville Hall. Looking around the property it was evident that a number of repairs had to occur; some of the windows had to be replaced, the front area needed attention and a whole new shower and bath area had to be added, along with a hot water system. One final addition was that a small two room apartment located in a building across the other side of the courtyard, that we called the gymnasium, was to be renovated for a cook and family.

Looking at the purchase over the years the deal was a messy one. In hindsight the process never looked or sounded real but the prevailing thought was that somehow we would soon move. In any event, the grounds and buildings of what was to become known as the House, were purchased by the Australian Board of Missions in late 1947, the purpose being to conduct a home for the education of 'part Aboriginal boys' from the Northern Territory. The Mission body was not able to find the total asking price of the land, so the Commonwealth government asked the South Australian Department of Education to pay the balance as well as about $1,600 in cash for repairs in return for a swap of other lands. A proposed road was closed, which gave more land to Glanville Hall. This made a total area of about 13 acres, allowing the sale to be completed for occupation by 1948. The cumbersome nature of the sale balanced around what the Church wanted and what the government needed. The Church wanted a trouble-free transfer of the land whereas the government and the local council were unable to say what their interests were and made the sale drag on until 1953.

The renovations and occupation of the newly named St Francis House went ahead. There was an addition of bathrooms, complete with a coke-fired boiler for hot water throughout, two additional rooms together with a bathroom and toilet for staff, and renovations to a small flat for the cook, Mrs Jean Almond (Jingle, as she was known). The dates of these events are vague in my mind but Jingle Almond, Jim and their daughter, Judith Almond (a young girl of about ten years of age) moved in. Of course Judith captured the attention of the older boys, but the real division between her and us was that our destiny was working class schools and the factory while the cook's daughter's was towards high school and the professions.

The Bishop of Carpentaria descended upon us for ceremonies to rename Glanville Hall as St Francis House. The bigger boys at the house had already been prepared for confirmation and the Bishop performed the confirmation ceremony at St Paul's Church, Port Adelaide. At the House the boys made a special road for the Bishop to drive his limousine along when he came onto the property for the official renaming ceremony. The new name was chosen by Father Smith. The choice was based on the personal nature of St Francis who was a man of humility and compassion. He humbly accepted his life of poverty, renouncing all his worldly goods and that was the philosophy he preached. His compassion also extended to animals, in particular, the weak and sick. Father and I built a bird bath that could be observed from his study, the structure of which made him very proud. I was also proud and had grown close to Father and more or less had accepted him as a father figure. Still, I could not understand our poverty, the rigour of religious education as well as that of public education, most of which went over my head.

In February the older boys returned from their Alice Springs holiday, with some of their relatives in tow. Soon, 11 more boys from Mulgoa arrived, including three from Alice Springs, Ernie Perkins, Richard Bray and Max Wilson. Ernie Perkins was Charlie's younger brother; Richard was Lawrie Bray's younger brother and Charlie's first cousin. Later, Lawrie became a great painter and Richard a talented Port Adelaide footballer. Finally the last boy, Max Wilson, was related to Robert Quartermaine, or as many knew him, Robert Tudawalla. There were some adjustments, mainly in our younger age group, as the pushing and shoving transformed into lifetime friendships, both social and political. One custom that simply came out of left field was that we always either shortened boys' names or completely emasculated people's names. I suppose this name-changing custom comes from deep within Aboriginal customs, but it also came from that belligerence to authority where a lack of confidence turns officialdom into informality. Many of these boys became men of consequence while others became tragic figures.

I became close to Charlie Perkins, Gerry Hill, John Moriarty and Vince Copley all of whom I have retained a lifelong connection with. I'll speak here about Vince who was born at Point Pearce sometime in the late 1930s. This Aboriginal government reserve was on the York Peninsula, some 120 kilometres from Adelaide. Its sister reserve was Point McLeay on Lake Alexandrina, which is adjacent to Hindmarsh Island at the mouth of the River Murray, where many of the people are related to Vince by tradition and blood. Initially, Vincent Warrior Copley grew up in South Australia but when his mother became ill with tuberculosis he went to live with his sister Winnie and David Branson in Alice Springs for a short period of time. But Winnie had her own family to care for and Father Smith agreed to take Vince. The Commonwealth had a say in fitting children like Vince and Brian Butler into care because the tuberculosis campaign was one of their programs.

Cop, or Fat Tarzan, as we called him, had an elder brother who died very young, and two surviving sisters Winnie Branson and Josie Agius. Josie married a great league footballer, Freddie Agius, and he played for West Adelaide, the team I followed. Although Winnie died young, she was instrumental in establishing the forward movement of the 1967 referendum and was significant later in national Aboriginal politics. I never knew until many years later, in fact not until 1988 when I was studying for my Master of Arts that Winnie's husband David Branson was of Marduntjara descent and had met Winnie when she lived in Alice Springs. Winnie knew my mother Eileen well; they both had worked together in the laundry at the Victor Harbour Repatriation Hospital located about 80 kilometres south of Adelaide.

During the following two years a number of significant events in my life occurred. The first was, I recall, that Peter Tilmouth, David Woodford and Charlie Perkins brought spears and boomerangs back from Alice Springs, things I could not recall seeing before. I was probably too young to remember bush relatives living close to the Native Institution in Alice Springs and using such implements to gather food. Peter, David and Charlie collected these hunting implements from Napperby and Bond Springs Stations where they spent the holidays. Their bush relatives lived in the stock camps at these stations.

St Francis House was about 500 metres from the Semaphore South beach and in those days it was largely deserted except for the mornings when horse trainers like the Hayes and Cummins families swam their horses. I remember the boys took their weapons to the beach, with me tagging along, and spent a lot of time throwing them. They began by attaching a *Kularta* (a throwing stick in Mardu) to the end of the spear and then throwing the spear an amazing distance; much further than without this implement. They taught me how to operate these two weapons together and I gradually became quite skilled. These beaches tended to have a build-up of seaweed and on the open sandy area we would build heaps of seaweed and have competitions at spearing these heaps. Soon however, it was time to go back to school but these were lasting memories.

The second major event at that time was buying new clothes at Semaphore the week before school started. The shoe shop was a place I had been to before but never with so many boys. The whole exercise took about two hours and all the shoes bought had leather soles. The boys going to Technical School had boots and the younger ones, including me, had shoes. I was sent two pairs of socks by my mother; the only time I received a present from her. By now my mother had married and was now Eileen Wickman. She and Reg Wickman her new husband moved to Alice Springs. The upshot of this was that the socks and trousers Eileen sent had to last for a very long time, at least two years. The socks were mended a couple of times and, in the end, the trousers had patches on both sides, like a pair of eyes in the seat of my pants.

It was likely that Father Smith was spending money he hoped to recoup from fundraising or from a less parsimonious Commonwealth regime. By this time the Chifley Labor government had introduced a new interpretation into the *Social Services Act 1941* (Cth) stating that Aborigines of mixed descent were 'non-nomadic'. Following this interpretation Aborigines of mixed descent began receiving social security payments such as child endowment and pensions. This subsidy enabled some mothers to pay the child endowment directly to Father Smith to buy school clothing, other needs and extras such as a train fare home to Alice Springs in the holidays. In any event we all got new clothes, but new clothes could not save us from what was to come in that our heritage was gradually whittled away.

The third event of significance occurred the day we turned up to begin our lessons at the Ethelton Primary School in the summer 1948. Everyone at St Francis House was up early in anticipation of attending the new school. Publicity about the new school attendees appeared in the daily press and some local bigots and parents were alerted to what the Church, or should I say Father Smith, was planning. Assimilation policies argued by the Commonwealth and ideas about altruism and 'race' were a common feature in newspapers. Father Smith favoured the notion that equality would emerge, not from ideologies drawn from legislation such as 'by reason of character ... intelligence and social development', as espoused in the 1941 legislation, but through social mechanisms and 'on trust'.

Whatever the case, all ideas were put to the test when we fronted up on our first day to Ethelton Primary School in the Port Adelaide district. Father Smith came with us and we marched as a group from St Francis House to the new school to be confronted by a howling throng of white mothers, fathers, and adolescent boys and girls barring our way in through the school's front gate. Father Smith was no man of force or violence; he left us some distance from the gate and passed with some difficulty and shouts of abuse through to the Head Master's room. The Head Master came out and addressed the 60-odd protesters and indicated that he would call the police if there was any attempt to stop these Aboriginal children from walking through the gate to be registered at the school. He had no illusions about forcing order; but Father Smith always sided with the boys' view when they had a couple of fights in the yard to settle their differences. Most Australians at the time probably accepted that the barriers to racial discrimination were social rather than legal. Father Smith tended to 'forgive' rather than rely on the 'rule of law' to control prejudice.

At the same time Mulgoa, the Anglican refuge in New South Wales, where we had been evacuated during the early war years, was in turmoil. The Church removed these people at the beck and call of the Military but ultimately failed them by not reuniting them with their people. The Church was driven to proselytising and tended to forget what the original purposes or commitments were to these refugees from the Japanese War. By the time hostilities ended some of the half-castes had returned to the Territory, but others remained in Mulgoa as refugees and had even become parishioners of St Thomas at Mulgoa! It may be argued that these Aborigines were happy to accept that the Christians were good people who protected and fed them when nobody else did, but the Church ultimately denied the rights of simple people and we still await entitlements of reparation in many ways!

The Church argued their educational ideas were more important than sending half-caste Aborigines back to their homes. Protestors accused the Church of denying this group their civil rights. Others argued that assimilation had already occurred, and that the children should be allowed to finish their schooling, allowing assimilation to further take its course. John Smith gives a spirited defence of the Church in his father's biography. However, John's work goes no further than accepting the Church's role in the assimilation process as fostering its own self interest. I am unaware of any action the Church took to protect people's heritage, to protect their human rights, their land rights or offer them compensation from the Anglican's stock of property wealth. The Anglican Church therefore still has much to answer for these events. There were older half-caste people who should have been repatriated and were never truly given the care for which they were promised and entitled. John Smith argues that the Church was in a no-win situation and it took time to resolve the complex issues. It was deemed that the only way out was to close Mulgoa in New South Wales and send the young boys to St Francis House to finish their schooling under Father Smith's guidance; and that is what they did. The girls were sent to St Mary's Hostel in Alice Springs. The Japanese War had affected many Aborigines, whose lives were never the same. White Australian people once more were more interested in revelling in their own windfall. The returned soldiers became Menzies cowboys –those who voted him in and later controlled the ex-service clubs and other conservative institutions – and in general despised Aborigines in any form!

In my case, my family was still reeling from the after-shock of the Japanese War. In 1947 Eileen and Reg's son Dennis was born at Victor Harbour. My mother was impetuous and was falling into situations from which she could never extricate herself. Many of her difficulties in life stemmed from her own upbringing, and while she had skills she could give to those who employed her, she lacked either commonsense or any idea of planning. I went to Victor Harbour in the winter of 1948 to meet Reg and to meet my brother Dennis for the first time. I never saw my mother, Reg, Dennis or Bill again until the summer holidays of 1950-51. I should mention here that as an adult Bill went on to serve in the Royal Australian Navy as a stoker for six years; including active service in Vietnam. I later speculated about the reasons why I had not seen my mother for such a long time. I thought that the assimilation policies of the Menzies government were one reason. As children of Aboriginal descent we would occasionally hear news on the radio about how the Commonwealth had reintroduced what they called the 'New Assimilation Policy' for Aborigines across Australia, which somehow were policies that affected us, our 'welfare' and education. Father Smith always pointed to the fact that we were 'wards' from the Northern Territory and the Anglican Church and Commonwealth government were responsible for us. We knew from our mothers that they had been affected by wartime employment and were paid less than white labour. I also knew from my family's internment at Balaklava that 'assimilation' meant that white people expected us to be like them: but we always knew we were not, and they made sure we were different!

The contradictory ideas about our relative importance and place in the world often perplexed us. Father Smith appeared in many ways to hold attitudes and values that were fair and reasonable to us, yet on the other hand he appeared more nationalist than others. For example, fund-raising was an activity we were always involved in. The staff and the boys were involved in raising money to contribute to the upkeep of the House twice a year. On one occasion we had a public exhibition night and our role was threefold: to perform a play called 'William Tell' as well as a gymnastic display; to help in running a 'fete' and finally to sell theatre tickets for a St Francis House benefit fundraising night. Almost every time these occasions arose the boys would get highly embarrassed. On the one level we performed the rituals expected of us in the general community such as singing the national anthem 'God Save the King', and after our play 'William Tell' had been performed we would lustily sing 'Land of Hope and Glory'. But we knew we were different in that we were always hungry, suffered the continual embarrassment of having holes in our socks and patches not only in our school shorts but also in our Sunday best. And to top it off, on many occasions we barely raised any money at all.

But for all the downsides we remained a close-knit group at the House, especially from outside attacks. When this happened we would close ranks, but there also were bitter short and long-lasting disputes among the boys. Let me tell you about outside conflicts. Most of us at the House had our own shanghai and we would go to the sand hills that stretched from the Glanville Fort to Escort House in the Grange. This was an expansive area of sand hills and we tended to fight anyone who encroached on our patch. One day the Port Adelaide boys led by the Wright brothers, Freddy and Jimmy, attacked us with sticks and bottles. A very dangerous business and we retaliated with our shanghais. We made our 'dingers' (as we called them) out of truck tyre inner tubes that were heavy-duty rubber that could shoot a stone a very long distance. All of the boys were rounded up and off we went to the sand-hills as a group to defend our patch. I did not see the Wright brothers for about two years after that incident in mid-1949.

The inside squabbles were both short and long-lasting. The first group to come from Pembroke Street in 1947-48, the older boys – John Palmer, Bill Espie and

Malcolm Cooper – had the wood on the younger boys because they could fight. Charlie Perkins and Lawrie Bray, who were first cousins, made up one tight group and depending on the issue and conflict would support each other. Then Vince Copley became a close friend of Lawrie Bray and would get caught up in any fights. Because I was much younger, I tended to be matched with boys of my own age like Ernie Perkins and his cousin, Richard Bray. The younger boys closer to my age had problems for one reason or another especially those who had came into the House at different times. On the whole, however, fights were few and far between and the general conditions at the House tended to send any real animosity among the boys, deep underground.

As I mentioned before, we could not escape nicknames at the House. Peter Tilmouth got his name 'Truck' because he worked each Saturday on a vegetable truck. When the Mulgoa boys arrived to join us in 1948, Jim Foster chose the name Truck; and it stuck. Jim Foster's nickname was 'Frog' which came with him from Mulgoa. Some of these older boys carried their biases with them and this was the case with Charlie and Truck. On one particularly fine Saturday morning in early 1949 Truck had given up his vegetable run and was working side by side with Charlie on a job near the cow shed at the rear of the House. Wally MacArthur was in charge of the work group. All of a sudden a dispute broke out and Charlie swung a full-blooded punch at Truck and hit him on the cheek cutting him below the right eye. As previously mentioned these kinds of disputes tended to divide along age and family lines; Truck was a friend of John Palmer, which meant that David Woodford immediately became involved. The argument Charlie had with Truck was over the roster duties; Charlie had long standing soccer commitments and Truck had changed them to suit himself. But these conflicts have to be understood in relation to families because they could and did affect dormitory sleeping arrangements, rosters, sport and other social relationships.

Other recollections involved room allocations of younger boys. It appeared to the smaller kids that when they moved into St Francis House that they were at a disadvantage regarding sleeping arrangements. The older boys occupied what must have been the original servants' quarters while the younger boys were allocated the original stable hands' quarters. As one of the youngest boys, I had one of the first choices of rooms; largely because I had moved in before the rest of the boys came back from Alice Springs in the summer of 1947-48.

Anyway, when the boys returned to St Francis House Vince Copley and Charlie's brother, Ernie Perkins, had the other two rooms upstairs in the southern wing, while Lawrie Bray and David Woodford had the last room on the south wing. David Woodford's mother, Millie, married Lawrie Bray's brother Norman Bray. Millie was a full sister both to Peter Tilmouth's mother Tilly Tilmouth and to the deceased May Hill, Gerry Hill's mother. Only in hindsight do I look back and ask the question: Why did I not know these relationships when I was young? We were kept in the dark and discouraged from knowing more about our Alice Springs relatives. The inference was that our future was with the white world.

In many ways it was the layout of the House that caused tensions too. Access to the bedrooms meant coming up the stairs that led to the tower through an annex to our three rooms. To get to the older boys' rooms you had to go past the pantry, which was in the main thoroughfare of the house, through the servery and up a flight of stairs. Other ways were either over the roof or by way of the fire escapes. We would use these pathways when raiding the pantry. The area around the pantry was like a honey-pot to the boys and many of us ended up in trouble for stealing things from it. Father Smith and family took the big forward rooms while the handyman, house and kitchen staff had rooms along the main corridor. Some of the cleaning staff of the House had been recruited from 'New Australian' migrant refugee camps in Europe, people outside called these workers 'Balts', a pejorative term I always thought was cruel. As a young boy I saw these people of Latvian and Estonian descent suffering much the same indignities as us. In the meantime, Jim and Jingle Almond came to live permanently at the House in 1948, while their flat in the gym building was renovated. Jim Almond never did take up his position as handyman because while waiting he took a job as a machinist at General Motor's Holden at Croydon, and while there, he lost his fingers in a machine accident. All these pressures added to the process of settling in and, as John Smith points out, his father was never a well man. We were never privy to the nature of his poor health, but he was wilting under the pressure to bring more boys down from the north.

By the time I was ten, in November 1948, I was acutely aware of the 'rigid controls' others in society had over me. News items about Aborigines made me and the boys I grew up with, sensitive to new ways the government would or could impose conditions on us. The news bulletins often contained information about how far governments would allow Aborigines to be educated, to receive full legal rights, how to behave, to enter licensed premises or even shops – where often we would be asked to leave for no other reason than the colour of our skin. These events had an impact on us and we would often hear about other Aboriginal boys who were the victims of discrimination.

News items gave white people ammunition as 'know-alls' to tell us what to do. As we came to know people more intimately they would reveal to us either our lack of civil liberties or our human rights, sometimes in advance of us knowing them. Fear of breaking these customary barriers or even laws, was a constant threat. When we played football we would be required to leave the training sheds immediately, similarly at swimming pools and picture theatres. On one of my mother's rare visits to Adelaide, I recall being asked to leave the Balfour's Cake and Coffee shop in King William Street in Adelaide. When we sat down there were still seats spare but we were nevertheless asked to leave.

Although Father Smith encouraged us to be proud of our past, the contradictions of religion and state policy played against their education theory and the relentless prejudices of white society. This was counterbalanced to some extent in that the boys were encouraged to write home on a regular basis. Writing letters meant that we did have some contact with relatives and we always hoped that this would improve our chances of school holiday breaks. On rare occasions mothers and siblings such as Bill Espie's brother Peter would visit. Freddie Archee, who later married my relative Myra Taylor, often came to visit as did Myra and Peter Taylor. Maggie Taylor, Myra's mother, was a close relative from Lilla Creek, so my spirits were always lifted when these visits occurred. Freddie was doing his electrician's apprenticeship and stayed at the Presbyterian Home for Aboriginal boys at Eden Hills, with Peter Taylor and others from around South Australia. When I wrote to my mother I would mention these visits and, later in life, she would recall these occasions when we met with Maggie Taylor at the Lutheran Mission Block on Gap Road in Alice Springs.

In 1950, my mother with her new husband and two young boys, Bill and Dennis, moved back to Alice Springs. My mother and Reg were overburdened with problems such as rent, accommodation and jobs. Eileen eventually got work as a cook and domestic and Reg as a labourer around town, but neither of them had capital for housing so renting was their only prospect. In the end even their prospects for renting were so poor that St Johns Hostel for boys gave my mother one room for a husband and two babies, plus a low paying job as a cook. But the marriage was under stress which meant Eileen neither had a place for me to return to in Alice nor the money for train fares, so I stayed at the House. Once again I was at the mercy and goodwill of the superintendent of St Francis House, and stayed there for the Christmas holidays once again.

But as the years passed the dream sold to our mothers came crashing down around our ears with a bang not a whimper. The image in everyone's mind was of an education of excellence. Father Smith's dream in 1945 was crystal clear in the minds of everyone who read about it in the *Adelaide Advertiser* or heard it from Father Smith's lips. Pembroke Street was in a bourgeois suburb of Adelaide that gave everyone involved a warm glow that success had arrived. By 1947-48 stresses began to show that assimilation was an ideology void of confidence. As the population of the House increased with new faces from Alice Springs and Mulgoa the image and the original idea was soon lost. There was a feeling that the House was being gradually transformed from a home for better education and care to an orphanage for motherless half-castes, a reform school for wayward half-caste children who were classified as 'welfare'.

It had taken more than a decade for Father Smith to fashion his ideas on solving the 'half-caste problem' through education. The wartime chaos in central Australia provided him with the opportunity to apply his belief that whatever he did would resolve itself in the end by faith alone. In spite of what the effects might have on us young children, he went ahead. His vision was grounded in a lot of hope. He hoped that the boys would cope away from their families; he hoped that the Church would find the money to feed the boys and his own family; he hoped that his own family would cope with the pressure; and his final hope was to find the money to pay the staff that came to work for him. In any event, 1949 was Father Smith's last year at the House, the year that his son John was born, the year I felt, rightly or wrongly, that he abandoned us for a new job and title: Canon the Reverend P MacD. Smith.

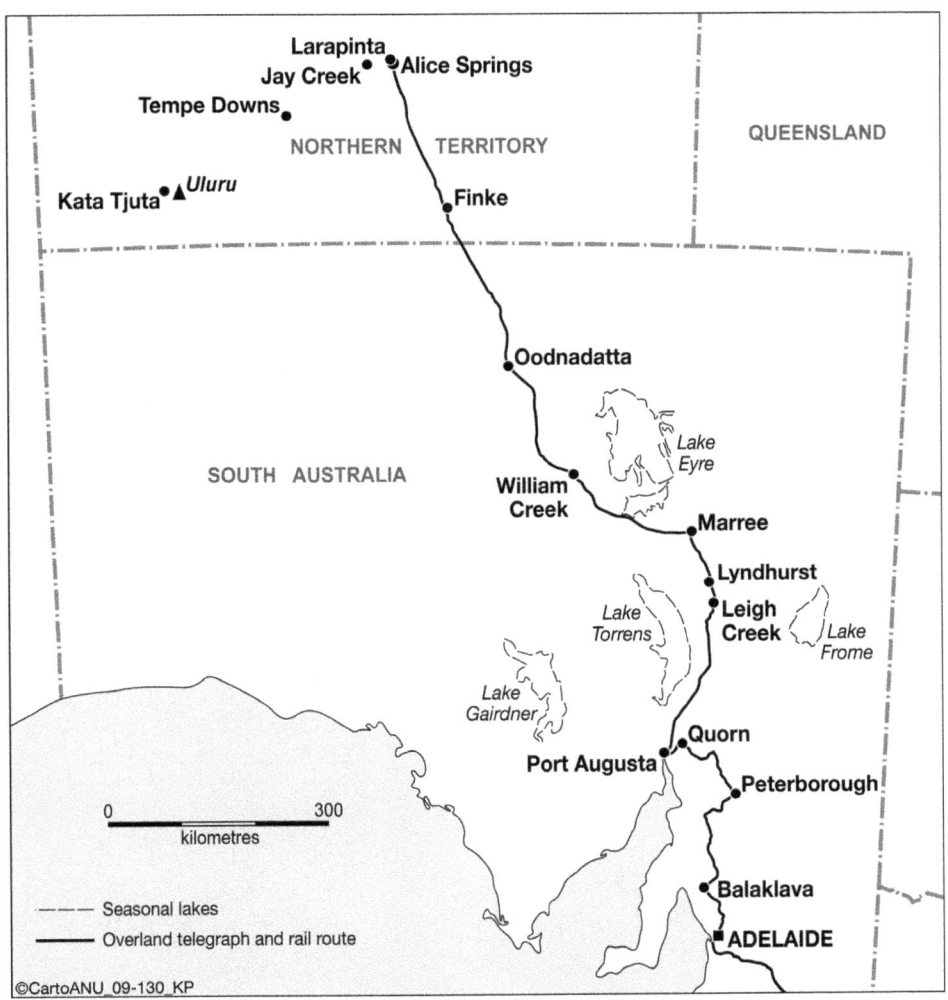

Figure 1: Map showing route of Overland Telegraph and railway including place names mentioned in the text. Courtesy of National Archives of Australia.

Figure 2: School children at first 'Bungalow', Alice Springs, 1914. Courtesy of National Archives of Australia.

Figure 3: [original caption:] Half-caste children sleeping arrangements, Jay Creek, 1929-32. NAA: 1928/59. Courtesy of National Archives of Australia.

Figure 4: Meal time at the first 'Bungalow', Alice Springs, 1929-32. NAA: 1928/59. Courtesy of National Archives of Australia.

Figure 5: Building new dormitories at Iwaputarka (Jay Creek) 1929-32. See wiltja in foreground. NAA: 1928/59. Courtesy of National Archives of Australia.

Figure 6: St Francis House on day of inspection for proposed purchase, 1947. NAA: A431/1. Courtesy of National Archives of Australia.

Figure 7: Father Smith and Frank Moy inspecting St Francis House for proposed purchase, 1947. NAA: A431/2. Courtesy of National Archives of Australia.

Figure 8: St Francis House, late 1940s: from rear left to right, Jim Foster, David Woodford (in hat), Laurie Bray, Peter Tilmouth, Malcolm Cooper, (front) Gerry Hill, Tim Campbell and Vince Copley.

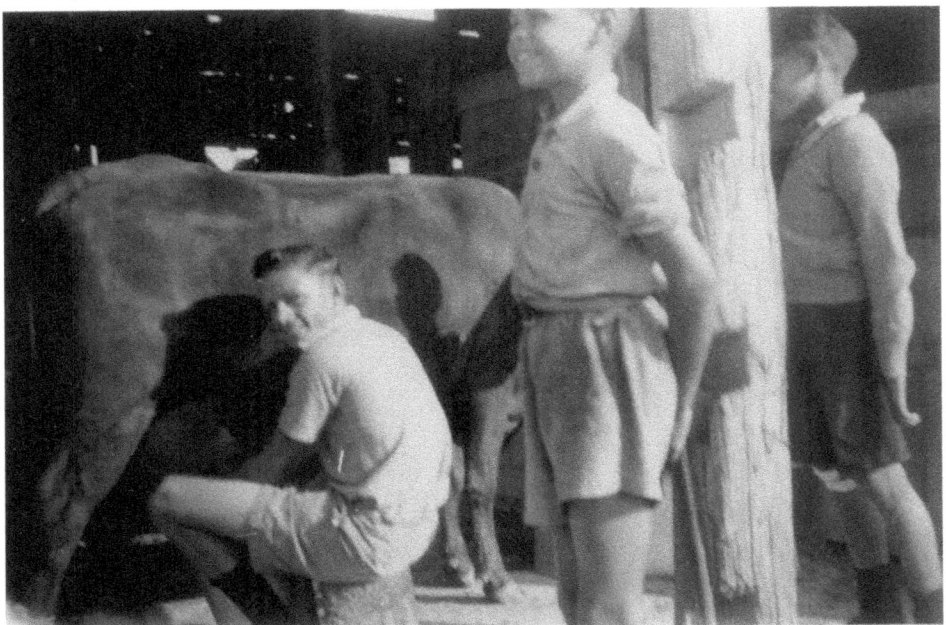

Figure 9: Mulgoa boys in cowshed, 1947: from left to right John Hampton milking cow while Tom Campbell and Ken Hampton look on. Courtesy of National Archives of Australia.

Figure 10: Mulgoa, New South Wales, 1949: from left to right James Stirling, Wally McArthur, Cyril Hampton and James Foster. Courtesy of National Archives of Australia.

Figure 11: Alice Springs railway station, 1952: self, my mother, Millie Glenn, Billy and Dennis at front.

Figure 12: Reunion of Amy Tennant, Millie Glenn and Mary Woodford at Rainbow Town, Alice Springs, 1951. These three girls were evacuated to Mulgoa at the same time as me.

Figure 13: My mother holding Sam, and Sandra on lawn at Administrator's Residence, Alice Springs, 1952.

Figure 14: Christmas 1952 at St John's Alice Springs: from back to front Jacky Campbell, Billy Briscoe (with hat), Phillip Bray in centre with Les Nayda and Harold Thomas (creator of Aboriginal flag).

Figure 15: St Francis House boys camping at Goolwa, 1953: from left to right Des Price, John Spencer, Denis Wickham (obscured), Jacky Campbell and Les Nayda (front).

Figure 16: St Francis House boys, 1953.

Figure 17: My brothers Billy and Dennis, at St Francis House in 1957.

Figure 18: Port Lincoln Soccer Representative side 1957. Self back row, second from left.

Figure 19: Croatia team, 1960. Charlie Perkins at back third from left, self fourth from left.

Figure 20: Charles Perkins with President of Croatia North Adelaide club, John Moriarty and self, 1960.

Chapter 5
Educated men or Christian misfits? 1950 to 1956

Let me begin by recalling how Father Smith's leaving affected me. Father Smith, as mentioned earlier, became a father figure not just to me but to some of the other boys too. Gradually as my eleventh birthday came and went I was beginning, like many of the other boys, to accept the fact that I was at the house for my own good and to get a better education. Along with the other boys I believed that we were there because our mothers had put their trust in Father Smith. My education continued as a series of failures even though the dream left by Father Smith was still the pathway for the good of Aborigines in general and in particular for 'mixed bloods'. We did know in advance of the Smiths' move but the big issue from the boys' perspective was the pace with which it all happened and the arrival of his replacement. While I did not display any outward psychological affects, inwardly, when I look back, I felt I became withdrawn and unresponsive to school and the other boys.

What possibly helped me cope with my feeling of loss was life on Semaphore beach, enjoying activities such as fishing off the jetty with Wally MacArthur, Vince Copley, Gerry Hill and John Moriarty. Soccer with Port Thistle junior's side also helped and would lead to a closer relationship with Charlie Perkins. But I kept the new boys from Alice Springs at a distance, boys such as Richard Bray, Des Price and Max Wilson. Some of the younger Mulgoa boys also got the rough end of my tongue too, like Wilfred Huddleston, better known as Boofer, and Tim (Bam) Campbell, Kenny Wesley and Kenny (Knobby) Hampton. Another outward display of my inner turmoil was caused by my general impatience with being lumped with younger boys because of my low grades at school. I certainly made a number of attempts to run away but soon after any escape, I lost courage to continue. In hindsight I always left the house a short time before meal-time and returned home just in time for meals!

In 1950 with Father Smith gone Charlie was regarded as one of 'the big four'. John Palmer had gone back to the Northern Territory too, and the new 'big four' were Charlie, Vince Copley, Ernie Perkins and David Woodford. My inability to cope spilled over into the winter of 1950, and I remember fighting with Charlie, Vince and Ernie. I do recall, however, that they teased me, and, in my own defence, I began throwing things at them. They were all bigger than me, and I got really angry with them, chasing them down the stairs from my dormitory towards what was the common room. In the end they evaded me and the only one who came back to console me in my distress was Charlie. At this time too I became conscious of Charlie and our friendship grew over time through sport. Charlie continued to have confrontations with other people such as Sergeant (Sargy) Jarvis (a part-time superintendent). Later these incidents revealed to me the tensions that were affecting many of us. We were mostly all unhappy but looking back, both Charlie and Ernie Perkins were never very happy away from Alice Springs.

My performance at school was affecting my whole existence. In 1950 I was 11 and spending my second year in third grade. This pattern of failure stayed with me throughout my schooling. Although I was older than my classmates my saving grace was that I looked much younger than my age. It was never about whether I was immature but more that I did not care and could never work out why I was at school because it all felt meaningless. Learning to read, write and spell was always a drag and as I mentioned before what I was good at was telling stories about what I did on weekends or on special occasions. The new Superintendent, Father Taylor, was very unlike Father Smith and knew little about our predicament and our past. In hindsight I recall I was not the only boy disturbed by the new Superintendent. It was a sentiment felt throughout the house. Out of this despair with authority my relationship with Charlie grew, in part, due to our growing fascination with the game of soccer. Many migrants, including those known as 'Balts' and New Australians, flooded the country and these people showed a great interest in us as individuals.

Charlie, with his brother Ernie, John Moriarty, Jerry Hill and I, began our soccer careers together and for the same team, Port Adelaide Thistle, or Port Thistle as it became known. In 1950 Port Thistle won the second division championship and was elevated to the first division. To qualify for the promotion the club had to have teams in the lower or junior division. Port Thistle management approached Father Smith for permission to rent a large field in the front area of St Francis House owned by the Church, and he agreed. Thistles had enough boys in the area to make two teams: a full juniors' team and a senior colts' team. The house boys filled the junior team and Charlie, 'Truck' and Harry Russel made the colts. From the beginning Charlie was a natural, as were many in the junior side, particularly Moriarty (Baggy) and Hill (Skrulyet). The boys from the house, to a person, played Aussie rules for Ethelton School or Le Fevre Technical School. I continued playing Aussie Rules for Ethelton Primary School on weekdays while Charlie did the same for Le Fevre Technical School. Charlie had great talent in both codes but I believe that he chose to excel at soccer as a way of evading the bullies at the House and as a way of venting his frustrations at Father Smith's leaving. He also resented the prejudice he confronted by those who played and organised Aussie Rules.

It is worth reflecting a little on Charlie's early life to gain an appreciation of why he chose to distance himself somewhat from the other boys and play soccer. Like me, Charlie was born at the Bungalow half-caste institution at the Old Telegraph Station just outside Alice Springs. Charlie was the ninth of 11 children of Hettie Perkins. As a young boy others often looked after him at the Old Telegraph Station while his mother worked on cattle stations, down the mines at Arltunga and later as a day girl in the three Bungalows around Stuart and Alice Springs. Following the Japanese attacks in 1942 Charlie's mother chose to stay in Alice Springs and work for the military. Unlike me, Charlie was not evacuated to Mulgoa and spent the war years as a young boy in Alice. This period shaped much of his life to come.[1]

Charlie spent some time at St Johns before going with Father Smith to Adelaide. However, the street problems of Alice did not go away and lingering bitterness often flared up, particularly between Charlie and John Palmer. Even though John Palmer had left St Francis House, Charlie's interest in soccer was a way, to some extent, of escaping from the ever-present bullying tensions in his life.

Out of all who knew him, I was Charlie's longest friend and although some may have at times been closer to him, or had greater insight into his personality than I did, I knew his life and times better than most. Perhaps, like Charlie, I kept losing my dearest and closest carers! Charlie often expressed his dissatisfaction to me about Father Smith's leaving us, as well as Church and government policies towards Aborigines in general. However much these events affected me, I'm sure that Charlie was equally affected, because we'd lost our specialness

Father Smith's leaving impacted on us all, but because I was the youngest I had to cope with being levelled at the house by recent arrivals that I did not know, even though I was related to many of them. I was no longer seen as one of the 'originals' with special knowledge on how things operated or as having any authority over younger boys. I now shared the same class at school with inmates who were much younger than me. I noticed that the new boys would treat me as a 'know all' and their attitudes came with their title of me as 'the Professor'. This really put me in my place, a situation that saw me become more of a loner.

However, I did have a few outlets away from the house. During my early time at Pembroke Street I was taken by Sargy Jarvis to Adelaide Oval to see West Adelaide play and even, in the late 1940s, to see Don Bradman. Sargy had met Father Smith at the Anglican Church in Alice Springs when he was posted there during the War. Father and Sargy became good friends and this continued after the hostilities. When Father moved to Semaphore Howard Jarvis tracked him down. At this time Sargy was a single man. He introduced his parents to Father

---

1   Perkins C 1975: 7-27. See also Read 1990: 1-50.

and the Smith family and soon we all ended up at the cricket. My connection to the Jarvis family continued as they had special South Australian Cricket Club membership tickets to all the big sporting games. Sargy Jarvis kept up the friendship until I left school, and meanwhile I'd go with the family to see England, the West Indies and India play against Australia. Having Sargy Jarvis as a friend with whom I could keep up these outings gave me a release from the tensions at the House. Before the war Sargy had played football for Port Adelaide with 'Big' Bob McLean but injured his knee on his return from the war, thus ending his football days. The Jarvis family all lived at Largs Bay, right near the Largs Bay railway station and owned an English car, a Morris Oxford. They would take me to football and cricket, and then onto their house after the game, have an evening meal, listen to the ABC Saturday sporting news and finally return me to the House. In my mind this special relationship was an escape from the mundane life at the House, Ethelton School and Church at St Paul's, Port Adelaide. Sargy was a favourite with the boys and often came to help out as a relieving superintendent.

Superintendents who followed Father Smith were discussed in depth among the boys, and I'll devote a small amount of space here to their period of control. All of us suffered in one way or another from Reverend Taylor's time at the House (Squizzy to us – the nickname of a notorious Melbourne gangster of the 1920s). He was an Anglican missionary who had spent time in Papua New Guinea and Malaya. Squizzy was a short, swarthy Welshman with a little dumpy wife we simply called Mrs Taylor and two children, a boy and a girl. These two children, sent to boarding schools in Adelaide, were kept at a distance from us and we never saw much of them. It seemed to us that when these priests came to dominate our lives, their wives did the dominating; they were more like ghosts always doing something else other than carrying out the duties that they had been placed there to perform. Squizzy, unlike Father Smith, never ate with us and the only time I ever had contact with Mrs Taylor was when I had to be treated for hepatitis, sporting accidents, gastro, cuts and bruises or was bedridden for one reason or another.

Soon after the Taylors arrived there was a severe outbreak of poliomyelitis. Many children in the Port Adelaide district were infected and so were some of the kids at the House. The first batch of boys infected were the two new Bray brothers Phillip and Robert, together with Glen Roberts, Gerry Tilmouth and Trevor Read. The Bray boys were related to Charlie and Ernie Perkins by marriage. Glen Roberts on the other hand was someone who was born in Arnhem Land and had been at Mulgoa with his mother Alice. When Mulgoa was closed, Glen went with Alice to St Mary's Anglican Hostel in Alice Springs but was sent south to St Francis for reasons which we were never told. The type of polio that the boys contracted seemed different to that of the children I had seen in the

Adelaide Children's Hospital when I went to have my tuberculosis immunisation injection. The children in hospital were strung up in big crates with ropes holding their legs up and some even in iron lungs. Phillip and Robert Bray were kept in a special room near the front entrance of the House. Most of the infected boys appeared to get over the paralysis fairly early in their confinement whereas Phillip and Robert's illnesses lasted for over 12 months.

When the polio epidemic was at its peak in-door activities were banned as quarantine barriers were put in place. Activities at the House were severely restricted together with those outside such as schools, picture theatres and public events, except football. I recall that much of the time we spent either on the beach or fishing off the Semaphore jetty catching 'Tommy Ruffs' and 'Mullet'. Another haunt was down at the Ethelton Swimming Club located near the CSR Sugar Refinery on the Port River. After our fishing expeditions we brought the catch back to the House, made a fire behind the boxthorn bushes, cooked the catch and stole potatoes from the pantry for a fish and chip meal. Another fishing haunt was the Port River swamp located at the back of the Ethelton 'dump'. The swamp was next to the Council tip where we went rafting at a location we called 'the deepy'. Some school days and many weekends would see us floating around 'the deepy' spearing flounder or flathead. So we did have a reprieve from the rigours of life under Squizzy Taylor's authority; but this time was all too short. It seemed to us that a far-reaching change had occurred but the solution never really dawned on us. All we knew was that life had become more difficult. Added to this was the drastic increase in the number of boys living at the House, from 17 in 1949 to well over 40 by 1952. In the summer of 1952-53, my own brothers Bill and Dennis made up part of the growing population of well over 50.

Taylor's period at St Francis House is remembered by all as a period of brutal repression. Taylor, I suspect, was a sadist who revelled in the power he exerted over a bunch of hapless half-caste kids. I have not been able to find one boy from the home who could say a good thing about Squizzy and his family. The period from 1949 to mid 1952 when the Taylor's were in charge was the most authoritarian regime at St Francis House. The first inkling that things were changing was that Squizzy used to control us with a one metre rubber hose. Squizzy would wake us up in the morning and give us ten seconds to be downstairs for breakfast. If his orders were not obeyed he would wait at the bottom of the stairs and flog boys indiscriminately, and with force. If you were hit by this hose it caused great swelling and this was not the only time he used it. He would hit boys when they were in the shower for taking too long; this overstay may have only been by seconds. In the showers and baths there was no escape due to the narrowness of the passages and I often had great red stripes on my legs and back as did other boys for taking too long to get out of the shower. This treatment was cruel and it got worse if fruit or other foods were stolen from the pantry. Everybody including the high school and working apprentices would be assembled in the common room and made to sit down at the school desks spread around the outside of the room. Squizzy would then hold court by walking up and down with the hose in his hand, and slamming it with great force on the end table. At times there were nearly 40 boys crowded in that common room shivering and highly intimidated for trivial complaints. Squizzy would use the loud hailer to assemble us. While seated in the study desks he would make us put our hands on the desks and he would slam the hose between our fingers. But Squizzy was not nearly so hard on himself. He had an intercom system installed by the Queen Scouts for his convenience; it was used to summon children to his study like a concentration camp.

We felt that we were mistreated and could do nothing about our circumstances. If any of the boys committed a misdemeanour the process was standard. The court and sentences were forcefully meted out by public exhibition. These courts and other floggings took place fairly regularly. As time went by complaints must have filtered through to the Bishop of Adelaide, who intervened. There was no inquiry but it was stated that reforms were in train and, I recall, that here we were at the Churches' and government's bidding, many without parental consent, being brutalised by church-appointed officials trusted to be humane. During my research for this book I was unable to find any reports or records of Taylor's or the next Warden's term – perhaps they have all been mislaid!

Things got worse with the arrival of Reverend Goff Sherwin in 1953-54. The Reverend Sherwin came to St Francis House after serving the Church in Papua New Guinea. He took on the role after serving in that region during the Second World War. We were told that Sherwin was an Australian army commando and had been involved in liberating New Guinea. It was said later that he came to reform the boys after the chaos that had been created during Squizzy Taylor's regime. By the time Sherwin arrived at the House there were still close to 40 boys. Some of the 'originals' had left for the Northern Territory while others were still boarding at the House, completing their apprenticeships. 'General Goff', as we secretly called him, was quite a big man of strong stature, large chest, a bald head and powerful legs that, when not in a cassock, were dressed in army-style khaki shorts. 'The General' reintroduced early morning rises, chapel mid-week, confessions on Friday night and stricter retirement times for all junior and apprenticed boys.

It is quite strange that when strict rules are clearly set down, boys will find a way to circumvent them. For example, on most Friday nights the Port Adelaide and Semaphore picture theatres had movies, a popular night out for the boys. During this time all hotels closed at 6pm, but there were always dances at the Port Town Hall and the picture theatres were almost always packed to the rafters.

'The General' would hear confessions between 7pm and 8pm. The older senior boys with girlfriends had a system of going to confessions early. After they would bribe the younger boys with money to make sure that when 'the General' did his night rounds the beds would be full, or so arranged that pillows were placed to fake occupation. If 'the General' was busy he would let the younger boys fill in for him.

Each dormitory had a fire escape and boys would file down these escapes to either meet their girl friends in the outer grounds or go to the Semaphore or Port pictures. All sorts of things were traded to help make the system work. Money held priority but food was a very tradeable commodity, clothing was another, and I remember getting my first long pants from Moriarty as a trade. Football boots, socks and jock-straps were favourites and I cannot ever remember the system breaking down. Some may have been caught in forcing the system during the week but that was not as serious. My 'Stanley Mathews' baggy soccer shorts were a trade and I think I passed on my long trousers to 'Skrulyet' Hill for a trade. The military regime of 'the General' lasted for a year or so before the next Superintendent came and life fell back somewhat to normal.

In the three years from 1953 to 1956 we had three lay-people, Mr and Mrs Morris Wilson and Malcolm Bald, as superintendents. In this period religion was not as strictly imposed and, it therefore took a back seat to most other activities. The first Superintendent was Mr Morris Wilson (Whicky Wilson to us). Whicky had mission experience somewhere in the Pacific but I never knew much more than that. Morrie, as his wife called him, was a big strong man with rusty brown hair, freckles and bow legs that made him walk like a duck. Morrie, as I'll call him here, was a personable man. I think he tried very hard to bring a more humane approach to the care of the boys from the Territory, recognising to some extent the trust of parents to fulfil a government policy paid for by Australian taxpayers. The policy never reached the quality of excellence it purported to be in the beginning and conditions never rose above a rudimentary level.

We wore the same cheap shirts, the same shoes that we mended ourselves, the same basic food and perpetual gifts from 'harvest festivals' as well as the same patched pants and socks. The same mothers' clubs would come to mend our clothes, sheets and pillowcases and tablecloths. Being the perpetual recipients of the niggardly charity of others was a demeaning experience. So too were our living conditions that endured for 11 years. I mopped the same old floor boards each week that Captain Hart had put in place in the late nineteenth century when Glanville Hall was built. Similarly, the bedrooms never changed as more boys came and the gymnasium was never built. The workshops remained in the same dilapidated condition left by Captain Hart. The courtyard that was set down in the days of horse and cart, where we learned to play soccer and cricket with stolen tennis balls, remained in its original condition. The assimilation policy achieved one thing for white society and that was making sure that the culture of our Aboriginal progenitors would be changed forever; and that that was achieved as cheaply as possible.

One great problem that Morrie and his wife (Turtle as we came to know her) had was how to treat the younger boys differently from the senior working and high school boys. Some of the older Mulgoa boys like Wally McArthur, and Harry Russell were indentured and successful apprentices, as were some of the 'originals' like Charlie Perkins, Malcolm Cooper, Peter Tilmouth and Bill Espie. They also paid board and so expected a measure of independence which Morrie and Turtle found very difficult to properly work out. It may have been Morrie's increased sense of authority at having both the Church and government behind him in making people behave in accordance with the policy of assimilation, and not just do-gooders 'serving the Church and the State'. But the worst thing that Morrie did in trying to establish his authority was physically to attack the boy's own true hero, Wally McArthur.

Before Wally came to St Francis House he was already a champion rugby player and runner. By the time Morrie Wilson came Wally was the hero of all the boys at the house and most learnt to play rugby league in an attempt to emulate him. The Mulgoa boys had played the game amongst themselves in New South Wales and at a higher level at Penrith and Mount Wilson secondary schools. For these schools they became champions; in particular Wally, James Stirling, Harry Russell, Jim Foster and Cyril Hampton. Later younger boys followed in Wally's footsteps: boys like Ken Hampton, Tim Campbell, Gerry Hill, John Moriarty and Wilfred Huddleston. St Francis House boys continued their association with rugby league by forming their own team called Semaphore junior colts. They also played rugby union for Le Fevre Technical School and it was there that Wally made history by setting the fastest running time by a schoolboy. He was even touted as an Olympic hope by amateur athletics officials. So Morrie had created a huge problem for himself without realising it. Wally McArthur never said what the real issue was but we do know that Morrie Wilson slapped Wally's face. Wally responded by telling Morrie that if he was not the Superintendent he would have retaliated. This response shows just how conditioned we had become and how we instinctively bowed to authority. After this Wally left the House and Morrie Wilson never regained the respect of the boys that he had once enjoyed. What followed was a series of revolts not just by 'the big four' but by both young and old boys.

To add to Morrie's woes, the South Australian Education Department sold off some of the land around St Francis House for a large housing project. Hundreds of what the government called 'temporary homes' were created to house needy and migrant people. This resulted in a number of issues as more people moved closer to the House. Port Thistle lost the use of the spare land as a soccer ground; more young women came closer to the house and, finally, it caused strife between the new populations and the Aboriginal boys at the House.

Port Thistle Soccer Club moved to a new ground on Robin Road about 500 metres away which was not a calamity in itself but it cut off the major advantage it had of signing up the new boys arriving at St Francis House. By 1955 many of the top players were poached by the burgeoning 'New Australian' clubs such as Port Adelaide, Juventus, Polonia, Budapest, the Dutch Club Orange and a team called International. By 1955 Charlie was a first division player while Moriarty was still at school and destined for an apprenticeship.

Many of the boys at the House, including myself, were influenced by the increased availability of local girls and young women. In the evenings once dusk fell and the after dinner meal chores, such as washing up for 50 boys and staff, was completed, boys could be heard escaping to the temporary homes where we would meet our girl friends or head for a prearranged location on the House property. There was a time gap of about one and a half hours between the end of meals and bedtime so plenty of cover existed for us and the girls. From the temporary homes you could hear the girls' mothers yelling at them to come home, searching the grounds of the House as a last resort. However, no real trouble or long term romances ever eventuated from these liaisons. Sometimes other encounters took place on Saturday afternoon matinees at the Semaphore picture theatres, attended by most of the school-aged boys from the House. The theatres were where 'race' came in and there it ended, but once the lights came on it was all over for a week as things went back to normal and the social divisions of both race and gender returned. Morrie Wilson, however, never bothered himself too much by the problems of discrimination. Like Father Smith he put more trust and faith in Christian morality rather than 'the rule of law', but his time at the House was coming to an end.

In 1955, Malcolm Bald, the handyman and Morrie's assistant took over as Superintendent. Levelling had returned as a way to understand government policy where Christian values were mistaken for liberal ones and our heritage was set down in international law; but these concepts were either overlooked or totally ignored. Later as a student of politics, it always seemed to me, when reading Menzies's American lecture on Australian law that the prime minister of the day had no sense of human rights, mainly because it was an idea espoused by European Fabian Socialists. Menzies believed that those who inherited British law were protected by the underlying principals of an outdated Magna Carta. Race politics in Australia, in Menzies's mind, was set to disappear under his watch.

Malcolm Bald was a local man from Largs Bay and the son of a fitter and turner who worked at the Osborne Power Station owned by the Electricity Trust of South Australia. He had attended the Le Fevre Technical School and was the second of three boys, all tradesmen of one sort or another. At the same time they were all members of the First Semaphore Boy Scouts and Malcolm (or Mal as we knew him) rose to become assistant Scout Master. We got to know him in about 1952 when five or six of the boys at the House joined his scout troop. The boys from the House were encouraged to join the Scouts mainly as an outside activity during the school holidays while the majority of boys returned to Alice Springs. It was in the Scouts that we got to know Mal as someone who was interested in Aboriginal politics and who showed an interest in what we could teach him about traditional life too. Poorer than your average Scout, we were helped by wearing cast-off uniforms from other branches and boys in the troop. The benefit that we saw was the end of year four-week or Christmas-time camps. The troop had a very large block of land at Mount Lofty in the Adelaide Hills and scouting activities took up quite a bit of our time during these summers.

Scouting had a deep attraction for the few boys who took it up as it offered a friendship we seldom experienced. Mal was a King/Queen Scout and an avid yachting enthusiast. He attended the Largs Bay Baptist Church and through his civic activities and connections he was offered the job of handyman and eventually the general assistant's position under Morrie Wilson. As time went by Mal became integral to activities at the House. At the same time he continued his scouting duties around the Port district.

One of the things that interested me greatly was Mal and his brother's fascination with cars and motor bikes. Lance Loftes, a local motor bike mechanic and sales dealer in second hand and new motor bikes, was one of Mal Bald's close friends. As Mal became more integrated into the activities of the House he bought an old Chevrolet fruiterer's van, stripped it down and it acted as a carriage for the boys. He also built himself a scramble bike and sidecar, working on his truck and racer whenever possible. At first he used the English Velocette motor cycle or Velo for short, as a single racer but later changed it around to take a sidecar. In his youth Mal raced as sidecar speedway and road racing passenger for Lance Loftes and this probably was the impetus to put a sidecar on the Velo and practice in nearby paddocks. Other boys were terrified of this machine but I got on gladly and he used me to practise on his reconstructed scrambler. When he came to the House he continued his activities and nobody seemed to mind. As it happened Mal Bald took us to Rowley Park Speedway and while this event was a big hit with us, we were an attraction to the white speedway crowd too. All this was very new for us after being cooped up by the priests, forever going to Church and mixing little with the outside world.

Morrie Wilson's more relaxed approach at the end of his term tended to flow on to Mal's attitude with us. He would take us up to Loxton and Renmark where we would camp in the Anglican Church Hall for the whole seven or eight weeks of the Christmas break. Fishing in the River Murray, swimming most days and spotlighting for rabbits and kangaroos at night, were all new and exciting. One day we were fishing at Harple's Bend, up river from Loxton, when a number of us boys – Gerry Hill, Richard Bray, John Moriarty and I – were sitting on a log when I noticed a tiger snake under the log. We yelled out to Mal, who grabbed his single shot 22-calibre rifle and came towards us where he could see the snake. Mal put the gun down low and took a shot at what he could see. Moments later the snake, a huge two-metre brute, burst from the log and before Mal could reload the snake turned towards us with raised head and hood like a cobra. Its intentions were very clear. I was the only one with a stick and as the snake reared its head to strike I swung out in a classic cricket hook shot to the leg, caught the snake just below the head and down it went. The snake had a broken neck, but at that moment all you could see was river-sand dust and this big fat body of the snake squirming in the dust. Mal and I were still close to the snake. He took another shot as he saw its head move and killed it. I swung around to see if any of the other boys were close but they had all bolted a good 20 metres away.

That was a good year for me. About 14 of us had gone up to Loxton that Christmas and the scare at the log was the first of two incidents involving snakes. The second involved me, Ken Hampton, Boofa Huddleston, Gerry Hill and from memory, Les Nayda watching a snake swim across the Murray. There were two men in a small rowing boat who were fishing on the other side of the river and they watched the snake pass them on its way to what seemed a distant spot up river. But somehow, the snake kept floating towards us and we dropped our hand lines. The only defence we had was a large log which Ken and I decided to grab and swung it towards this large tiger snake that appeared determined to land where we were fishing. Luckily for us the snake dived under water and it must have been another 20 minutes before we saw its head come up near the top of the water and go down again. We were moving around, now with a shorter stick yet it was another five minutes or so before it decided that it had had enough and swam back to the other side of the river.

Some days later John Moriarty, Gerry Hill, Richard Bray and I, all strong swimmers except Fig, as we called Richard, decided to swim across the Murray River. The current was quite strong as we set out on a race. Hill and Moriarty were well in front but I could hear Fig grunting, as I turned around to see where he was I could sense he was struggling and as I turned a second time, down he went. I yelled to Hill and Moory (Moriarty) who were both some distance away that Fig was in trouble and I dived to search for him. The Murray River is the colour of strong milk coffee, but down I went and suddenly something grabbed me from the back and I swung sideways and spun him around, grabbed him in turn by the neck and made my way up to the surface. Fig was in trouble, coughing and spluttering, as I made for the shoreline. Hill and Moory caught up to me pulling Fig up the bank to safety. Mal Bald was livid when he heard the story and Fig copped the biggest telling off I had ever heard Mal give. I still feel that had I not been so close to Fig he would have drowned. Although Fig never became a strong swimmer he went on to have a great football career with Pioneers in Alice Springs, Port Adelaide and Exeter.

Meanwhile Malcolm Bald became the Superintendent of the House in 1956 even though a government inspector had recommended earlier that his employment as a handyman and sports facilitator at the House be terminated because he did not have the appropriate skills or experience. It is, therefore, ironic that the recommendation by a Northern Territory administrative welfare officer was not only overlooked but that Mal later went on to become the Superintendent! Perhaps it highlights where we stood on the social ladder and how little the Church really cared in those years to instil forms of transparent management.

After I left the House I never saw Mal Bald again until the year of the referendum on constitutional change for Aborigines in 1967. He was then living on an isolated farm between Murray Bridge and Karoonda in South Australia with two young boys. I later heard that sometime between then and the early 1970s he left South Australia for the west following two prison terms; and while there I heard his life was cut short in circumstances I leave for other historians to investigate. It is only in hindsight that I recall a number of incidents that were sexually inappropriate while he was in charge of us. Mal would often take the younger boys out to secluded locations at Torrens Island and Outer Harbour where we would all swim. The mangroves were about 30 metres deep providing ample cover for Mal to sit on the bank and watch 15 or so young boys slide naked down the muddy bank of the Port River. I leave my readers to draw their own conclusions about his character. Suffice it here to say that his downfall made me realise how vulnerable the boys at the home were when we were subjected to the care of a number of misfits who were supposed to look after us both physically and spiritually. There were other incidents over the years of the staff behaving inappropriately, such as overzealous touching while supervising the boys' bathing at night. These were people employed by the Church and the State.

Late in 1956 I left St Francis House for Mrs McGee's house at Semaphore South, after spending Christmas in Alice Springs with my mother. During this holiday I spent a lot of time listening to stories relayed by my mother and her sisters Eddie Kenny, Maggie Taylor, Ruby Tilmouth, Nora Laughton and lastly Hetti Perkins who had looked after these and many of the other half-caste girls in the three bungalows around Alice Springs in the period between the wars. Some of my memories returned with their help. When I left St Francis House I could barely read and write; I had spent much of my school life repeating year after year until I was too old for primary school. When I left for the last time I was nearly 18, a Christian lad believing the world was full of good Christians. My livelihood lay not with my education, as Father Smith believed, but with my sporting ability alone, but that could have happened anywhere. My heritage had been attended to by nobody and its reparation came only in part and for that I had to tread a very long road. The beginning of that journey came mostly over the next four decades, the story to which I now turn.

Chapter 6
Life after St Francis House, 1957 to 1964

The general thrust of race policies in the 1950s was 'new assimilation'.[1] For Liberal and Country Party politicians this was the status quo, which was for us to conform to the idea that Aboriginal culture, language and peoples would soon disappear, and we would become like other white people on the continent. When this meltdown was complete our citizenship would be reinstated. This notion harks back to Macquarie's little known proclamation of 4 May 1816 stating that all Aborigines in the British-claimed area of the continent would be British subjects and would be equal before the law.[2] And, in order for this to be achieved the dominant society provided taxpayers' money for us to disappear into the morass of white society. However, we wanted our heritage, wealth, land and a fair share of the human rights that flowed from the 1949 United Nations Declaration of Human Rights and other United Nations' covenants.

It was in this milieu that I left St Francis House in the summer of 1956, a failure as an educated Aborigine, thousands of miles away from my birthplace and my people's culture. It was not just assimilation policies keeping me from my heritage but the ignorance and prejudice of Australian society and politics. The Anglican Church forced me to be a good Christian, but I was a misfit in Australian secular society. I had no place to stay when I left St Francis House and would have been homeless if it had not been for the kindly Mrs McGee, the woman who washed our clothes and bedding at St Francis House. She offered me board in a room on the back veranda of her home at Semaphore South. I gathered together a few clothes and my football gear and left behind my two brothers Dennis and Bill at St Francis House.

Mrs McGee's house was between the Ethelton dump and the Grange railway station. As I remember, the area was mostly saltwater swamp and the remaining sand flats were used to stable the Cummins' and Hayes' race-horses alongside the mangroves. When the 'king tides' came in on one side of the Port River the sea came right up to the Grange Railway station.

Mrs McGee's husband Bill was a waterside worker and had all the attributes of someone who had spent most of his life as such. He worked intermittently, drank heavily and it could be timed almost to the minute that he would arrive home full

---
1 Gale 1972: 57-58.
2 McCorquodale 1987: 19.

of grog five minutes before the seven o'clock radio 5DN or 5AD evening news, having been tossed out of the Admiral Hotel near Black Diamond corner at Port Adelaide. Bill, like most wharfies, was a ruddy-faced, hard-working man who never scoffed at the most dreadful jobs that the Stevedoring company would ask him to do. Almost daily, if he was able to talk, Bill would recite the vulgar wharfie jokes he had learnt that day on the homeward bus. Notwithstanding his appearance, Bill was a most amiable man, drunk or sober.

For a wharfie Bill was unusual because he owned his own house and was able to support his ten children on his and his wife's incomes. Independence was Bill's lore and that was instilled into all his children. Bill was a Port Adelaide football team supporter and as predictable as most wharfies were in their politics. He hated the Liberal-Country Party and the Liberal Premier Tom Playford and Bill was someone who could pick the composition of Port's football team on Friday evenings at the Admiral Hotel without fail.

Bill wanted me to become a wharfie but I was not up to taking his advice and spent a few months doing casual work such as stacking wool, loading timber, truck driving and unloading wheat ketches around the Port Adelaide harbour. Not long after I got a job on the railways and was lucky to move to a room at a Rosewater boarding house close to the railway Round House in the Port marshalling sheds. By early 1957 I had passed my fireman's entry exams and worked on the Adelaide suburban and country passenger freight runs that took me as far north and south as Port Pirie and Border Town respectively.

By mid March I had transferred to Murray Bridge as a fireman on the school and freight train runs. When I arrived the Murray River was in flood and the main journeys were to take school children back and forth to Tailem Bend, twice a day. Although I was working for the South Australian Railways I was still a ward of the Northern Territory and South Australian governments. It would be over a decade before I would be a full citizen of Australia.

I was later posted to Port Lincoln on the Eyre Peninsula, which has a harbour on Spencer Gulf. Here I was accepted by most of my work- and sporting mates. Of these I was closest to the migrants, who were both workmates and soccer friends. I fired engines for a Jewish bloke called Jack Asher and a Hungarian migrant called Mat Giezler. Both these men were very out-going men with broad and worldly minds.

Very few Aborigines lived in the town of Port Lincoln when I landed. Mainly because they had poor education, thus poor job skills, and were still under the control of the Aborigines Protection Board. Out of sight out of mind! Most white people, therefore, were either oblivious of what society was doing to Aborigines or gave very little thought to their circumstances. There were one or two Aboriginal families such as the Roderick, Betts and Burgoyne clans moving in and around Port Lincoln, mostly playing football for local teams. The Roderick twins, both engine drivers, worked alongside me on steam engines while the Burgoyne men played football for Wayback or Minindie football clubs.

Part of my job on the railways was shunting the wheat trains around the marshalling yards and pushing the wheat cars out onto the wharf. One day soon after my arrival a big bloke named Charlie Oliver jumped on the engine and said, 'Can any of you blokes kick a footy?' I said nothing at first but Jack Asher, the engine driver, said, 'Hey Charlie this bloke's a Blackfella; he must be able to play. Every Blackfella I know is football mad, and I've seen some beauties up at Peterborough, where I come from!' When I told Charlie that I wanted to play soccer, he blurted out, 'What, that's a Sheila's game isn't it?' He jumped down from the engine and shouted at me: 'Come to training on Tuesday night! OK?'

I found out later that Charlie was a scuba diver around Boston Island, where he photographed sharks and took others out to do the same. He looked and sounded tough so I went along to train with Souths and made the first team with Charlie Oliver when the season opened. I enjoyed the life as a fireman and playing footy. Souths went to the top in 1958; I was selected to play for Port Lincoln, and my photo now hangs with others in what Port Lincoln people call their 'Sporting Hall of Fame'.

When I went to Souths I knew many of the white players who worked for the railway and got on well with them. I was certainly more interested in girls and I was particularly interested in the migrant women who followed soccer. My weekends were busy; I played cricket or Aussie rule on Saturdays and soccer on Sundays. Nevertheless work dominated my life and I often had to struggle to get back for the weekends.

I had already left Port Lincoln when I learned that my uncle, Rupert Maxwell Stuart, had been arrested for the murder of a white girl at Ceduna just before Christmas 1958. Rupert was the son of my mother's grandfather, Paddy Stuart. As a small boy of about two or three Max was in a half-caste institution with my mother, who cared for him there. It is not difficult to imagine my feelings when I heard the news. It came at the time when I was about to resign from the railways, move to Adelaide and sign up to play soccer for Beograd for the summer season. Because Max was a relative of mine, I followed the case closely until I left for England in late 1961.

Max's story begins on the 20 December 1958, when a nine-year-old white girl named Mary Olive Hattam was murdered on the beach between Ceduna and Thevenard. Days later Rupert Max Stuart was accused of raping and murdering the young girl. The case gained national notoriety for a number of reasons including the significant impact it had on the politics of South Australia, the press, legal and court systems and of course Rupert Max Stuart himself. It probably is a fair statement to say that under most circumstances white Australian country town people despised, loathed and resented Aborigines of any complexion. In particular in South Australia, many country people hated the fringe camps created by Aboriginal workers who lived there while tending the 35 to 40 kilometres of wheat stacks created by the Second World War wheat hoarding. This phenomenon created work rejected by whites for others to do.

Since whites dominated all forms of the labour force they rejected the burdensome, tiresome and heavy labour of lumping wheat-bags all day in the hot burning sun unless forced by profit or necessity to do so. This strenuous work left a gap for poor Aborigines to earn a living as an alternative to the wholesale burning down of native scrub for payment in kind such as sugar, flour, tea and an occasional sheep carcass. Max was an outsider on all counts; he was not a local but was born of Arrernte and Marduntjara heritage. His ceremonial and religious tradition was Arrernte through his father and Lutheran Christian through his Mardu mother, who was also related to my grandmother Kanaki, Kutju Kungaru.

There were a number of troublesome issues surrounding the charging of Max, issues that sparked the nation's interest and subsequently resulted in a Royal Commission into the way the police extracted the evidence to charge Max, how the record of interview was written, the English used by Max to express his ideas of admission to the crime and finally his footprint in the sand near the murder site. Max was largely convicted on the identification of this footprint. In his statement Max said that he was near the murder and saw it but denied that he was the murderer. Death by hanging was the initial sentence but was later commuted to 'Life'. The commutation process was long and laborious, and in my view, was a factor in the eventual downfall of the long-standing Playford Liberal-Country Party government. It also reflected badly on the Lutheran Church, some Aboriginal witnesses as well as the news media and the legal profession.

Ironically Max's saving grace could well have been his unconventional religious background. Well before Max went through Arrernte lore he would have come into contact with a number of religious creeds, including Presbyterians, Anglicans and Roman Catholics all vying for his baptism. That he claimed Catholicism but failed to commit himself probably saved him from the inevitable outcome of a death sentence. How did this come about? At the time there were a number of religious bodies involved in one way or another seeking political and religious salvation for Aborigines by collecting both full-bloods and half-castes together to feed them, attend to their sores or clothe them.

In Max's case there was a Roman Catholic mission at Charles Creek, a reserve created by the Northern Territory administration as a refuge for the remaining original Arrernte families whose culture was destroyed by the take-over of their lands. Max's parents stayed at Charles Creek out bush, as well as at a camp near Heavitree Gap when they came into the township of what was then Stuart. Paddy Stuart, Max's father and a police tracker, went to town regularly from the Finke region but he and wife Nada also stayed at the Presbyterians' camp at Mbartuwarintja which was near what is now Flynn's Memorial Church. At the time of his trial Max gave his religion as Catholic which to him could have meant either Anglican or Roman Catholic. However, whatever the religious technicalities of the Nicene Creed, it is quite likely there was some confusion about confessions and priests, which in turn saved Max's life.

Priests of all denominations began visiting Max and listening to him as they did with other inmates on death row. One doubting Catholic priest, the Reverend Father Thomas Dixon, saw a legal weakness in the way police had bashed Stuart in order to extract a confession on the assumption that they could get a conviction result by 'cooking the data'. However, the police misjudged the press and the groundswell of religious scepticism about the state processes. The state in the form of Tom Playford's Liberal-Country Party also misjudged the political capital of Max's treatment by white police and the justice system; including whether Max was guilty or innocent.

Father Dixon did not see Max until he was on death row and as a result of these meetings he later revealed in court evidence of Max's possible innocence. Father Dixon claimed that Max did not kill the Hattam girl and that aspects of the police case were unsound. He based these claims on his experience as a missionary of Arrernte, Unmutjara and Luritja peoples and the close contact he had with these groups. Unless you can either speak an Aboriginal language or have lived close to people who speak Aboriginal pidgin English it is hard to follow what is being said. In pointing out cultural differences such as language, Father Dixon was able to raise a political storm about the trial and police brutality. Police indifference to justice overlooked these important impediments; they wanted nothing more than a quick and easy trial without pesky priests or interfering notions of justice.

Soon after Father Dixon became involved, others were drawn into supporting Max's search for freedom, or should I say, his life. His death sentence was commuted to life in jail and he was later paroled. At the same time the Aborigines Progress Association also began showing an interest in Max's predicament. The Aborigines' Progress Association was a political organisation formed by Malcolm and Aileen Cooper, whose members included Aileen's sister Nancy Brumby together with Aboriginal friends Geoff Barnes, and Maude and George Tongerie. The organisation worked out of their temporary government home at

Taparoo and was where we met on a regular basis. Aileen had a number of sisters and Aboriginal women friends while Malcolm had the backing of Aboriginal men friends: some of whom were boys from St Francis House, including myself, Charlie Perkins, Jerry Hill, John Moriarty, David Woodford, Harry Russell, Tim Campbell, Ken Hampton and Wilfred Huddleston all of whom became members of the Association.

Millie Glenn, my mother's sister who cared for me at Mulgoa, was also involved. Millie had been a cook at St Francis House, but, at this time she was a hostel manager for Aboriginal girls at Millswood. The girls from the hostel attended high school in Adelaide. Millie and these girls all attended gatherings organised by the Progress Association. It was formed to voice protests against the Australian government as well as the racist and oppressive laws under which Aborigines in South Australia lived.

Malcolm Cooper worked at the Imperial Chemical Industry depot Osborne branch and later became a prominent Port Adelaide footballer playing many games with the great Foster Williams. Aileen was a Colebrook Home girl from Pitja Pitja country and had worked as a cook and domestic at St Francis House where she met Coop, as he was known. The Tongeries were brought up in the Oodnadatta orphanage, then the Colebrook home and Eden Hills. Aileen, Maude and George all came from northern South Australia and suffered the same discrimination as we and others did. So far as the Progress Association was concerned, any Aboriginal person could join this body.

Most of the St Francis House boys mentioned previously remained in Adelaide and suffered in many ways from the prejudices of both government and white society. These boys quickly became involved in one way or another with the Association. As individuals we had issues of our own but two things were uppermost in all our minds. First, we wanted to be political, to change the oppressive legislation under which we lived. This included the abolition of the exemption clause in the Act that forced us to hold a 'dog tag'. The clause meant that we had to apply to the protector to get an exemption from the *Aborigines Act 1934* (SA) and in doing so deny our race and Aboriginal heritage. Most Aborigines rebelled against this law and refused to recognise it. Second, we wanted to live freely as Aborigines with rights the same as those people we worked and lived with. We had already been politicised somewhat in the late 1940s as a result of the British weapons and atomic testing projects. We would not lose these attributes and even though to some extent we went our separate ways, the social and political consciousness we clung to brought us together in one way or another.

In 1959 the Progress Association and the Aborigines' Advancement League and possibly Mrs Duguid's women's body were the only local Aboriginal organisations around. Although we knew some of the white people in the League, that organisation was really the political arm of the Presbyterian Church. Dr Charles Duguid was its main spokesperson but the St Francis House boys preferred the Progress Association. The feeling at Coop's organisation was spirited. Members were both angry and full of plans for action. Resolutions were sent to Donald Dunstan, the Labor member for Norwood, libertarian bodies, feminist bodies and from memory an Adelaide lawyers' body operated by Cameron Stewart, who later became Chief Justice of South Australia. The Association met regularly and I attended when I could break with railway and sporting commitments.

On my return to Adelaide I lived at a boarding house a few streets behind my old primary school in Ethelton. The Exeter Aussie Rules Football Club offered me the chance to play with them alongside other Aboriginal boys I grew up with such as Wilfred Huddleston, Ritchie and James Bray, Tim Campbell and Harry Russell. Exeter found me a labouring job at a government foundry on the Port River and I worked there until about August of 1961. The foundry belonged to the Department of Water and Sewerage, and while appreciated by me as an income, it was one of the worst jobs the Port Adelaide district could offer. But the members of Exeter football club had supported me in getting this labouring job at the foundry, so I was happy to stay there until I went overseas.

In the 1959 football season I played for Exeter in the Aussie Rules amateur league A-grade side. The team that year was successful and went to the grand final, playing against Adelaide University to whom we narrowly lost. In this same season I was selected to play for South Australia in the National Amateur Australian Rules Carnival in Perth. Two other Aboriginal players were selected from Exeter, Richard Bray and Wilfred (Boofer) Huddleston. I played my last Aussie Rules game for Exeter in the 1959 grand final and subsequently returned to soccer. John Moriarty and I signed to play soccer for Beograd in the summer-night football season. These matches were played under lights at Norwood Oval. Charlie Perkins had recently returned from England and was instrumental in taking Croatia to the first Division and enticed me to play the winter season with them.

In the winter of 1960 Aboriginal politics and soccer were my passions. With Aboriginal politics high in the minds of the South Australian polity through the Stuart Case, the Aboriginal Progress Association (APA) took on the task of changing the *Police Offences Act* 1953 (SA) by using Dunstan's capacity to put up a Private Member's Bill. In 1959-60 we met Dunstan on several occasions at his home on Norward Parade to make plans for a wholesale onslaught on the *AboriginesAct 1934* (SA). Significant changes were made ultimately by the

Liberal-Country Party. The old *AboriginesAct 1934* (SA) was swept away as Liberals began recognising that Aborigines wanted change and were clamouring to dispose of welfare support.

Playford wanted to do away with the status quo and dismantle the Aboriginal Affairs Board together with the old system of Protectors in regional areas. Playford wanted Aborigines to be just like everyone else in society. At the end of Playford's vision Aborigines would be left with nothing; no land, no heritage, no wealth and no identity. This system in my view would have led to the disappearance of Aborigines and to what Playford saw as 'integration', another spin on 'assimilation'. This would have led to no specific government agencies for Aborigines and they would have to 'fit in' with other Australians. Playford had in his mind the idea that 'proof of Aboriginality' was to be an entry in a 'Register' (or 'stud book') still to be created. The state administration would alone decide if a person was fit to be deemed a citizen and then that person could be removed from the register. More than that, under discussion was the concept that any person whose name appeared on a register could be confined or removed from Aboriginal reserves. Dunstan was concerned about the new Act and asked us for advice on our thinking on these matters.

Our view was that Playford was pursuing a backward step and we rejected the idea of a register, and in general opposed the removal of any Aborigine by police under any circumstance from their reserves. What we saw was the blatant withdrawal of people's privacy if police had a capacity to have at hand a register to check our race and promptly remove, detain or incarcerate any person listed in it. We wanted the return of our civil liberties, a capacity to declare ourselves to be an Aboriginal person. In turn we wanted the return of our land, freedom of movement and protection of our cultural heritage.

On weekends Charlie, Moriarty and I would either go to soccer club cabarets or to hotels such as the Hendon Hotel that held dances in the saloon bars. It was here that Charlie first met Eileen Munchenberg and her friend Yvonne who was visiting from New Zealand. From the start Charlie was besotted with Eileen; not many white women accepted Charlie and from the word go he felt confident with her. Charlie and Eileen were married in the September of 1961 in Adelaide. After they were married Charlie talked about going to Darwin and even wrote to the Northern Territory administration about a job prospect. He was totally shocked when they dismissed his keenness out of hand and only offered him a job as a bush mechanic. He never forgot this contempt. When passing through Sydney he was offered a signing with the Pan Hellenic soccer club and he and Eileen decided to stay put. In Charlie's mind too was the thought of going to university.

I stayed in Adelaide playing soccer for Croatia, transferring to Polonia in 1961. But by the end of winter I decided to go to England to try my luck as a professional soccer player. I arrived there in October as buoyed as ever thinking that I was heading for a career in the home of world soccer. While playing in Australia I assumed getting started in an English club would be easy but got a shock when I found myself playing with boys much younger than myself. The weather was like mid-winter in Australia and many of my clothes were of summer weight. The trial I had for Hemel Hempstead was not a good one mainly because the wind and rain were too fierce and the muddy fields did not suit me. They asked me to play for an amateur side called Hemel Hempstead Rovers which I did and fared better. As the winter drew on I became more and more fearful that I would injure myself; my confidence was plummeting. I stuck it out in Hemel for that winter and moved to Preston in mid 1962.

However, one aspect of Hemel Hempstead that would have a profound effect on my life was meeting Norma, my wife to be, at a local dance hall. We met early in 1962 and were married in the autumn of that year. I think to start with Norma was fascinated with meeting someone from Australia. Her brother John had spent some time working at the Rum Jungle uranium mine in the Northern Territory in the 1950s and had always spoken well of his time in Australia, and in particular well of the Aboriginal people whom he had come across. To some extent this allayed the apprehension that Norma's parents, Beatrice and Ernie felt about us eventually returning to Australia.

Norma's family was originally from Willesden, a suburb of London, where she was born during a Second World War air raid. Norma spent the first ten years of her life in London attending first Leopold Road infants' school and later Oldfield Road primary school. The family left London in the mid-1950s just before Norma went on to secondary schooling at Apsley Grammar School in Hemel Hempstead. Her family background is quite diverse. Her mother Beatrice came from a transport/carrier family-owned business and was financially well-off until an accident killed a young neighbour and injured her father. As the story goes, the grandfather was never the same after the accident and died a few years later. Beatrice was 15 at the time of his death.

Beatrice was one of 12 children but it seems that none had the business acumen to successfully carry on the family business and tales abound of houses being sold cheaply to buy fur coats for wives! Beatrice had seven sisters and she was very close to all of them – Minnie, Louisa, Alice, Annie, Charlotte, Grace and Christine. Norma grew up listening to her mother and aunts regularly getting together and socialising with each other. Because they knew each other so well situations could be discussed in half sentences – the recipient knowing what was coming and in this way young ears were spared the finer details. Beatrice was also very close to her four brothers – William, Mick, Tom and Charlie.

Brothers Tom and Charlie lived close by during the war years, and the story goes that Charlie carried Beatrice and Norma, as a newborn infant, from the neighbours where she had been born to their flat while it was snowing. The godsend was that Tom filled the coal cellar up for her; between the brothers they looked after Beatrice and her young family while Ernie was away at war.

Ernie, or Pop as I always called him, also came from a large family. He often talked about his brothers Harry, Jim and Jack and sisters Sophie, Mary and Minnie. His father earned a living as a labourer and died when Ernie was just 21. Ernie's mother known just as Gran was a larger than life figure in Norma's life when they lived in London. Every Sunday Pop would take Norma to visit Gran who lived in nearby flats with Pop's sister Minnie and family. After they would go for a walk, weather permitting, along the canal to the local pub, the White Horse, where Pop would have a drink and then together they would hurry home for Sunday lunch.

Beatrice and Ernie were married in the early 1930s and started out their life together renting a small flat and sharing facilities in Harlesden, London. Like many of their generation the Second World War disrupted their lives when Pop was called up to go in the army. He served as a sapper in the bomb disposal unit and spent most of the war at John O'Groats in the north of Scotland. Norma's brother John was five when war broke out, and as the bombing intensified in London most children and some adults were evacuated to the countryside. Beatrice and John were both evacuated for a short time to Lord Carnarvon's castle in Wales. After six years in the army Ernie resumed civilian life as a slater and tiler. He worked for many years for London Transport and on the move to Hemel Hempstead worked as a glazier for Hemel Hempstead Housing Commission.

In mid 1962 I left Hemel for Preston by train with some confidence but nowhere near as much as I once had. I had my first trial game for Preston North End at their training ground on the outskirts of the city. I lived at Deepdale and got a job in a factory near Preston's ground. The truth hit me when I began training that most of the new players were again very young. I made the thirds and ended up playing reserves and thirds. But other events were overtaking my life. I took a short break to return to Hemel Hempstead where Norma and I were married in the local mediaeval church of St Mary's at Apsley. It was in a magnificent rural setting and this coupled with the fact that the church was made of flintstone made it very special. Her best friend Elaine and cousin Jean were our bridesmaids, along with Norma's brother John as the best man. We celebrated our wedding at a local hall with family and friends. Next day Norma and I left Euston station on the Flying Scotsman train to return to Preston.

Life after St Francis House, 1957 to 1964

I settled into a routine of playing on snow, ice, mud and rainy days. Just as I was getting used to the conditions I badly injured my ankle which took months to heal.

At about the same time we decided to return to Hemel Hempstead mainly because we were expecting our first child and Norma wanted to be nearer her family. While Beatrice was hesitant and fearful of the fact that Norma and her new grandson were eventually going to leave England, she and Ernie were always very good to me. Soccer was not paying me any money so I quickly got a job at a steel fabrication factory called Dexion. I found the job easy and soon became part of the production team and learned to enjoy eight and 12 hour shifts.

In 1963 our first son Aaron Charles John was born at St Pauls Hospital in Hemel Hempstead. He was a small baby at birth, little more than two kilograms, but soon flourished with lots of love from all those around him. Aaron was a very contented and agile baby who learnt to walk when he was just nine months old. He was a lovely baby whom the family all adored. We left England when Aaron was just 12 months old and looking back it must have been very hard on Norma's parents to see their only grandchild heading off to the other side of the world.

Charlie had phoned me a couple of times to persuade me to return to Sydney rather than Adelaide. We arrived in Sydney on the P&O liner *Iberia* in April of 1964. Charlie and Eileen met us at Circular Quay. England was for me a great success and I came back to Australia to where I spent some of my early life in the Church of England refuge. Meeting Norma and the birth of our first child were my greatest achievements. However, I also count living with Beatrice, Ernie and John as a success because as a family they always made me very welcome and through them I came to appreciate some of the foibles of the English way of life.

Chapter 7
Race relations, work and education, 1964 to 1968

I returned to Australia in 1964 to find Aboriginal issues in New South Wales very different from those I left behind. In South Australia bureaucrats identified Aborigines as being persons of 'full-blood', others of Aboriginal descent were regarded as 'state wards', mainly those who were living on southern reserves. Then there were those people of Aboriginal descent who were classified as non-Aborigines because they had been given a State government exemption from the Protection legislation. Persons holding an Exemption Certificate had what was known in common practice as a 'dog tag'. And finally, there were those people of Aboriginal descent who refused to conform to government policy because they believed it would demean them as 'honorary whites' if they did so. The exemption system in New South Wales was more that of failed assimilation policies. Despite the government's parsimony, there were benefits for some individuals. Although the *Aborigines Protection Act 1909* (NSW) existed, the Welfare Board was not totally blind to the idea that urban life together with social conformity needed a measure of economic resources. There were no fringe benefits for education but there was for housing in city urban areas. On the downside Aborigines were not permitted to create organisations in opposition to government policies. However, some organisations deemed illegal under the *Aborigines Protection Act 1909* (NSW) did exist but were not prosecuted. The Aborigines and their friends who ran these organisations were courageous and enlightened people.

This chapter is not only about my re-education, but about race relations and how it shifted between racial politics and socialisation practice. I arrived in Sydney with Norma and our infant son Aaron late in April 1964. Norma's parents, Beatrice and Ernie, had waved us off with heavy hearts at Southampton. One of the ports of call was Naples, where we went ashore and I recall pushing Aaron around in a stroller that squeaked all through the main street of Naples much to the amusement of everyone. Finally as we walked across the street at a set of traffic lights the stroller collapsed. I took it apart as best I could and put the contraption into a large hopper down a side street. We made other port calls at Cairo, Port Said, Mumbai (then Bombay), then on to Fremantle, Adelaide, Melbourne and finally Sydney.

I could see Charlie Perkins and his wife Eileen from the top deck as we docked at Circular Quay in Sydney. They greeted us warmly and took us to the Baltimore

Hotel on the Esplanade at Bondi beach. This hotel was very basic but we were only there for a couple of nights before securing a small flat at Gladesville in north Sydney. I began looking for work in the Gladesville region, but Charlie phoned to tell me a position had become available at the Canterbury Council in Campsie. The job was an opening for an Aboriginal person and I took the opportunity to apply.

Aboriginal people in New South Wales were then campaigning for fair rents across the state and for a better employment deal. The political 'fair rent' campaign began on reserves in rural areas, however, most of the unemployment was in large regional areas and cities, like Sydney, where the campaign was well and truly under way. Aboriginal leaders campaigned for the state to be more vigilant about utilising Aborigines, including local governments, who tended to shy away from employing Aborigines. The position I applied for was open to any Aboriginal person with a fourth form certificate. It was as a clerk in the Health and Building Department of the Canterbury Council and had been vacant for over six months without any takers.

Charlie dropped me at the council chambers in Beamish Street, Campsie where I met the chief health and building inspector, a Mr Dave Watkins. He interviewed me and asked about my background. I told him that I had not been to high school and had a poor education record. I explained to him that although I did not qualify for the position I was willing to get a driver's licence and go to night school to get the necessary qualifications needed for the position. This was good enough for Dave but it had to be cleared with the Town Clerk and the Mayor because the offer was unusual and political. The Council was an inner city Labor council and had made the offer because they wanted to support Aborigines in New South Wales. Issues at the time included high rents on reserves and the concomitant drift to the fringe camps, high levels of poverty and poor health and high rates of Aboriginal unemployment.

Aborigines had been protesting since the second decade of the twentieth century. From the sheep yards of the Riverina, western wheat and cattle properties around Walgett to the Sussex Street Trades Hall in the 1930s and on into the 1960s, Aborigines had raised their voices. Aboriginal shepherds and shearing workers had protested about inequalities and poverty as early as the 1890s. They continued on into the 1920s and 1930s when, with Communist Party helpers, Bill Ferguson began lobbying the Protector of Aborigines under the guise of Christian gatherings. From 1938, apart from the war years, the Aborigines Progress Association had held annual meetings during a time when the White Australia Policy was in full force.

Following the post-war boom, housing rents increased and resulted in many Aboriginal people fleeing to the rent-free fringes of New South Wales country towns. Welfare could be denied once Aborigines left the reserves. This caused social problems in the bush and the fall-back was casual market gardening labour or official employment at long distances from family. Reserves became crèches where women and children stayed waiting for returning partners, many of whom never returned. Housing protests intensified during the 1930s, throughout the 1950s and on into the early part of the 1960s. The rent strike became a fully-fledged protest movement in the early 1960s as wide-scale pressure on the Aborigines Protection Board mounted. While supporters attempted to shore up a flagging New South Wales Labor Party, I was returning from England to take advantage of the ferment of the time.

To begin my employment in good faith I began a correspondence course for the fourth form certificate under the Wyndham Scheme. I failed on the first try and so in February of 1965 I began classes at night. I took four subjects – history, geography, English and science – as a strategy to pass the certificate. To gain entrance I had to be assessed by the Sydney Technical College's psychologist, whose report said that it was possible for me to study for the certificate. They also remarked, however, that it was doubtful whether I could go any further and university qualifications would be, for me, 'a pipe dream'. At that stage any thought of university was a long, long way off as I persevered with the night time study and was successful at my second attempt. The Canterbury Council was happy that I had passed and almost all the staff cheered me when it happened. My confidence by this time was increasing and I succeeded in getting my driver's licence without difficulty.

The next hurdle was the clerical tasks. At the beginning of the job I was semi-illiterate with few reading skills and this flowed on to my capacity to write and spell. Both were very poor. Once I got to the front office a fellow officer George McGrath had the responsibility for teaching me all the duties of the position. George treated me exceedingly well. He was a very popular person who had begun work for the Council as a cashier and had transferred to the building clerk's job some years earlier. In early 1964 George planned to travel around Australia with a friend, meaning his job would become vacant. George had the patience to teach me how to make building applications, how to enter these into a special register that needed to be correct for legal reasons, how to assist building inspectors by posting back people's conditions of approval and, finally, how to file applications correctly. When applications were approved it could involve a few hundred dollars, or huge amounts if for works associated with complexes like the Roselands shopping center costing millions.

It goes without saying that I had to have my wits about me. There were other pitfalls in this position such as handling the public. Building forms had to be filled out by people who like me could barely read and write, so in the first few months, George basically held my hand. Ratepayers can be irate for any number of reasons and they would be easily upset if I gave out the wrong information on the phone. Again, George helped me by showing me how it was done and I 'learned by doing'. Another duty was the filing. Filing, most people would suspect, was a simple job and in general this is so, but the Council system was complex. The first application after Council opened for the year on 2 January, took the number 1/1965 and so on. This system was an instant ready reckoner so that plans could easily be located. With care the system could be kept free of chaos but it could just as easily be thrown out of kilter, and it was not easy to locate an error. It was easy to blame others but I often made mistakes with the numbering system and corrections were embarrassing. But George taught me how to beat the system, and I did so many times.

The Council had a very popular and sophisticated library network that stretched from Punchbowl north to Earlwood, and from Burwood and Strathfield south to Revesby and Narwee. Each suburb had its own branch and three or more librarians kept the very efficient system going. Each branch had to be paid and supplied with all the things libraries needed and that was my job. A hand gun was kept in a wooden box beneath the cashier's counter and each pay day I would collect it, and the money box, and go to the central administration, where another clerk checked the pays and handed them over to me. After lunch each fortnight I would pick up the librarians' wages and off I would go to pay the library staff. I would take a different route each time, trying, as George taught me, to act and practise a kind of hide and seek from would-be bandits seeking to rob me. They never did fortunately. At this time we did not have a car and often to give Norma and Aaron a ride out I would pick them up from where we lived in nearby Clissold Parade and take them out while I did my library run. This slightly unorthodox behavior of taking the family for a ride never got out of hand and I constantly worked to improve my service to the ratepayers and council hierarchy.

Clissold Parade was literally at the back of the council chambers in Campsie and while we lived there Norma would often take Aaron to the park near the swimming pool on Cook's River. In the winter he played in the park and during the summer they would swim at the pool. Norma's mother Beatrice visited that year from England and during this time we bought an old weatherboard house in Cardigan Road, Greenacre, near Bankstown. We were overjoyed. This was a particularly memorable time for us as we had been living in rented flats often moving every three months for one reason or another; mainly because landlords did not like young children. To have our own house was very special, particularly for Aaron, who had a garden to play in for the first time. He was so excited the first morning that he couldn't eat any breakfast. All he wanted to do was play in the garden.

Not long after moving into Cardigan Road my mother rang in despair and asked if I would consider looking after my youngest brother Sam, aged 13, and put him through school in Sydney. She said he was uncontrollable and had been banned from attending school in Alice Springs. I was taken aback to begin with because at that stage there was already myself, Norma, my young son Aaron, and John, Norma's brother, living in our two bedroom small weatherboard cottage. John had arrived by boat from America earlier in the year and went on to live with us for two years while working at the University of Sydney as a lab technician – he has since maintained that this was one of the most enjoyable jobs he ever had. I suggested to my mother that Sam be told that he was coming for a holiday. I also suggested that if he was able to fit into the family we could extend his stay, put him through school and try and make the future for a 13-year-old boy a little brighter. Sam arrived shortly after, carrying a packet of Benson and Hedges cigarettes in his pocket and wearing 'winkle picker' shoes with the soles parting at the front. When we arrived back from the airport he went straight to the lounge room and stretched out on the floor almost filling the whole room. Norma, John and I looked at each other wondering if the scheme we had agreed to was foolhardy. But after a couple of weeks things settled down, and like a miracle, Sam asked if he could stay and continue his education in Sydney. I enrolled him at South Strathfield High School and with a lot of encouragement he did very well, even topping the class in a number of subjects – a far cry from the cigarette-smoking unruly lad that had arrived 12 months earlier. It was the start of a long fatherly attachment that I feel towards Sam.

In 1966 I took on fifth form part time. I would go to night-school classes at the Bankstown Technical College four times a week straight from work. The plan was to do two subjects a year: first year mathematics and geography, second year history and English. Mathematics was my weakest subject and I was tutored in this subject by Jack Kendall who had helped me pass my school certificate. Jack came twice a week and on weekends nearer to exam times. Jack was a great friend, and a graduate in chemistry from the University of Sydney. He lived near Hornsby and had a chemical equipment factory in the North Ryde area. He would come to Campsie and later to my house at Greenacre to help me with my mathematics. Jack also helped enormously at the time we were trying to buy Greenacre. We were short of $200 and Jack arranged for his solicitor to lend us the money from a trust fund he managed. A condition of the trust fund was that I visit the hospitalised lady owner at her nursing home in Strathfield. I was very happy to do this and was forever grateful to Jack for his help. With Jack's help I passed the Bankstown leg of the fifth form certificate.

Although my focus was on getting educated, Aboriginal politics was always a part of my consciousness but it had become more social than political. Each lunch time in 1968 I would walk from the Technical College in Ultimo to the

Foundation for Aboriginal Affairs at the top end of George Street. I would take the lunch Norma cut for me and make a cup of tea and listen to the older Aboriginal men's stories about their biographies, their lives from the places they had migrated from, why they had done so and what they were now doing with their lives. Men like Doug Scott, Chicka Dixon, Roy Carol, Candy, Harry and his brother (Booma Nulla) Williams would gather around about mid-day at the Foundation, and were generally there when I came for lunch. On some days they would bring their families in and I would meet them, and on occasional weekends Norma, Aaron and I would go to concerts at the Foundation. On other occasions my family and I would go directly to Charlie's home in Glebe. Other days I would study at home and if it was hot we would all head for Coogee beach or Wattamolla to escape the stifling Sydney heat.

We all loved Coogee and Maroubra but my son Aaron especially loved it. Aaron had a special rock pool he loved to play in at Maroubra, and Norma and I would walk along the beach. The surfies would fascinate Aaron as they either carried or dragged their surfboards along the sand. Some would carry the board on their heads and pass us going the other way; Aaron would drag his make-believe-board along copying the surfers. On many occasions such as when Aboriginal visitors from interstate came to see Charlie, he would contact us and we would all go for the day to Wattamolla, a great swimming beach in the Royal National Park. I recall visits from John and Rita Moriarty, Vincent and Brenda Copley and later, my cousin Ian and Peggy Lake.

The Foundation was not only a focus for my lunchtime meetings with New South Wales Aborigines, but more importantly it was the genesis of my life in national Aboriginal politics. The Foundation began in Walgett as a reactionary movement by stalwarts like Harry Hall and the Morgan family but it took on a more liberal approach when it was established in Sydney. These families were cattle and stock-workers, many of whom had migrated to Walgett from further west during and after the Second World War. The population drifts created two factions: one made up of Kamilaroi descendents and reserve Aborigines to the south and east and the others migrating from the west in the Lake Eyre basin region.[1] In the first instance, white people dominated the positions on the Foundation board. Its political and social focus was the provision of a liberal thinking approach in which Aboriginal people could believe in a life outside of welfare.

Ted Noffs of the Wayside Chapel was an evangelical Methodist preacher who drew Charlie to him and introduced him to Harry Hall in the early 1960s. Ted was a 'new age' Christian who moved around rural New South Wales talking to Aboriginal groups who were looking for some kind of political connection

---

1   Horton 1994: 530-531.

outside the institutionalised churches. Harry and other Aborigines in Walgett found life on the periphery of the Labor government's power-base difficult to penetrate in small numbers and found Ted Noffs an ally in gaining political traction. The State Labor government had reigned for 20 odd years and it was generally difficult for Aborigines to bring to their attention problems such as high rents, unemployment, and poor education and housing in rural areas. Ted, along with Professor Bill Geddes and the Liberal Party's north-shore 'Blue Rinse Brigade', began supporting a new approach to Aboriginal affairs with an emphasis on greater freedom and liberty, reform of the legislation and liberal opportunities for Aboriginal people. A new wave of political action involving wide support was building and the Foundation for Aboriginal Affairs was the end result. At the time these influences were difficult to detect but the ideology was unmistakable. So opaque was its message that it gathered up Aborigines from both the left and right of the political spectrum. The ideology encompassed ideas of developing an Aboriginal view-point of class in which Aboriginal entertainers, budding entrepreneurs, successful sporting identities, trades-people, boxing identities, trade unionists (both left wingers and political misfits) and white and black students, all of whom wanted change in allowing people to move up the class ladder free of racial prejudices.

This mosaic of support was diverse but at the same time the Foundation, the Federal Council for the Advancement for Aborigines and Torres Strait Islanders and other Aboriginal bodies amassed political support of a nationalist kind. Although I had no real political connection to the Foundation I supported the organisation for its forward-looking approach to welfare. Equally, I supported its altruism and its courage to take on a moribund Labor regime bereft of compassion or new ideas, in particular, in areas of the politics of race.[2]

The Foundation developed in the early 1960s at a time when Aboriginal people were dissatisfied with living under the *Aborigines Protection Act 1909* (NSW). They had initially migrated to fringe camps and rural towns, but were often under threat by local councils and thus many were forced to move on to Sydney for work. The Foundation picked up on this migration and initiated programs to help people settle in Sydney. Many Aboriginal women like Flo Grant, Shirley Smith, Eileen Lester, Joyce Clague and Lily Kunoth supported the Foundation on the basis of their involvement in family welfare and issues such as appearing for children in court. However, Aboriginal men like Roy Carol, Doug Scott and Herbert Simms appeared to me to support the Foundation for more commercial reasons such as supporting boxing contracts, trotting activities and running Aboriginal artefact shops.

---

2   Perkins 1975: 99-106.

Shirley Smith or 'Mum Shirl' as everyone came to know her, was a Catholic and wanted Aborigines migrating or in strife with the law, cared for in a more personal way. She argued that too many in welfare agencies had became overly bureaucratic, asking too many questions of Aboriginal people needing help and a meal. Flo Grant was a nurse's aid and Eileen Lester was a trained nurse who came from the Warburton Ranges in Western Australia, married a white man and migrated to Sydney during the Second World War. Similarly, Lily Kunoth, like me, had been evacuated, as a refugee from the Japanese War, and was drawn to the Foundation by her traditional relationship to Charlie. Joyce Mercy was already a member of the Federal Council for the Advancement of Aborigines and Torres Strait Islander national political body, and had secretarial skills. All of these women, including Eileen Perkins and my wife Norma, acted as auxiliary workers on fetes and fund raising activities.

Climbing up the Australian class structure was virtually impossible for Aborigines, but some managed a small ascent. The assumption was that if you made it at sport, as a member of the military, as a poet or a writer, you were on the way up. Roy Carol, who later trained my youngest brother Sam, was a champion boxer. Roy was against the exploitation of young Aboriginal boys by other boxing promoters. He had a small gymnasium in Chippendale and a contract to provide boxing bouts at the Marrickville RSL. Doug Scott, a relation of Roy's, worked for many years on the building of the Warragamba Dam and had amassed a team of trotting horses. Doug clearly aspired to become both a famous racing owner/driver as well as the seller of Aboriginal arts and crafts in Sydney.

Chicka Dixon, a waterside worker, was a reformed alcoholic and a highly prominent political activist. Chicka came from Wallaga Lake on the south coast of New South Wales and was related to other well-known Aborigines such as Burnum Burnum (Harry Penrith), Herb Simms, Ken Brindle, Ted (the Fox) Thomas, Ross (Jirra) Moore and Bobby McLeod. Already a prominent left political activist in Aboriginal politics, Chicka was motivated by Bill Ferguson and Jack Patten and was equally inspired by Charlie Perkins and wanted reform services to deal with Aboriginal alcohol addiction. He also wanted a place where Aborigines could get off the street for even a small amount of time to clean themselves up and have a meal. The Foundation tended to meet, or aspire to meet, all these and other needs. In particular, Chicka and Roy wanted the Foundation to implement a service that met young Aboriginal people arriving from the country and then helped them find a place to stay and get work quickly.

For those who had few class aspirations, the Foundation believed it could find solutions. Daily country trains would bring in people who were new to Sydney and would subsequently get lost and fall foul of criminal violence. The Foundation also created opportunities for musicians and young sports persons by entering teams in all kinds of sports. Rugby, of course, was a prominent sport and links to sporting bodies were assumed to be a strength. The Foundation did most of these things and also linked in with student bodies both state and national and was instrumental in supporting the statewide 'Freedom Ride' led by Charlie Perkins in 1965.

This event was also supported by the Walgett Branch of the Foundation.[3] The 'Freedom Ride' embodied student radicalism and Christian socialism. The protesters wanted rural whites to be fair to Aboriginal groups and allow them to be included in the use of town services and have equal access to all public amenities – a kind of 'mutual obligation' process. The Freedom Ride put great pressure on the then New South Wales Labor government when about 30 University of Sydney students hired a bus and toured western New South Wales country towns highlighting how overtly Aborigines were being discriminated against. How, they asked was it possible for white society to do what it did, given the protections Aborigines were entitled to under international law? Ultimately they traveled 3,200 kilometres and exposed widespread problems by observing the 'conditions of life' of Aboriginal people in rural areas. The students argued that townsfolk in the many communities they visited were breaking international law by basically refusing to live side-by-side with Aborigines and this conflict had become a universal culture of intolerance.

Like the Vietnam war, the Freedom Ride brought Aboriginal disadvantage and exclusion right into the lounge rooms of wealthy 'first world' whites to expose the 'third world' on their door step. It highlighted the futility of the *Aboriginal Protection Act 1909* (NSW) and the overt discrimination that Aborigines suffered in country towns – the most obvious was that Aborigines were banned from using most public facilities and services. The most prominent and newsworthy target for the Freedom Ride was discrimination at local swimming pools. Owners of these facilities and white townsfolk banned Aborigines and their children. The most lasting images of this period are those of Charlie and a group of Aboriginal children enjoying themselves in the local town pool on a very hot country-town-day. I remember clearly the return of the Freedom Riders and the press's reaction to the event. I was part of the returning 'sandwich team' along with my wife Norma, Eileen, Neville Perkins (Charlie's nephew) and Gary Williams (an Aboriginal university student whom Charlie billeted). As the Freedom Ride bus pulled up outside Charlie's house in Glebe we had a large trestle prepared, full of food and drinks to serve the protesters and the press.

At the time the incumbent New South Wales Labor government appeared oblivious of the level of discrimination in country towns. The Freedom Ride bought this out into the public arena and put the issue on the political agenda.

---

3   Perkins 1975: 74-91.

Faith Bandler was a rabid Labor Party supporter, but of a haughty type, Ken Brindle held to definite petty bourgeois traits, while Herb Simms was more of a Christian socialist. Then there were others such as the anthropologist Bill Geddes, who tried to introduce the idea of a 'chocolate coloured world'. He clung to a harmonious view of the world in the face of angry Aborigines who wanted 'Black Power'. During the mid-1960s Charlie Perkins was seen by some Labor supporters, including Faith Bandler, as a Liberal Party stooge who was definitely en route to the upper classes. But he confounded people who tried to pigeon-hole him as a Liberal rather than a Labor supporter. In truth, he was neither, but he chose a moralistic posture, a kind of evangelical populist where his *raison d'être* was to be a spokesperson for Aborigines and although dressed like a top line Italian professional footballer, he identified as, and spoke like, a fringe-camp river-bank black. Charlie's powerful ego allowed him to be not just 'Bolshevik' but at the same time a 'Menshevik'. These traits came to the front in the Freedom Ride. This modus operandi stayed with him throughout his later working life as a public servant.[4]

For over half a century local governments had pushed Aboriginal camps way-out over their boundaries as a means of escaping the responsibilities to service them. Rural whites owned all the land, the rural pastoral properties; they controlled the schools and town swimming pools and ran the town councils. They therefore commanded all the wealth and prosperity of the regional areas. They controlled the primary and public health systems, the libraries, hotels and businesses. Aborigines, totally without power, possessed the poorest health, were least educated and lacked incomes and any form of wealth. So entrenched was the culture of racism that it took riots, bombings and demonstrations to awaken public awareness. The change of government from Labor to Liberal-Country Party failed to dislodge the hold of truculent rural white 'red neck' society. Not until the re-election of a more enlightened Labor regime under Neville Wran in the 1970s was it possible to say that racism in rural New South Wales had come under either some 'rule of law' or social control.

When people from the bush came to Sydney in the 1950s they went to the sand hills and bush lands around La Perouse. This was the old Aboriginal living site traditionally called 'Bunabri', and ironically located at the place where all their problems of colonialism began – off Botany Bay. Race prejudice lay at the heart of Aboriginal poverty. Monopoly of lands by whites had, for a long time, ensured and guaranteed a failure to reorganise Aboriginal economies. Political monopoly guaranteed that white society would deny Aboriginal rights to the

---

4   Perkins C 1975: 74-98.

franchise thereby symbolising Australian racism.[5] Race laws made it easy for whites to oppress Aborigines across the continent that cemented in time their historic indifference.[6]

Looking back to the mid to late 1960s, a deep division emerged along a fault line with the Labor supporters on the one side and the Liberal right on the other. Charlie, with his ability to attract publicity, quickly flushed out Labor supporters trying in both state and national arenas to gain political credence. Labor in Sydney had ruled for a long time and was edging towards decay while at the national level searching for a means to escape opposition. It is hard to deny Charlie's influence, together with his alliances, to get the financial and political support needed to create a new organisation based on liberal and socialist philosophy. But the rancour continued for a long period in this era.

On the one hand, Ted Noffs was a great believer in Martin Luther King's capacity, often likening Charlie to King, to move American blacks to see their destiny in political liberation born of self-interest. Noffs supported the idea that Aborigines with resources could search around and find what was achievable to create an organisation of their own making. In the first instance the Foundation raised its own funds to build a form of symbolism that showed that Aborigines wanted change. On the other hand, the Communists in New South Wales had shown Aborigines that if they had the will to rise up against tyrannical landlords it was possible too to do other things. The 'Rent Strike' in New South Wales that progressed in the 1950s, for example, rolled onwards to a movement that exposed the poverty among Aborigines when they left the reserves to adopt a pattern of living they knew well: to head to rent-free land on the fringes of white country towns.

Although New South Wales Aboriginal people had a history of protest they lacked interstate unity of the kind liberal nationalism needs. The Aboriginal people behind the Foundation drew from their own efforts to do that and I could see them doing it. Charlie already had strong links to the Federal Council for the Advancement of Aborigines and Torres Strait Islanders (I'll call it the Federal Council). It was through Charlie that I first met Dulcie Flowers, a Torres Strait Islander woman with strong links to the Federal Council and Queensland Aboriginal politics. Dulcie was married to a Sydney classical musician and held fund-raising nights at her home in Earlwood in Sydney. There I also met Ken Brindle, Faith Bandler and Jack Horner. Brindle was a Kinchela boy and a recently returned soldier who fought in Korea and Malaya. He was a New South Wales delegate to the Federal Council. Bandler alleges that Kinchela Boys' Home was a New South Wales government institution where children coming

---

5   Stevens 1971: vols 1-3.
6   Rowley 1986.

in contact with both the Aborigines Protection Board and the law courts were sent either for some trivial parental misdemeanor committed against the *AboriginesProtection Act 1909* (NSW) or charges of summary offenses and/or crimes of some description.[7] But it was more likely that most were committed as either 'uncontrollable' or as 'not being under proper care and control'.

Faith Bandler was an executive member of the Federal Council, a woman of South Sea Islander descent, and of considerable political standing in the Labor Party. Jack Horner was a kindly man, who, some ten years earlier, had been transfigured and enlightened towards Aborigines by his face-to-face contact with African racism while in England with his wife Jean. Jack and Jean struck up a long and ongoing contact with the Federal Council and both were executive members.[8] I met up with Dulcie more so than with the others, whom I only encountered at Federal Council's Easter conferences in Canberra each year from 1965 to 1968. The Foundation was never an affiliate of the Federal Council but Ray Peckham, Harry Hall and Charlie were the three people most instrumental in raising the political poverty issue in New South Wales.

The foregoing discussion reveals the immediate national contact that individual Aborigines such as Charlie had with both the Foundation and with the Federal Council. Faith Bandler did not seek Charlie's views when she wrote about her recollections of the Federal Council's activity with Bobbi Sykes in 1989, which I think demonstrates the ideological schism between them.

I have already spoken about the Freedom Ride, but for me the three other issues of particular note in this period were: the 1967 Federal referendum to change the Federal Constitution regarding Aboriginal rights; the Federal Council's growing internal and external conflicts building up to the split of 1970, and my matriculation from the Sydney Technical College to the Australian National University. The origins of the 1967 referendum lay in a series of public debates about whether parts or the whole of the political system should control Aboriginal affairs and how it ought to be done. Questions about Aborigines and Federation lay in the notion that the states should control all people (including non-citizens) within its borders. This was one political task of what is known as separate powers, where states kept their colonial right to control citizens. These rights were granted to Aborigines by Macquarie's Proclamation in 1814, but were gradually removed and eroded as colonies created their own draconian laws to control Aborigines. Control of Aboriginal peoples remained with the states after Federation. The Commonwealth, having no constitutional power to make laws for Aborigines, kept out of the issue. I have already explained in an earlier chapter how it dealt with Aborigines in the Northern Territory, and Baldwin

---

7   Bandler 1989.
8   Horner 1994.

Spencer, as early as 1911, called for the Commonwealth to take over Aboriginal affairs. In the three decades to the 1930s, state and territory administrators looked to assert their control over, on the one hand, growing welfare problems among Aboriginal groups in all states, particularly the growing population numbers, caused by expanding pastoralism, while on the other hand, growing cultural breakdown among Aboriginal groups as urban poverty raged.

Following the Labor government's abortive 1944 referendum attempt to take control of Aboriginal affairs, Robert Menzies had no stomach for an additional try. People like Les Haylen, the Federal Member for Parkes, Jessie Street, Bert Groves and Faith Bandler all pushed the Menzies Liberal governments to take control of Aboriginal affairs under a petition launched on 29 April 1957.[9] All attempts to persuade Menzies failed as he continued to espouse the view that change would result in creating Aborigines 'as a race apart'. This issue came up over a decade later in the 'Gerhardi and Brown' Federal Court case, but for different reasons than those implied by Menzies.[10] This was a court case, the details of which I won't go into here, involving a New South Wales Aboriginal clergyman who went to the Pitjantjatjaraku lands in the 1980s without a permit. The South Australian government objected and charged him; a court case ensued and Brown was fined for trespassing.[11]

The years 1961 to 1965 saw arguments put by whites in general and politicians about whether to support or not any constitutional changes, to either publish counts of Aborigines in the national census by repealing section 127 or by changing and amending section 51 (xxvi) so as to allow the Commonwealth to make laws for Aborigines. Myths flew around in abundance – including many about Aborigines getting the vote – but what it showed was the inability of Australians to move independently with the times. In 1965, eight years after the petition was launched in federal parliament, Menzies agreed to meet a Council delegation. The Liberal-Country Party government resolved to hold the Referendum but set no date; Menzies retired in 1966, leaving the implementation to the incoming Prime Minister Harold Holt. The date was set soon after for 27 May 1967. All government actions in law, politics and economics have an effect upon people's lives and I discuss the consequences of the 1967 referendum, in a concluding chapter.

Whenever governments decide to spend money in their own interest, ideas tend to follow, and that is what happened in Aboriginal affairs after 1967. Dr HC 'Nugget' Coombs was appointed the chair of the government's Council for Aboriginal Affairs (I'll call it the Coombs Council), together with the politically

---

9   Bandler 1989: 88. See also Taffe 2005: 37-38.
10   Bandler 1989: 65-66. See also Taffe 2005: 104-106.
11   McCorquodale 1987: 76.

conservative anthropologist WEH Stanner and BG Dexter, Secretary of the Office of Aboriginal Affairs. Their brief was to fix what was understood to be the 'half-caste problem' first, and then later deal with the 'full-bloods'. They may not have used these exact words but that is what they meant. Nevertheless, the Coombs Council made no attempt to define what they meant when they called people Aborigines.

On a personal level, my work in the Canterbury Council had broadened by 1967, and I moved from the building to the pay-master's section, where I was responsible for calculating the garbage collectors' and refuse tip operators' wages together with other council charges. Later in the year I was approached by my benefactor, the New South Wales Aboriginal Education Council and offered a scholarship through the New South Wales Aboriginal Education Foundation. The scholarship was to attend Sydney Technical College on a full time basis to complete my matriculation in one year, and with Norma's blessing I agreed. This was a bit of a windfall for me and I had no idea where this would take me. In 1968 the Canterbury Council gave me leave without pay to enrol in four subjects: English, geography, history and second-level mathematics, all under the new Wyndham Scheme. I passed the four subjects, but not at a high enough level to be accepted by the University of Sydney. Not to be defeated, I applied to other Universities and was accepted by the Australian National, the Tasmanian and New England universities. I accepted the most attractive and took the offer from the Australian National University in Canberra.

The New South Wales Aboriginal Education Foundation still exists today. I was recently reminded, at Kevin Rudd's Sorry Day speech on 26 February 2008, by Trixie Davies, an Aboriginal woman from Sydney, who clearly remembers the day I was given the award. It drew tears to my eyes when reminded of the event 40 years earlier. She recalled that it was Djon Mundine, the art entrepreneur, and I who received the awards. It was an emotional night for Trixie too. From there I still had a very long road to hoe to where I wanted to go.

However, the more educated I became, the more I was steadily drawn into the circle of Aboriginal politics that I thought I had left behind in Adelaide. One of the enduring memories of this time is that I began to appreciate what New South Wales Aborigines had experienced for nearly 200 years under British and Australian governments. My Northern Territory Aboriginal family had only experienced this same destructive process for less than half that time. I recognised in myself a definite resistance and I could see it plainly now in Sydney. It was not just cultural, it was a resistance, not just about politics but also it was about economic and social non-conformism.

I moved from Sydney to Canberra in early 1969 and stayed in a college at the Australian National University while my family went to England for a well deserved holiday. They returned in June and we set up home in Canberra. In hindsight Canberra seemed as though it was an inevitable location for the family. I went there seeking a tertiary education but we all got much more than that.

Chapter 8
University and Aboriginal politics, 1969 to 1971

Canberra was not initially a daunting prospect for me, mostly because in my mind I was deluded that my education problems were all behind me. On arrival in the national capital I went straight to John XXIII College at the Australian National University and was given a room. From memory, this was a Roman Catholic College run by the Jesuits and the Dean I recall was the Reverend Dr John Eddy, who later figured prominently in my life. It was here in John XXIII College that I began my 40-year long association with university life.

I began attending lectures and in my spare time looked for accommodation for us as a family. I rented a house in Dickson which was within walking distance of the university, and looked forward to my family's return from England. Norma liked the place I found and we all settled into life in the national capital. One of the enduring memories of this time was Norma bringing a game of Monopoly back from England. It became nightly entertainment for the Briscoe and Perkins families. By this time Eileen and Charlie had three children, Hetti, Adam and my god-daughter Rachel. The Perkins family would arrive at our house in Dickson and Monopoly would be on for one and all: that was until one night when Charlie got soundly beaten and out of frustration the Monopoly board went up in the air – houses and money went everywhere! We still laugh about that night.

I felt lucky because I could combine my studies and political interests, mainly through friends living in Canberra as well as those who came to the capital on government business. Life as a student at first appeared straight-forward and I enrolled in four subjects: economics, statistics, accounting and political science. For me these subjects conjured up the idea that they would bring me status I'd never had before and people might listen to me both as an Aboriginal person and an economist. These subjects also seemed important and fitted in with my notion that the way ahead meant that in only four years I would be someone to be reckoned with in political life. This, I thought at age 31, was the way that things worked and that it was just a matter of time, of which I had a great deal.

My studies continued and I did reasonably well at mid-year examinations. During the mid-year break we went to Adelaide for a reunion with the St Francis House boys, celebrating Father Smith's eightieth birthday. At this time I had given very little thought to the Church's underlying weakness and rationale in removing us with or without our mothers' consent to educate us in Adelaide.

I discuss my change of heart later but on this trip we all went off happily to Adelaide to see friends, many of whom I had not seen for over a decade or so since leaving the boys' home.

We had a Volkswagen car at the time, and drove there and back via the Riverina and Murray Valley route. Aaron was old enough to absorb every changing and exciting new event during the journey. Norma and I took it in turns to drive the 17 hours from Canberra to Adelaide. We took the direct route over the Hay plains but from Renmark we digressed through Morgan travelling down through the top end of the Barossa Valley from Eudunda to Adelaide. In Adelaide we stayed with Norma's great school friend, our bridesmaid, Elaine Ziersch and her husband Geoff. Norma was keen to catch up with Elaine and meet her new baby son Christopher so the trip was an all-round favourite. The St Francis reunion was held at one of the boy's houses. Father and Mrs Smith were overwhelmed to see so many of their 'boys' grown up as adults with families of their own. I was also able to visit Millie Glenn, my mother's sister, who had cared for me as a young child during the war at Mulgoa in Sydney.

We journeyed home from Adelaide after a week via Murray Bridge, Loxton, Renmark and Wentworth through to Canberra. A couple of events on that trip are dear to my memory. One was when we stopped on the banks of the Murray River to have lunch; we looked around and saw this huge crate of oranges that had been dumped on the side of the river. At first we took just a couple to eat with our lunch – but – they were the juiciest and sweetest oranges we had ever tasted and we could not resist filling a large part of the back seat up with oranges for the rest of the journey. The other fond memory is that of following a rainstorm from Narrandera to Wagga Wagga with Aaron counting frogs on the highway as we travelled. It was dark and we could clearly see the frogs leaping in the headlights of the car all the way home.

While studying I felt confident that I could also be political. I occupied positions on the magazine *Identity*, the Aboriginal Housing Panel, Aboriginal student politics and the Federal Council (generally abbreviated to FCAATSI). Housing for Aborigines was a huge problem right across Australia. In part, this was because of population growth and, in part, because sedentary living without shelter made people sick and caused innumerable deaths from exposure. The states possessed a politically parsimonious policy in regard to Aboriginal housing. They built houses that white people wanted but that Aboriginal families found inappropriate. Lack of funds for maintenance was a common state administrative response – build houses for Aborigines and then just leave them alone, was their refrain.

Colonists inherited this racist attitude from their British roots of two centuries ago and it solidified their racial prejudices. My mother grew up under similar conditions and on many occasions I returned to find her living in a tin shack with a dirt floor, unlined walls with nail holes everywhere and doors that let flies and vermin in as they pleased. The housing panel enabled me to use my knowledge of poverty to travel extensively to both urban and rural areas, and to remote communities like the central and western desert regions. As a student I became deeply involved in Aboriginal issues and travelled to a number of conferences that included both government and FCAATSI business as a student delegate.

It is worth looking at some of FCAATSI's history not only because I was involved but because it was a major player in Aboriginal political reform. From FCAATSI's inception in 1958 the guiding ideas focused on 'advancement'. To many of the Aborigines involved, it seemed contradictory. Less than a decade after its beginnings the ideological flaws began appearing in FCAATSI's policies and it was under serious political attack from within. This unrest was underpinned to some extent by the fact that all the states within the Federation had draconian legislation that concentrated Aboriginal communities on reserves and missions, many of which were run by religious orders.

Legislation such as the 'White Australia Policy' operated under laws built on the myth that 'people of colour' produced societies with inherent 'racial' problems and undesirable social diseases. In the minds of white people, 'blacks' were devils, filthy, diseased and incapable of becoming like Europeans. So those white people already here not only prohibited 'black' persons but also those of swarthy Mediterranean descent from entering Australia under highly racist legislative criteria.[1] I use the term 'racism' here as one in which dominant societies use political power, in any form, to oppress groups in their society because of their 'colour', in particular; and because of their differences.[2]

FCAATSI built its aims on 'advancement' and gaining white paternalistic acceptance, and in so doing lost sight not just of international laws but missed a critique of Australian laws, and the white majorities practising the culture of racism. The revolt against racism was not just by Aborigines but by society in general. Nevertheless Aboriginal youth was the catalyst that, in their naivety, began to erode FCAATSI's underlying prejudices. What Aboriginal youth wanted was to change Australia's racist laws and to declare illegal acts that contravened international laws.

At the 1968 FCAATSI Easter conference, signs of confusion appeared. In hindsight, Aborigines at the conference were unsure who the delegates were and how much voting power Aborigines possessed. Aboriginal members and visitors could see that they had the balance of power in numbers. In the

---

1   Tavan 2005: 7-31.
2   Fredrickson 2002: 9.

circumstances FCAATSI's constitution ruled the day because all of the many Aborigines who turned up, but who were not delegates of a particular union or organisation, were not allowed to vote. As usual, the Aboriginal session drew about 100 participants who came from all states and the main issue focused on 'Land Rights and compensation'. South Australia already had land and compensation legislation but its laws had limitations. This particular year the Aboriginal delegates asked FCAATSI to support a publicity campaign for remaining states to grant land and compensation for loss of lands. Some focused on tribal lands, others wanted their mission and government reserve lands while those removed by previous generations wanted compensation to purchase land in urban areas for housing and employment.

That Friday evening Dr HC 'Nugget' Coombs gave a keynote speech on Aboriginal leadership. There was distinct scepticism about what Coombs stood for. Aborigines were impatient about what progress the Commonwealth, and in particular, Coombs and his Minister WC Wentworth (who was also present at the conference), had achieved following the 1967 referendum success. Joe McGuinness, the then President of FCAATSI, responded by saying that Coombs had not taken much notice of Aboriginal points of view and feelings. On the Saturday, I recall, there was general acceptance of Executive member Frank Engel's ideas to create a Trust Fund to give Aborigines more power over their own lives. But these were not ideas warmly accepted by most white people on the floor of the conference. Aboriginal dissent seemed a form of ungratefulness of the perceived good they had accomplished for Aborigines over a long period of time. And Faith Bandler showed certain complicity with this viewpoint.

Land Rights was on most lips the following year, but not on Minister Wentworth's, nor on his Party's collective mind. Liberal conservatives like Wentworth either rejected outright Aboriginal economic and political interests or hung steadfastly on to the notion that Aborigines had no claim on anything. At the same time students were rallying around the Gurindji claims for land and better working conditions, but left a gap in the collective minds of Australians. Faith Bandler and Jack Horner drew public criticism from many Aboriginal people for their lack of understanding of Aboriginal political issues.[3]

A later writer blamed the changing of FCAATSI's position on its lack of intellectual and ideological foresight. 'Land Rights' was a difficult proposition for FCAATSI members, which had until then focused on 'advancement' and not 'political change'. Even some members like Joe McGuinness could not grasp the gravity of the demand for land and its attack on the British notion of land ownership. Faith Bandler, as acting General Secretary, feared upsetting white society and the Council's meagre outside support, that is, the truculent white

---

3   Taffe 2005: 210.

Australian land owning upper-class.[4] Land demands tended to be too hard not only for the political and legal minds of FCAATSI, which feared this demand was revolutionary, and confrontational, but also for some Aboriginal executive members.

I recall Gordon Bryant discussing Ken Brindle's brutish nature, manners and attitude outside the Telopea Park High School's assembly hall where the conference took place. Bryant indicated privately that he not only vehemently disliked Brindle's brutishness and threatening manner but more that Brindle had no understanding of Aboriginal affairs outside New South Wales. Brindle, Bryant claimed, was more interested in being popular in Redfern. Bryant was right in some respects that Brindle was more interested in his ability to control crowds at the Big E (slang for The Empress Hotel, the Aboriginal haunt in Botany Road, Redfern) rather than Aboriginal politics in general. But there was another side to Brindle in that he wanted land for a cultural centre and sporting club and that is where Bryant revealed his own paternalism and lack of local knowledge. Brindle also found jobs for people and was extremely close to Department of Social Security officers; his other interest was looking after the Redfern-All-Blacks rugby team.

Charlie Perkins complained on the conference floor that FCAATSI was out of touch and that meetings should be held in the Northern Territory where members could really appreciate Aboriginal demands for Land Rights in an attempt to escape poverty. The conflict between Perkins and Bandler intensified in that period but mostly behind closed doors. Perkins had moved to Canberra and Bandler remained in Sydney, where she operated the FCAATSI office not far from Trades Hall in Sussex Street.

FCAATSI members listened to Aborigines who came to their conferences but did nothing to abate their real concerns. Aborigines believed the main agenda for FCAATSI members was the election of a Federal Labor government and because of its weak ideological perspective a resolution to have a 'Land Rights' campaign fell flat. This bought to the surface the concept that the return of Aboriginal lands frightened white people, allowing television commentators to observe just how land and pastoral lobbies reacted to Aboriginal spokespeople like Burnum Burnum. But in reality white peoples' fears were even more deep-seated in that they rejected the idea that Aborigines on missions, including those of mixed descent off reserves, could have any heritage claims. Most white people believed that land claims would bring the whole legal land structure down when in reality all Aborigines of any description wanted was a plate of food each day and to be like whites!

---

4   Taffe 2005: 208-10.

Some white FCAATSI spokespersons argued, as the historian Sue Taffe writes, that Aborigines were their own worst enemy because they could not understand what they wanted themselves. And even more revealing is that Aborigines were often unable to attend meetings to articulate what was occurring in their society. This exposed how little power Aboriginal Presidents such as Joe McGuinness really had in the organisation. Charlie Perkins continually complained to Faith Bandler about Joe's position but failed to impress her or other executive members. This captured the hostility between them. Later Charlie confided in me that the Council should have paid his fare to every Council meeting rather than leaving him out, only producing him when it was 'convenient to Council'. Changes to the executive in 1968 caused a deepening of the rift of the inability of Aborigines to articulate what they thought about their lives. Most Aborigines believed that, because of FCAATSI's failures, the Australian polity was unable to comprehend how they felt about their social and cultural circumstances including what they wanted from state and federal legislators.

Almost nothing changed in 1969 as most whites supporting FCAATSI, through finance or friendship, saw 'advancement' as meaning a 'multiracial coalition' and not social justice or anti-colonial redress – mirroring the notion argued years before by Professor Bill Geddes at the Foundation for Aboriginal Affairs. Most Australians believed that their rights were supreme and the United Nations post Second World War Declaration of Human rights reflected this 'brave new world'. There was little doubt that it resulted in a better society for white people but left virtually nothing for Aborigines. Little had changed since the British gladly handed the land over to Australians at Federation, and Aborigines got nothing. They were to be beyond all understanding of what it was to be human, to be beyond material gain, owned nothing and were to inherit nothing from their dead ancestors!

Social justice in the 1960s was a concept barely reaching the academic journals or the daily print media but it was a term used by lawyers, particularly those following international law. The silence of the anthropologists in dealing only with those people defined as possessing pure Aboriginal culture – the so-called advocates maintaining their lofty cultural illusions – was intellectually stultifying. As agents of government they worked when government money flowed. The only voice who understood the Aboriginal historical predicament on civil rights, legal rights and Land Rights was the Australian National University political scientist Charles Rowley, who was refused full membership to the Australian Institute of Aboriginal Studies. Rowley understood the rigour of change from colonial politics to Australian nationalism and how it affected all people of Aboriginal descent – not just those who served the interests of the anthropological discipline. Rowley also recognised that Aboriginal problems were political and not just economic and cultural questions.

Barrie Pittock had read the signs too, and was telling the FCAATSI executive that change had come and Aborigines wanted more than the Council had previously stood for. Pittock, a Quaker, had investigated the conditions of blacks in United States penal institutions. As the interest in, and by, the World Council of Churches and the United Nations intensified, these two bodies developed policies, including covenants, on oppressed and landless Indigenous peoples and began looking towards people affected by post-colonialism like Australia.4 These issues of Aboriginal 'autonomy', executive involvement and control sizzled beneath the surface as FCAATSI bore the brunt of growing Aboriginal radicalism. The 1968 annual conference shifted its ideology from 'advancement' to more complex ideas like Aboriginal autonomy, leadership as well as Aboriginal control of their organisations and future.

Ken Brindle has been credited for bringing Aboriginal leadership further into focus but I recall more Denis Walker, Bruce and Joe McGuinness, John Newfong and Kath Walker as the ginger group calling for overall change and greater Aboriginal leadership. Anger and dissent was fuelled by the failure of FCAATSI to either properly fund the 'All Aboriginal Land Committee' or to give the concept its full and spirited support. It appeared to those Aborigines present, myself included, that they did not know where it was going. This left participants at the 1969 meeting stunned, a position that tended to last all year while issues of Aboriginal leadership, autonomy and control dominated intellectual thought.

Although the Easter conference of 1970 was predicted to be the ideological battle-ground, few could have forecast what would happen. In addition, there was the elephant in the room – the Commonwealth Office of Aboriginal Affairs – and nobody was able to predict what impact it would have on the discussions! The development of Federal policy was in the hands of Coombs, Stanner, Dexter and the bumbling Federal Minister Howson as much as with Aboriginal spokespersons around the country. Everyone, including the Church, was vying for the moral high ground. While Aborigines around Australia were looking for inspiration from international political sources, FCAATSI looked to Barrie Pittock and Kath Walker for solace while Australians looked to the security of their own land titles for safety. But it was the Church and anthropological theorists that government relied on to articulate Aboriginal perspectives to the Advisory Council in 1970.

My critique of anthropology, and its disciples, is based on the fact that anthropologists dominated policy from the early part of the twentieth century until the new millennium. One such actor was Professor Bill Stanner who had returned from overseas in the late 1940s and was appointed as a reader in comparative social institutions at the Australian National University. Stanner was looked on as the heir apparent to Baldwin Spencer and Frank Gillen. Stanner offset any real Aboriginal political unity when he drew a long bow in his 1968 Boyer Lectures, *After the Dreaming*.[5] He successfully constructed a picture of a moribund Aboriginal society with nothing left of its culture and without capacity to either fight back or rebuild. On a number of occasions Stanner tended towards posturing as an amateur historian, not the anthropologist that he was, but relying on his Tory histrionics. He began his Boyer Lectures recalling Phillip's landing, his attempts at 'consultation' and his lasting legacy of failure. Stanner could not bring himself to talk of 'racism', because he believed Australian did not stoop to such prejudice, preferring to brand it as 'racial relations' drawing Aborigines into the bad half of that relationship.[6]

Stanner's private role as an anthropologist and conservative political actor was to ensure that in his and his colleague's minds Aborigines were defined as those who managed to retain a pristine culture. He held that any change to that pristine culture would render them without an ancestral claim on their heritage.[7] The catharsis Aborigines faced, according to Stanner, rendered them unwilling to put their claim and they could, therefore, do nothing but 'flock into [white] settlement'. Stanner believed that the 'natives' stories' ended in the first decade of British occupation.[8]

Australia's anthropologists were the first to sign-post the distinction between people of mixed European, British or other races and those they claimed as their own clientele, the people of 'full-descent'. Stanner always talked about Aborigines but these people had no names, no biographies and we knew nothing about their lives, what they did and the worlds they lived in. Australia knew very little about them and knows little still. Baldwin Spencer, the creator of Australian anthropology, had maintained that half-castes were the destroyers of Aboriginal culture and they must be got out of native society, or words to that effect. Stanner himself did not produce much major work from his own research and did not speak an Aboriginal language publicly: the very thing he hypocritically accused others of not doing. These days he is held up as an Australian intellectual icon and neither Aborigines nor white society appears to questions this.

In the early 1960s the Menzies government gave anthropologists huge Commonwealth funds to create a special organisation exclusively for antiquarians – the Australian Institute of Aboriginal Studies (AIAS) which later included Torres Strait Islanders in its title (AIATSIS). The Institute backed the anthropologists' faith in conservatism, and their moribund humanities discipline. To this day, anthropology has never questioned its monopoly. Anthropologists

---

5   *Stanner* 1972.
6   Stanner 1972: 7-8.
7   Stanner 1972: 8-11.
8   Stanner 1972: 11-15.

were able to double-dip in a way unavailable to other academics. If they failed to get a government research grant they could then make their bid to the Institute for a grant. Stanner's criticisms of historians helped to ensure that they were not granted membership of the Institute for some time, ensuring that until recently biographical and historical collections were limited. In addition, this club for anthropologists has remained silent on outside Aboriginal politics. So to come full circle: Stanner was in an ideal position to protect his interests as the anthropological representative of the Council for Aboriginal Affairs. His view of Aborigines as those of full descent prevailed. Consequently many Aboriginal rights and much of their heritage were forgotten.

Coombs's Council for Aboriginal Affairs was reticent in promoting democratic political structures in Aboriginal society. He and his Council members Stanner and Dexter preferred to continue what state government bodies had done before and following Federation: protectionism and assimilation. Freedom of association was absent from state legislation and was strictly forbidden even in the face of democratic trade union and equal wage struggles by the Northern Territory Ordinance.[9] The Council did nothing about the Aboriginal labour question until well into the 1970s when it created the community development employment programs. Stanner, working in the northern areas of Australia, made only non-committal comments on the struggles over equal wages, often after the event. The comments he made were mainly about lawyers, not freedom of Aboriginal labour, a struggle which had been raging since before the 1920s. Once 'Land Rights' came up as a political issue, anthropologists resisted giving political advice to FCAATSI nor did they offer their affiliation.

Aborigines across Australia thought that 'Land Rights' would mean a Land Rights Commission to work through the return of traditional lands to all peoples who were owed a birth right. However, the appointment of an anthropologist to advise Woodward made certain that Aborigines who no longer practised their traditional culture as they themselves defined it, would get nothing. This anthropological strategy ensured that limited benefits went to non-tribal groups even though they had moral and legal rights to their heritage and land. Aborigines and their democratic interests were sidelined until the 1980s when the Hawke government moved to create a new commission to be a supreme representative governing council for the Indigenous peoples.

These understandings, impressions and events set the stage for the catharsis that beset FCAATSI meetings before and after the election of the Whitlam government in 1972. This story had its origins as the Easter conference of 1970 loomed; most Aborigines interested in what was happening in FCAATSI knew that the World Council of Churches would soon be providing funds to support the growth and

---

9   Stevens 1974.

development of a national Aboriginal political body. Others have given their views on the workings of FCAATSI in the early 1970s, but I want to concentrate on the internal 'split' as I recall it. At the time I was a student living in Canberra and attended the meeting as an Australian National University representative for the National Student Union. The numbers of Aborigines present is hard to gauge but it was certainly more than in 1969.

Issues of Aboriginal political rights dominated along with questions of control, leadership and autonomy. I distinctly recall the early sessions were mainly about Commonwealth grants to Roper River and Willowra cattle stations. Spokespersons for these groups wanted support for their moves to buy back their traditional land on cattle properties. Dexter Daniels and Martin Jumpatjimba asked especially for their land to be bought back under a Commonwealth pastoral grant and got a resounding vote of support. The Office of Aboriginal Affairs was having a real impact both on land and constitutional questions and it was significant that Dr Coombs would speak that evening on the question of 'autonomy and leadership'. Kath Walker raised discussion on the constitutional question that all Aborigines be given full voting rights in FCAATSI business. To support these notions we were all given candle-lit torches and marched from the Telopea Park school hall to Parliament House where a number of speakers talked on 'Land Rights'.

The following day both Aborigines and Commonwealth officials tried to persuade and influence the conference to hand over power to Aboriginal people. People like Kath Walker, Doug Nicholls, Charlie Perkins, Phillip and Jacob Roberts, Len Watson and John Newfong all indicated that Aborigines were ready and willing to take control of FCAATSI. Talk by most whites and a few Aboriginal state delegates likened the push to 'Black Power' which alienated some FCAATSI delegates who took a more conservative line echoing the idea that politics was about compromise. However, compromise was not a sentiment in the minds of most Aborigines, who wanted nothing less than a take-over.

FCAATSI was in turmoil as Joe McGuinness, Jack Horner, Ken Brindle and Faith Bandler tried to change the nature of the discussions and move past the question of constitutional change. Executives also tried to console the majority, but had there been an open vote Kath Walker's motion would most certainly have been carried. But back room dealings, led mostly by Bryant, Bandler, Brindle and Horner, succeeded in delaying election of new office bearers, and the constitutional question of Aboriginal autonomy was back on the agenda. This political strategy was designed to take advantage of the fact that many Aborigines had left the conference and the delay meant that the constitutional question was defeated. Doug Nicholls and Kath Walker called for a further vote of those present, rather than a delegate vote, asking those who supported the defeated motion to move to one side and those who did not, to move to the other side of the hall. Others recall this as a:

> rift [which] marked the effective end of the Federal Council as a body that brought together diverse representatives from all over the country: both Indigenous people and non-Indigenous supporters such as trade unionists, members of churches and religious bodies and peace activists.[10]

The final nail in the coffin for FCAATSI was driven in with Labor's victory in 1972. The balance of power in Aboriginal Affairs changed subtly, and sometimes not so subtly. The new Minister Gordon Bryant's long involvement with FCAATSI gave him a sound understanding of the ideology, workings and membership of the organisation; he was fully aware of the current schism within the movement. One of the first things he did was to bring together members of the old, mainly white FCAATSI guard, together with the new young Aboriginal radicals. Bryant then performed what would now be called classic wedge or divide-and-conquer politics by symbolically sidelining the old guard from any further policy discussion within government by taking the radicals out to dinner to seek their counsel. In so doing he left the white members out in the cold. Gordon Bryant went on to create what looked to be a representative body of Aboriginal advisors in the form of the National Aboriginal Consultative Council. However, this body was not one democratically elected but one carefully selected by the Office of Aboriginal Affairs staff. Democracy went out the window and bureaucracy took its place.

Stepping back a little, the period from 1970 to 1971 for me involved two significant events: the creation of the 'National Tribal Council', and my family's move back to Sydney. First, the National Tribal Council. After the 1967 referendum, Joyce Clague and Don Dunstan went to Geneva and came back with the impression that when South African liberation movements had achieved their goal, Aboriginal aspirations would be the next agenda item. To temper this impression Kath Walker attended a World Council of Churches conference on racism, returning to Australia with her eyes widened and her resolve stiffened to root out FCAATSI's paternalism and assimilationist programs. She had a steadfast supporter in Barrie Pittock. Thus the 1970s 'split or rift' had a next stage – the creation of the National Tribal Council. This body was funded by contributions from the World Council of Churches and was modelled on the existing Queensland Tribal Council. It was created following a vitriolic struggle of Aborigines wanting to take-over control of FCAATSI. This push included backing John Newfong as General Secretary. In September of 1970 the first

---

10 Taffe 2005: 260.

annual Tribal Council conference was held. I was appointed as the Council's Minister for Health, a position I held until October 1972. While these political fractures persisted and dominated my thinking my education was affected and I failed miserably the end of year university exams. I then enrolled at the newly created Canberra College of Advanced Education where I studied and passed three subjects, English, systems theory and organisational theory. But my meagre scholarship was proving more and more difficult for a growing family to live on, leading me to apply for a Liaison Officer's position at the Foundation for Aboriginal Affairs in Sydney.

In April of 1970 I attended a conference on Aboriginal drug and alcohol dependency. While there I met the young Gary Foley, an Aboriginal political activist from Sydney. Gary was born in Grafton in New South Wales and had parental links to Gympie in Queensland. He had spent his youth in Coffs Harbour and migrated to Sydney as a drafting apprentice.[11] He spent time at an adult education employment program at the University of Sydney's adult education centre. The program was financed by Commonwealth Social Security funding, and managed by Allan Duncan, a white lecturer, and Ken Brindle. Foley talked to me about what was happening in Aboriginal politics in Sydney, how he had come to Sydney and what the political climate was like. Foley told me that the Foundation needed staff with a capacity to be able to change its policy away from a welfare body bent on providing services to the poor and destitute. These were admirable tasks, but Gary wanted me to get involved in the creation of a legal service for migrating Aborigines from rural areas who were being harassed by squads of police in the inner city area.

I returned to Canberra not with study on my mind but the urge to take the job in Sydney. In June and July of 1970, I went to Perth in Western Australia for the National Tribal Council Conference and up to the Warburton Ranges to look at Aboriginal housing conditions at the local mission. The National Tribal Council had by this time received funding from the World Council of Churches.[12] As Health Minister, I reported on the state of Aboriginal health and the Council supported my idea that primary health care funds be budgeted to help establish independent primary health arrangements. Other Council members backed this concept, well aware that many communities known to them were without access to medical and health services. Rural white people could access specialist treatment in regional centres when their bus or plane travel was funded by Commonwealth rural health subsidies. Why was it that Aborigines could not access these primary and secondary health services, I wondered? I answer these

---

11 McGlade 1994: 374. See also Duncan 1971-76: 1150-1174.
12 Howie-Willis 1994c: 764-765.

questions later, but as I was really only one of a few people in the organisation that had any semblance of understanding about the Australian health system at the time, our expertise was stretched.

In September 1970 I was successful in gaining a paid position at the Foundation for Aboriginal Affairs in Sydney. We left Canberra all packed up in the Volkswagen with light hearts looking forward to a new chapter of our lives back in Sydney. At the time the chairman of the Foundation for Aboriginal Affairs was Professor Geddes. Geddes was a New Zealander who had married a Maori woman and they were both original members of the Foundation's board. Professor Geddes was head of the Department of Anthropology at the University of Sydney, where Charlie Perkins had majored in anthropology in the middle of the 1960s. They had become political allies in developing the Foundation's welfare and political strategy. One of the original key policies developed by Geddes and Charlie had been the idea of having a property wholly owned by the Foundation on George Street, Sydney. Now that was achieved. There was an underlying ideological current among those running the Foundation. Geddes supported a liberal approach to race relations that favoured a multi-racial board which raised its own funds through public donations. The liberal position was to bring into practice new 'race relations' ideas together with 'economic opportunities'. Most Aborigines supported these liberal views but it caused some friction with the left-leaning Labor Party supporters. The socialist view favoured government funding with a totally Aboriginal board practising self-determination and was supported by FCAATSI radicals, the Glebe Labor factions, the Aboriginal trade unionists and the University of Sydney student movement.

The other *raison d'être* of the Foundation was to be an organisation with considerable political clout that Aborigines could learn to run. The idea was that when the Foundation made a public announcement it would be a rallying cry that others in New South Wales and ultimately Australia would listen to. That was the theory when I arrived, a theory that had lasted from the early 1960s when funds were first raised for the purchase of land and the Foundation's operations. In 1970 I still believed that the organisation was a force for good and opposed what most thinking Aboriginal people in New South Wales saw as the abominable practice of 'assimilation'.[13]

The move back to Sydney had disappointments initially both on the home and work fronts. We moved as a family back to our old weatherboard home in Greenacre. The house had been rented out while we were in Canberra and when we returned we found a big hole in the lounge room wall along with a very sad looking house. It was a big frustration for both of us, but more so for Norma

---

13 Rowley 1971a: 383-450.

because she had struggled for years to buy furniture for the house and had gone back to work to buy new carpets that were now ruined. Norma was never fully able to see the house in a better light and we began to look for another home.

While all this was going on I began working as the Foundation's field officer. I had a great belief that the Foundation was all those things I've already spoken about, essentially a place of hope and opportunity for Aborigines. The first three managers were Aborigines – Charlie Perkins, Chicka Dixon and Herb Simms – but by the time I started there was a white ex-Commonwealth public servant as manager, Peter Taylor. I was not immediately disillusioned, throwing myself into the new job. At the same time we began looking for a house closer to my work. But it was not long before other Aboriginal members of staff started expressing their disappointment about their wages and the way they were being treated.

Much of my time in the Foundation's office was spent providing welfare assistance such as meal tickets to destitute Aborigines to eat at a grill cafe in George Street. It is likely that when the Foundation was first established the main focus was this welfare role rather than pursuing liberty for all Aborigines. But by the time I came to work there things had become more complex. There was a general feeling of disquiet about the way Taylor and the Foundation executive were running this once important organisation. So strong were the Aboriginal staff member's feelings that a strike was called. A week later I was sacked. I was now out of work and spending my time fund raising and doing social welfare tasks for the National Tribal Council. While not working in the community I sharpened up my home renovation skills.

We were more fortunate with the new house search than I was with the job. We found a house that we both liked in Summer Hill, an inner city suburb of Sydney with good rail transport links. It was a semi-detached full brick house of Federation style with dark red brick, slate roof and terrazzo front verandah. The outside was in very good condition but the inside needed renovating. I neither regarded myself as a renovator, nor a handyman, but I had learned some maintenance at the boys' home and applied these skills. Two of the bedrooms were in need of major repairs including joists and new floor-boards. After repairing the floors I sanded and varnished them back to their original Russian white pine origins. We painted and re-papered the walls in the dining room and prepared the kitchen for an update. An Aboriginal friend, Jerry Bostock, helped paint the main lounge and second bedroom. But the renovation work was endless and more and more my time at home was reduced as other demands increased.

Part of my job at the Foundation had been familiarising myself with aspects of Aboriginal politics and organisational activities between La Perouse, the City and Glebe. Gary Foley introduced me to the Aboriginal Legal Service Committee and we met each week at the Presbyterian Church in Botany Road, Redfern, about five doors up from South Sydney Community Aid. The legal service committee was made up of white and Aboriginal members. Most of the white members were lawyers and included people like Professor (later Justice) Hal Wootten, Ross McKenna, Eddy Neumann, Bob Debus, Paul Lander, Gordon Samuels and Peter Isaacs. The Aboriginal members were Paul Coe, Gary Williams, Gary Foley, Billy Craigie and me. These meetings often included visiting Aboriginal men from country areas as well as students who were associated with the Aboriginal Education Foundation and the Allan Duncan Adult Education program at the University of Sydney. My ties with the legal service were to open up a new chapter in my life.

This was a time of great excitement and change following the repeal of racist laws in the late 1960s. By the early 1970s rural New South Wales reserve and fringe camp Aborigines were flocking into Sydney looking for work opportunities and a better way of life, and that's a story I elaborate upon in the next chapter.

Figure 21: Our wedding, Apsley Church, United Kingdom, 1962.

Figure 22: Herb and Ruth Simms at their Sydney home, 1965. Herb was the Director of the Foundation for Aboriginal Affairs in the mid 1960s.

Figure 23: Norma's parents, Beatrice and Ernest Foster visiting Australia, 1966.

Figure 24: Picnic at Wattamolla, Sydney, 1967: Eileen, Charlie and Hetti Perkins, Vincent Copley, me, John Moriarty and my son Aaron in front.

Figure 25: My mother at Melanka Hostel, Alice Springs, about 1970.

Figure 26: My Mardu family, circa 1970: my mother's two brothers Percy and Intji are on the far left, and Uncle Cydika Warri.

Figure 27: Charlie Perkins and me at apartheid demonstration at Australia v South African Rugby match Sydney Cricket Ground, 1971.

Figure 28: St Francis House reunion, 1967: Father Smith second row, second from left.

Figure 29: Djabangardi. My Australia Party campaign photograph 1972. Authorised by PJ Graham, Mitchell Street, Darwin.

Figure 30: Federal election, 1972: George Bray and family and my campaign manager Len Smith in shorts.

Figure 31: Briscoe and Perkins family on holidays at Malua Bay, New South Wales, 1978: back row, from left to right Adam, Eileen, Aaron, Hettie, Norma, John, front row, Charlie, Rachel (my goddaughter), Lisa and me.

Figure 32: Farnham House, my son Aaron, Gary Foley and Kelly (Farnham House resident), 1983.

Figure 33: Self and Fred Hollows at the time of his Australian of the Year award, 1990.

Figure 34: My sons Aaron and John, mid 1990s.

Figure 35: My son Aaron and his partner Meredeth Taylor, 1993.

Figure 36: My daughter Lisa and self at her admittance as an ACT solicitor.

Figure 37: My PhD Conferral, Canberra, 1997: from left to right Sam (Jupurulla) brother, self, Michael Johnson, Norma, Roz and John Moriarty, Gabi Hollows, Mike Lynskey and John Balazs.

Figure 38: My grandson Mitchell Taylor-Briscoe and me on a cricket break, Canberra, 2001.

Figure 39: My brother Bill and Gerry Hill, Canberra, 2001.

Figure 40: My cousin Mary Ross (nee Kenny) and Aaron, 2000.

Figure 41: My sister Jennifer Summerfield at Umuwa Pitjantjajara Homelands where she is a health worker and traditional artist, 2004.

Figure 42: Launch of my book Counting, Health and Identity: A history of Aboriginal health and demography in Western Australia and Queensland 1900-1940 at the Sydney Writers Festival, 2004: from left to right Julia Moriarty, Rosa (my goddaughter), Norma, Anna and Ruth Hollows and Kate Balazs.

Figure 43: Australia Day AO Award with my son Aaron on lawns of Government House, Canberra, 2004.

Figure 44: Australia Day AO Award 2004 at Government House, Canberra 2004: from left to right Governor General Michael Jeffrey, Dr Tom Gavranic, Millie Glenn, me, Norma and Mara Gavranic.

Figure 45: My brother Sam with his sons Sam and Leeroy, 2008.

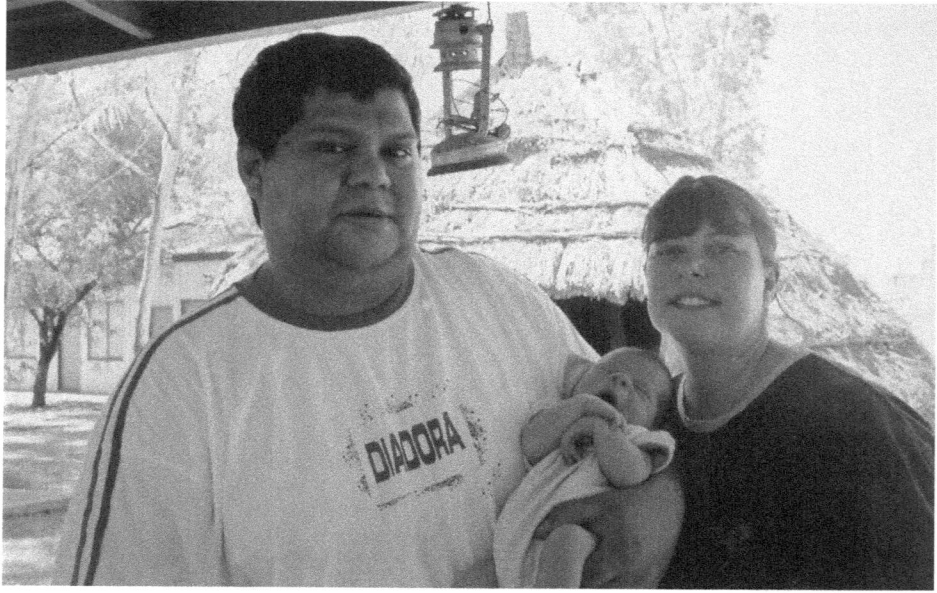

Figure 46: My daughter Lisa, partner Shaun Wilde, and baby Jack at Glen Helen, 2005.

Figure 47: My eldest grandson Mitchell, 2009.

Figure 48: My grandson Jack and me at Malua Bay, New South Wales, 2008.

Figure 49: This is where it all began for me – Pembroke Street. I still recall my mother leaving me here in 1945. Self with friends Elaine and Geoff Ziersch, 2009.

Chapter 9
Redfern and the early 1970s

Being unemployed in Sydney with a family and a wife to support were frightening thoughts. This was the second time that I had put myself in this predicament and I did not relish telling Norma what had happened. We had only recently returned to Sydney and our savings were meagre; the future for us looked grim financially. But as it sometimes happens in life we made one of our biggest commitments at a time when we had least money. One of our major concerns was the growing number of primary schools that Aaron had been to mainly due to our instability. We decided that although we had very little money what we had would be well spent on stable schooling for Aaron and we enrolled him at Trinity Grammar at Strathfield in the south-west of Sydney. It was one of our best decisions and Aaron loved the school and did very well both at his school work and as part of the school's sports teams.

For me the next couple of years were jam packed with action and motion. In the months following my sacking from the Foundation I spent much of the time raising funds and promoting the National Tribal Council; mostly in Sydney. One of our biggest fund raising events was selling second-hand clothing to Aboriginal families in and around Redfern and La Perouse. In Canberra, Eileen Perkins had organised a fund raising drive by asking for good quality clothing, games and toys which she then sent up to us in a very large truck. We stored everything in part of our bedroom and a sunroom at the front of our house. This gave me some funds to promote the new Aboriginal national body that was created on the basis of 'self-determination'. And I owe a debt of gratitude to Chicka Dixon, Tommy Williams, Ozzie Cruse, Herb Simms, other Simms families and Trudy Longbottom, all from the south coast and La Perouse for their help in this venture. At the same time I was working on a voluntary basis for the Redfern Aboriginal Legal Service which gave me the opportunity to familiarise myself with the organisation's objectives and people on its inaugural council.

Early 1971 was a time when everything was happening in Sydney, and in particular Redfern. The Aboriginal Legal Service, or just the Legal Service as it came to be known, was created on the back of growing radicalism of the rural Aboriginal population migrating into the city. The thinking behind this radicalism was the need for legal protection for rural Aborigines, who bought with them a lack of understanding of urban European culture. The nature of this growing political radicalism was highly demanding of Australian society in general: although the gullible Australian press wanted to believe something more sensational, basically it amounted to Aborigines fear of a culture of police brutality and white lawyer self-interest.

I worked closely with the newly appointed secretary of the Aboriginal Legal Service Ross McKenna, and assisted him in bringing the objectives of the organisation to as many Aborigines as possible. At this time legal services for poor people in New South Wales were based on what was called a 'public defender' system and operated by people applying to the courts for the appointment of a lawyer. In theory the system should have worked but as is often the case the reality was different. Many people coming in contact with the courts, such as jailed prisoners or their family members, applied for legal representation but often found it difficult to access. The system propped up both an illusion of justice and an assumption of freedom and liberty. The reality was that overworked and ignorant police officers out of convenience often handed out 'plead guilty' advice to those charged, telling them they would be treated leniently. The other method was for the accused to front the Magistrate, who would ask the accused if he or she had legal representation and if not a lawyer at the bench would be asked to take the case on a minute's notice. If nobody volunteered the prisoner or plaintiff would be asked to complete an application that was often too complicated for those with poor educational backgrounds to fill out. It was a very archaic system that lacked a guarantee of either human rights or justice.

The new liberal approach by the legal service was to be different. It was constituted to be able to raise its own funds and, where necessary, arrange for free legal services and representation for any Aboriginal person in need. A liaison system was implemented where a person with local racial or ethnic knowledge would seek out the person charged and offer them free legal representation.

I had been a regular visitor to Long Bay gaol on Foundation business, and now that I was no longer employed by the Foundation I decided to poach their activity. Each Monday and Wednesday I would call at the watch-house and ask if the Aborigines there had lawyers to represent them. If the answer was in the negative the guards would let me in to speak to prisoners in small confessional type boxes inside the prison. This was how I established a rapport with the guards. Equally this was how I became known at the Bay and would sometimes talk to five or six Aboriginal people who had no legal representation. Our system worked well and the process started immediately after I talked to the client and it was far more efficient than the public defender system. I would then go to Ross McKenna's office in the Arts faculty at the University of New South Wales at Kensington and we would arrange for lawyers there and then. The following day I would revisit Silverwater, Parramatta and the Long Bay gaols and outline to inmates what they could expect from our service. I gave them notes on what was happening, what the charges meant and the name of the lawyer who would be representing them. In addition, I contacted their families, took family members to see them, took families to court and gave them money for smokes and reading material.

I quickly built up a working relationship with locals such as Shirley Smith, or Mum Shirl as everyone called her. I first met Mum Shirl in 1965 as a volunteer at the Foundation and through Ross McKenna I reacquainted myself with her. Mum Shirl had had a long association with prisoners at most of the adult and children's remand centres around Sydney and in my early days at the legal service she proved to be an invaluable link between the service and Aborigines in custody. I had already met some of the inmates I represented at Long Bay gaol during my time at the Foundation needing welfare or on Friday nights at the discotheque run by the late Matt Silver and his Black Lace band. The lawyers we drew on I found were really great people and the system appeared to work from the outset.

In February of 1971 the inaugural Legal Service council meeting took place at the student roundhouse at the University of New South Wales. I still had no paid work and we were living off $200 Professor Hal Wootten had loaned the family. I applied for the position of Liaison Officer and recall attending an interview of about six people at Hal Wootten's office in the weather-board rooms of the law faculty. I had met only two members of the committee previously: Hal Wootten and Paul Coe the resident Aboriginal member. The interviewing committee asked me a few questions about Redfern but mostly focused on two things – did I think the Legal Service was a valuable contribution to Aborigines' wellbeing and did I have a car of my own? The answer to the first question was that since the 1967 referendum Aborigines were migrating in huge numbers to urban areas and in many instances were unable to adapt lawfully to their new situations. In the case of Sydney there were few lawyers in a position to take clients who either could not or would not pay. Migrating Aborigines often did not have employment and after coming into contact with the law had little knowledge of how systems worked and gained little comfort from police and prison guards. Rather, they were regularly picked on by police, often with no reason. The answer to the second question about my own transport was that I owned a Volkswagen that was both easy to maintain and cheap to run. The committee had other people to see and I was told the outcome would be known in a few days. Later that week I learnt to my great relief that I had the job.

I began the new job the following week with two other people, the new secretary, Anne Weldon (nee Coe) and the full-time non-Aboriginal lawyer, David Collins. Anne was a very efficient and placid person who came from the Cowra area. She was of Wiradjuri descent and had good links with the community. David Collins had been working as a commercial lawyer with a North Sydney firm and was a great person to work with. Defending and working with Aborigines was a very challenging job but Dave knew nevertheless almost instinctively what was needed. It was Dave who managed the office and he got on very well with both Anne and me. What impressed me most was his capacity to get the best lawyers to work on the tasks allocated to them. I also saw him operate in court and he was always impressive. He had a very nice approach to Aboriginal people and taught me a lot about dealing with police and lawyers at the same time. I have always wondered how lawyers can contain themselves with civility while at the same time protecting the interests of their clients. My role as a community advocate came easily to me and the learning component, which I always enjoy in a job, came in the form of learning the ropes of being an articled clerk to Dave. My Canterbury Council work stood me in good stead for that task and my tertiary education prepared me for research and report writing. I believe my biggest achievement and success was the ability to work directly with families and the people who knew them.

Two case examples will suffice to highlight the work of the legal service: first, a case involving a bank robbery at Dubbo and second, the case of a man accused of escaping from police custody. As they say in all good stories, real names will not be used. In the first example I got a frantic phone call from the mother of an Aboriginal young man who had held up a bank in a town out west and he was now on the run from police. He was in hiding with a friend, terrified to give himself up, fearing that he would be bashed as a recidivist. His mother, on the other hand, was fearful and panic stricken that the police would shoot him in an attempt to capture him. I told the woman that I would contact Mum Shirl (Shirley Smith) and meet her at her home in Newtown. I found Mum Shirl and we contacted a lawyer. The lawyer advised the mother that the best course of action would be to try and persuade the young man to give himself up in the hope of getting a fair go. The mother agreed and Mum Shirl and I picked up the young man and took him to meet the lawyer at the Legal Service office in Botany Road, Redfern at the rear of the South Sydney Community Aid. The young man agreed to have the lawyer represent him. Mum Shirl and I visited him on a regular basis while he was in custody. We also took his mother to see him and attend his trial. He received a custodial sentence but this was the last time he offended and I believe that because of other rehabilitation services in custody he reformed and has since shown great leadership in the community.

The second example concerned an even younger Aboriginal youth who was involved in an escape from custody while being shifted from one country penal establishment to another. I cannot recall the full details of the escape and how it was allowed to happen but the boy not only escaped but he bashed a police officer before running into thick bush. Mum Shirl came to my home in Summer Hill and told me that the boy was the eldest son of an Aboriginal woman from the Young area and whose father had died. The young man had already been through the Children's Court a number of times. However, he really was the bread winner and the mother was desperate to stop him being mistreated and spending more time in jail, leaving the family destitute. From home I contacted Dave Collins and he quickly came to our aid. He went to the Redfern Police Station and arranged for the boy to give himself up to police and at the same time ensured that senior officers were involved and underlined the fact that we wanted to help and not hinder the police. This approach resulted in a good outcome and I saw him in Long Bay gaol a few times before he went to court again. This is a well known case and I will not discuss it any further, except to say that the family was reunited some time after the event and the youth went on to build a good life for himself in his own community.

I relate these events not just as examples of good news stories but rather to highlight the fact that the law promises minority groups the same treatment as everyone else. However, history and practice reveal that this had not always been the case and the Redfern Aboriginal Legal Service created a new liberal approach to legal aid for Aboriginal people. Coercive institutions exist because societies living without liberty fail to take account of the 'rights of human beings', Peoples' rights can be overrun by war but they can and do get overrun in societies that believe it cannot happen in their patch. We know it does! Aboriginal legal services were curtailed by the Liberal-National Party governments in the late 1970s and again after 1996 mainly because of mistaken belief that they acted against the government's interest.

While there were good news stories there were also incidents that went very wrong, created by circumstances beyond anyone's control. One such incident occurred one Monday morning when Dave Collins and I went to pick up an Aboriginal man at his brother's house in Eveleigh Street, Redfern. He was to be at Redfern Court for the early session. These terraced houses were very small places and as I went into the tiny front room I could see there must have been 25 people sleeping in the room with barely a space between each body. I could see our client in a far corner and told him I was there to take him to court. He said he was too sick to go, so I left. On the footpath outside I lamented to Dave Collins that this was where the legal service had lacked real depth because if people were sick the service itself would come under attack and would be unworkable.

The issue of its client's poor health was a major concern for the legal service and was intensified by the issue of population distribution. Up until the 1960s the majority of New South Wales Aborigines had lived in rural areas, however, by the early 1970s large numbers of youth who were high-school educated were deliberately leaving reserves to look for better jobs in the city. When they came to the city they either stayed with relatives, in empty houses or at refuges. For the most part large populations were pushed out into state housing at Blacktown, Campbelltown and west of Parramatta and came into town on weekends to access cheap entertainment in concentrated locations like Redfern and Kings Cross. They were expected to use mainline standard health services but in many instances failed to do so until it was too late. This seething problem quickly alienated these young migrants who were looking for a better life rather than the torture of everyday living under control on government reserves.

The problems of 'culture-shock', poverty, missed opportunity and alienation coupled with ignorance of white culture exacerbated Aboriginal peoples' health problems. Somewhere around April of 1971 I called a meeting to talk about general health problems but more particularly about the lack of medical practitioners in areas where they were most needed. At the back of my mind was the fact that the Australian primary health system was fundamentally based upon a patient's relationship with a medical practitioner. But more often than not general practitioners moved out of slum areas such as Rosebery, Erskineville, Newtown, Chippendale, Surrey Hills and Redfern when poorer folk moved in and were unable to pay for consultations.

With the drying up of primary health care Aborigines were dependent on centralised health structures based in large hospitals. Often when health monopolies occur they undermine age-old structures and the weak and poor are the ultimate casualties. Casualty was the word because it was the poor and weak that used emergency hospital services when they needed to see a doctor. The mindset of many rural Aborigines was to keep away from towns and government agents and only call for medical assistance when an illness or disease had reached the chronic stage. And when this happened they often saw a different contract doctor each time resulting in a less than satisfactory lasting relationship with a general practitioner. Redfern was a veritable desert and even if there had been doctors there it was unlikely they would be general practitioners offering their services to non-paying customers. The only option was therefore the outpatient services of hospitals.

It was in this milieu that I called a meeting to thrash out the possibility of establishing a general medical practice service for Aborigines in Redfern. Nothing like this had been done in Australia before and so it was a big first! But sometimes luck and serendipity come together. Late one Friday night as I was leaving Hal Wootten's law faculty office I bumped into Christine Jennett, a sociology student who was a member of the Communist party and the Gurindji committee. On this night she had come to see one of her tutors about the Gurindji land question and I mentioned to her the meeting about setting up a medical service. She was unable to come but knew of some doctors who were concerned about health problems in Aboriginal stock camp communities in the Northern Territory; they might be interested in helping. I advertised the meeting for the following Thursday.

Eight people were at the meeting – Mum Shirl, Dulcie Flower, Len Smith, Reverend Wesley and John Russell from South Sydney Community Aid and two late comers Dr Paul Beaumont and Professor Fred Hollows – the Gurindji committee doctors. Fred and Paul were ophthalmologists who worked at the University of New South Wales Eye Clinic at the Prince of Wales Hospital in Randwick. Fred was head of the clinic and Paul was a graduate student in Fred's teaching department.

Basically I was outlining to the few who came that medical practitioners had vacated the poor areas in the local suburbs. Fred spoke rather impatiently to begin with, saying that Aborigines did have access to general practitioners who would service them on demand. This attitude angered me and I began to spell out the difficulties Aborigines faced. I told Fred about the Aboriginal populations migrating from destitute rural government reserves, that they came for work, which they were little prepared for and how they slept in empty houses. When they got sick general practitioners were nowhere to be found in the local suburbs because they relied on paying clients and there were few able to pay, black or white. Many of the sick would wait for near death conditions, and then would either be taken to hospital by ambulance or to casualty for emergency treatment. I reiterated the notion that Aborigines were entitled to the same relationship with a medical practitioner expected by other Australians. In addition, Aborigines and their children suffered from diseases other Australian had only heard about in third world countries: diseases such as worms, impetigo and anaemia which led on to serious social problems like missing school and work.

Fred was silent; but Paul Beaumont said, 'We could round up a number of doctors to work for nothing'. Fred responded, 'We could get some free drugs from the Prince of Wales Hospital: but where would we operate from?' John Russell and Reverend Wesley piped-up, 'We have a shop on the other side of the road and you could have that rent free.' Mum Shirl said, 'A few people such as the Brigidines from North Sydney could operate a transport group.' Dulcie Flower said, 'I know a few Aboriginal nurses around the traps and we could also be responsible for bringing in and managing the patients.' I then said, 'Look we need to have a controlling body that is both community-based and democratic.' And so the first Aboriginal Medical Service was born. We all decided to call the first General Meeting in two weeks' time. I indicated that we did not really want an exclusive body but one that was open and transparent. I added that we needed to elect a governing committee and get the backing of the community. But Fred wanted to get things going immediately. That was the kind of man he was – impetuous! He began by saying: 'Look, we can begin the process now and have something to show how it works by the time the General Meeting takes place.' John Russell opened the shop the next day and

Fred came in the afternoon with a truck full of boxes of medicines and medical equipment, all brand new. The service was not yet constitutionally established but was nevertheless off and running.[1] The idea soon spread and today there are Aboriginal Medical Services all around Australia. They all have their genesis in that Redfern meeting of 1971.

Many people in Aboriginal affairs during this period linked their struggle to the South African question, which was quite possibly due to the increasing Roman Catholic influence in the World Council of Churches. The Aboriginal Legal Service, and in particular its young Aboriginal radicals, initially criticised the anti-apartheid movement for not being active against Aboriginal dispossession, poverty and oppressive government treatment. However, it was not long before these same activists – Gary Foley, Paul Coe and Gary Williams – were deeply immersed in encouraging Sydney and New South Wales Aborigines to get involved in protesting against the South African Springboks sporting teams touring Australia and New Zealand.

Everywhere the Springboks played Aboriginal leaders were standing up to protest against white South African treatment of blacks. They linked the South African struggle with Australia's treatment of Aborigines and the Legal Service was in the forefront in getting as many lawyers as they could to protect the interests of those arrested at the demonstrations. My cousin Charlie Perkins and I were there, on the eastern or Paddington side of the Sydney Cricket Ground, when a great wave of people went over the fence. We all surged forward in an attempt to stop police arresting demonstrators. I could see lawyers I knew such as Eddie Neumann and Bob Debus along with Ross McKenna as well as Fred Hollows being dragged across the Cricket Ground to a cavalcade of 'Paddy Wagons'.[2] The lawyers had special collar badges on so they were able to go up close to the police vehicles. The violence was at its highest just before half time. As I left the field I could see large numbers of Aborigines and supporters wearing Springbok jumpers and yelling 'Aboriginal Land Rights now' being abused by Australian Springbok supporters, a vision I have never forgotten. The police charged and threw most of them into their wagons. Ten or 15 Aborigines were arrested and the Legal Service defended them all along with many white people.

White Australians in the 1930s were generously contemplating giving vast tracts of land in Western Australia to Jewish Zionists as well as setting aside land for returning soldiers. Australians thought of Aborigines as dying out without either investigation or enquiry. Now as the Land Rights campaign was accelerating in 1972, noticeable was the absence of so-called advocates of Aborigines among the

---

1   Corris 1991: 99-107.
2   Corris 1991:109-118.

anthropologists, who were still verbally and intellectually paralysed. Aboriginal heritage was never a philosophy proposed by anthropologists and this thinking dated back well into the 1920s. Until that point many anthropologists were 'acquiring' sacred objects and bark painting for their own private or museum collections. Aborigines were objects to be studied and when they died out the land would be opened up for mining, irrigation or other uses by whites.

Aborigines were still — except in Redfern — out of sight and therefore out of mind. The Aboriginal perspective on traditional land, their places of birth on missions and their communities were given little credence. This included those on non-government unsupervised settlements and fringe camps who thought deeply and significantly about 'their places'. Liberal-Country Party ministers of the Crown and governments everywhere fought bitterly with Aborigines to block not just their rising political radicalism but their struggle for ownership of places of significance.

It was not the earliest indication of Aboriginal nationalism. As far back as the early 1960s, the Yolngu 'bark petition' was presented to the Federal government to indicate that big companies could not take wholesale whatever lands they wanted without some reckoning of the rights of Aborigines.[3] This political standoff was to end up in the High Court when an Aboriginal group, Millirrpum and others, opposed Nabalco Pty Ltd and the Commonwealth of Australia. It was lodged in 1969 and came to judgment in April 1971. Aborigines lost this case. The judge declared that Aborigines do not own the land but they belong to it. Aborigines were seething with disappointment and loathing against Australian society with a truculent government opposing them in every way.[4]

On 25 January 1972, William McMahon the Prime Minister and leader of the Liberal-Country Party coalition made a long-awaited public declaration in Cairns, Queensland. McMahon, it was thought by at least most Aborigines, would make a sensible statement and come to grips with not just the Aboriginal political question but would recognise the wide ambit of rights that Aborigines had historically been denied. Instead, McMahon made a declaration totally against Aboriginal interests. He proclaimed that there would be no 'Land Rights', no recognition of prior ownership and that assimilation would remain the order of the day. Aborigines would receive equal benefits and no lesser treatment than other Australians.

I was in Sydney at the time and I recall the despair and desperation of McMahon's Cairns speech. Aborigines were shocked and disappointed. They thought that because of 'Nugget' Coombs' closeness to McMahon he would see the rightness of Aboriginal claims. Instead McMahon fell in with the Country Party 'red

---

3   Howie-Willis 1994a: 100-101.
4   Howie-Willis 1994b: 130.

necks', whose idea of self- and national interest totally excluded Aborigines. That day the message went around that a meeting was to be held at Chicka Dixon's house in Darlinghurst. At the meeting John Newfong spoke about his contact with Aborigines in other states and his outrage at decisions like the Gove Land case, as well as the blindness of Liberal-Country Party perspectives towards Aboriginal health, poverty, unemployment, Land Rights and racism. He raged that post-colonialism was an absolute blind-spot in Australia's foreign policy that grew out of its imperialism in this region, and within the British Empire. African and Asian leaders, he pointed out, had continually spoken about Australian racism and in particular the oppressive policies towards Aborigines. Such international opinion was always ignored. A number of others such as Paul Coe and Gary Foley spoke about their disillusionment with McMahon, and Liberal and Country Party Ministers such as Ralph Hunt and Peter Nixon. They suggested that some form of action should take place and it should be in Canberra the following day. Chicka Dixon said the Waterside workers had small amounts of funds from which he could draw to support a Land Rights protest in some way.

> There are people in Canberra who would support a protest, in particular, on land rights and anti-racism. And, if we could get a small number of protesters to Canberra to protest about McMahon's political recalcitrant attitude towards Aborigines, the support would flow.[5]

Chicka broke the stunned silence by adding that People like Charlie Perkins, Stewart Harris, Eric Fry, John Merritt and other Australian National University academics would help to sustain it for a few days. Chicka said he had been in touch with Charlie Perkins, who had suggested that it would be a good idea if we erected a couple of tents on the lawn outside Parliament House and called it 'The Aboriginal Embassy'. Most there thought it was a great idea and a number of people volunteered. Billie Craigie said, 'We'd go [pointing to Michael Anderson] immediately if we were given money for petrol.' Chicka agreed to get the petrol money and said that trade unionists and Charlie Perkins with Bertie Williams (the actor Bindi William's brother), would meet them at the site with tents and sleeping bags. The Aboriginal Tent Embassy was born!

A car was dispatched about nine o'clock in the evening from Sydney for Canberra with Michael Anderson and Billie Craigie on board. Little did we know then what a storm we had set in motion until we opened the morning newspapers. We were on the front page of almost every state and national (and even some international) newspaper in spite of it being Australia Day 1972.[6] Like the proverbial snowball that increases in size as it rolls down the hill, the

---

5 Howie-Willis 1994d: 774.
6 TheAustralian, 26 January 1972: (editorial). See also Taffe 2005: 273-275.

protest soon gained momentum and grew into a crescendo during the weeks following Australia Day. The protest swelled, not just for Aborigines but for much of the Australian population. The Liberal-Country Party coalition made matters worse by adopting a truculent posture, using legislation to define and protect the Parliamentary precinct. They planned and executed a process to both demolish and dispose of the embassy and I believe this was the spark that lit a great and lasting fire under the Liberal-Country Party itself.

Those were the days of action and confrontation. And I was very much involved in raising money through the Aboriginal Medical Service to fund buses to take protestors to Canberra. Each week I would notify people through community radio and arrange for funds to be dropped at the Medical Service. I would take the hat around to collect donations at locations like the University of Sydney when Aborigines such as Paul Coe were enthusing students about the Aboriginal Embassy. Eddy Neumann and Ross McKenna, executive members of the Medical Service, took charge of the money. When I was returning from one of the Aboriginal embassy demonstrations with my brother Sam my Volkswagen seized-up, leaving us stranded at the halfway point between Canberra and Sydney. I managed to get some old sump oil from a nearby farm and continued on to Marulan where the car died completely. There was a petrol station and wrecker's yard nearby where I sold the car for $120. Sam and I went straight to the highway and thumbed a lift to Summer Hill.

But things were coming to a head at the embassy and the Liberal-Country Party government was having none of it – especially outside their Parliament House. In late February as the turbulence grew so more and more people descended on the lawns outside Parliament House to defend the Embassy. I believe I was among the first group of protesters to chant the mantra, 'What do we want? Land Rights! When do we want it? Now!' I also sang out this chant at the Australian National University Student Centre – mostly with a big loud hailer! I knew many of the students having studied there in 1969 and was able to coordinate much support from them.

And it did come about! Probably the time that stands out most in my and a lot of other people's minds is the day the police tried to dismantle the Aboriginal Embassy. As the protest took effect I recall myself, Mum Shirl and Stewart Harris and many others being swamped by the onslaught of hundreds of police.[7] As more and more police arrived, Stewart Harris tried to calm things down by telling them that they should respect Aboriginal people's rights both to demonstrate and to put their case to government. Aborigines made speeches and as the police readied themselves to move in and remove the embassy Mum Shirl made her now famous speech telling the police that Paul Coe was her

---

7   Stewart Harris was chief correspondent in Australia for *The Times* London.

nephew and woe betide them if they laid a hand on him. The next thing I saw was the soles of Mum Shirl's shoes as she was overwhelmed in the marauding police barricade, followed by the waving tent as the surge of police dragged it away. As quick as a flash another tent replaced the stolen one and bodies, loud speakers and police were everywhere. Next I could hear shouts behind me as Denis Walker lay flat-out on the ground with Bobby Sykes yelling out for an ambulance while Gary Foley screamed with loud hailer in hand, 'What do we want? Land Rights! When do we want it? Now!' It was generally accepted when the rhetoric and dust settled that the embassy was a very creative Aboriginal protest that had made a significant impact on the Aboriginal psyche, confirming and affirming Aborigines' sense of identity.

Over the years there has been much discussion about if and how Aborigines fitted into the British heritage or the 'ANZAC' conception of Australia. In the 1990s Prime Minister John Howard dismissed the 'frontier violence' model of the Aboriginal past, implying that it was a slight on the traditions of Australian identity. Aborigines on the other hand argue that Aboriginal nationalism has nothing to do with the legends of white society's settler colonies of the nineteenth and twentieth centuries or of the two world wars of imperialism. Aborigines have their own interpretation of the past. Aboriginal nationalism grew initially out of traditional tribal family struggles against colonial expansion and later the emergence of 'black nationalism' in the post Second World War years. In the second half of the twentieth century 'Land Rights' formed the basis of the opposition to assimilation policies.[8]

As Gough Whitlam's star began to gain ascendancy he saw that something was happening in Aboriginal affairs but could not quite see the political implications of 'Land Rights' and could only envision his path to the prime ministership. Even before Whitlam came to power in December 1972 he had lobbied 'Nugget' Coombs to accept the job as his advisor. Coombs told me and other Aborigines at a conference that he would not accept Whitlam's offer unless substantial policy arrangements were announced regarding Aborigines. Coombs was still pressing Whitlam on the night of his major policy speech on Aborigines to instigate a Royal Commission to determine the kind of model that 'Land Rights for Aborigines' would take. Coombs missed the subtlety of Whitlam's capitulation because he, like Whitlam, meant 'Land Rights' only for Northern Territory Aborigines. Coombs later persuaded Whitlam to include the central desert lands for consideration by the Woodward Royal Commission.

Like Prime Minister Bob Hawke, a decade or so later, who yielded to Brian Bourke on the 'National Land Rights Plan', so Whitlam hoodwinked Aborigines into believing that there was uniformity within the policy offer: but there was

---

8   Rowley 1986: 1-22.

not. This reality did not become evident until Justice Woodward was appointed to inquire into how land models for Aborigines in the Northern Territory would be fashioned. All those people who heard Whitlam outside Parliament House and the Aboriginal Embassy in mid 1972 had no hint of what was in Whitlam's mind when he promised 'Land Rights for Aborigines'. We were naive and had no ear for complex political policy so we listened to false promises by which we were easily swayed. This was the first time I had been on the same podium as Gough Whitlam and I still wonder how I got there. Blinded by the heat of the political moment, the disappointments of the Gove case, and ten years of promises over the high levels of infant deaths[9] in the Northern Territory, Aborigines accepted Whitlam's offer.

From as early as the 1960s Labor oppositions had seen some profit in linking Aboriginal issues to its altruism. Infant mortality was in one sense a blunt axe used on Liberal coalitions but they never really looked past the emotive issue of Aboriginal babies dying. Coombs, when Chair of the Council for Aboriginal Affairs, failed to articulate that Australian governments were in fact holding fast to assimilation as an economical and social 'race' strategy. Whitlam, on the other hand, must have felt anxious that 'Land Rights' would afflict white Australians with the loathsome idea that Aborigines would take their titles to land by stealth, and that such a policy would never elevate Labor to government. Coombs was later to tell a gathering of Aborigines at a conference that Whitlam still had doubts in his mind when he articulated his 'It's Time' policy speech in November of 1972. During this speech Whitlam stated that he would implement Land Rights and instigate a ten-year Aboriginal health plan to solve the high mortality of Aboriginal children.

With an election looming, Whitlam held fast and left Coombs sweating until the last minute to avoid a political backlash. Whitlam knew full well that deep-seated Australian racism had no conscience in its obligations to Aboriginal people. The 1967 referendum was proof enough that while urban people supported the passing of the referendum it would be the rural white land owners who would rise up and prevent Aborigines in the states (as they did later with 'native title') from granting laws and compensation to protect Aboriginal rights. Many Aborigines like Charlie Perkins, thought that Labor could never be trusted and this scepticism was behind his attack on Whitlam at a hotel in South Terrace, Adelaide, when Whitlam gave a publicly recorded speech. Charlie let the press know of his disappointment and that Whitlam would not satisfy Aboriginal people's hopes of political and economic prosperity. It was at that press conference that Charlie announced his run as an Australia Party candidate for federal parliament, in spite of his health. The enthusiasm was there but he was suffering from chronic kidney failure and in late July he asked me to

---

9   Smith L 1980: 1.

take his place to run against Sam Calder for a House of Representatives' seat in the Northern Territory. I agreed and he prepared my way with the leader of the Australia Party the maverick businessman, Gordon Barton. My experiences are laid open in the next chapter.

Chapter 10
The Northern Territory, 1972

The 1972 Federal election was a time of heightened tension among interest groups in Australia. The Liberal-Country Party coalition had been in power since 1949 and all politically minded people sensed a change. All except those in power. Aboriginal poverty, high infant mortality rates and the question of Land Rights left Aboriginal leaders wondering how they could contribute in the political milieu they were confronted with. Charlie Perkins had been telling me for three or four years that he wanted to 'get rid of this government', in particular to show his contempt for the Country Party. Charlie at the time was an Assistant Secretary in the Department of Aboriginal Affairs and in spite of his role as a bureaucrat he was intimately involved in Aboriginal politics. So was I. On many occasions he would express his confidence that change in Aboriginal people's living conditions were just around the corner while at other times he would be filled with despair.

The time frame between accepting the nomination to run for the Northern Territory seat and leaving Sydney was very tight. As a family we had to sell the Summer Hill house to finance getting to, and living in Alice Springs. I had to resign from the Legal Service, make contact with the Australia Party base in Darwin and prepare my thinking for an election campaign. One of the first things I did was to speak to my colleague Len Smith to seek his views about if, and how, I should run my campaign. Len was a PhD candidate in sociology at the University of New South Wales, but living and working in Canberra at the time. He encouraged me to take up the offer and stand for the Northern Territory elections saying that he would come to Alice Springs to help with the campaign. Len also had the dubious honour of being with us when we spied a car that we liked in one of the distant car yards along the Parramatta Road. We went back the next day and bought the car – a gold and black Holden. There was little time to agonise over decisions!

One of the memories that sticks in my mind was that on the morning we were leaving Sydney Tommy Coe arrived to take home two great big old style armchairs that we had promised him. Bob Debus, later a Minister in the state and federal Labor governments, had given us these chairs. They were massive, and Tommy just picked them up and put them on his shoulder as though they were dining chairs and walked out the door. Tom was Paul and Anne Coe's relative whom I came to know through Mum Shirl.

And so as a family we left Sydney in the new car — Norma hadn't even driven it at this stage — and headed for Adelaide. Once there we arranged to buy a caravan when the funds from the house sale went through and have it shipped to Alice to live in. We drove to Port Augusta where we put the car and ourselves on the Ghan train. The train journey was eye-opening for the family as we passed through the native bush and grasslands of the Flinders Ranges beyond into my peoples' lands of central Australia. For Norma the biggest culture shock was arriving to find Alice Springs station had a dirt platform — a far cry from the Euston station of her youth. We were met by Malcolm Cooper and family, who kindly let us stay with them overnight.

The arrival of the caravan was some way off and initially the family had nowhere to stay. The issue was critical as I was booked to go to Darwin the next day to make contact with the Australia Party, which left the family without any accommodation. However, by a stroke of luck one of my commitments that day was to visit the director of the Institute of Aboriginal Development, Jim Downing, about visiting reserves he was familiar with as a pilot. Jim and his wife Shirley sensed our despair and very kindly offered the family the use of the front verandah. It was a life saver. The area was very small but we had the basics of mattresses and bedding along with an esky and eating utensils. After a few days Aaron started at Traeger Park School with the Downing children. He immediately settled into life in the Territory.

Like many first time visitors to the Top End, the heat hit me. I met up with members of the Australia Party at the Darwin Hotel, which was a picturesque cream painted building with new foxtail palms surrounding wide open verandas. I could feel the coolness of the place as I walked towards the open saloon bar at the rear, from which you could see the wharves and the blue-green Arafura Sea. I met the Australia Party delegates who greeted and treated me very well. We went through the itinerary they had compiled and I fitted in easily with their philosophy and plans. The great issues in the Territory were self-government, quality education, health, the economy, immigration and race relations. I also added Aboriginal 'Land Rights' as a key issue for the Australia Party. The plan was that I would start in Darwin and visit communities as far down as Hooker Creek (later Lajamanu), the Barkly, Arnhem Land and Port Keats, as well as communities around the coastal areas in a three-day program.

The area around Alice Springs was to be tackled in three sections. I would fly out to Uluru, Kata Tjuta, Apatula and Papunya and Lake Nash, then to Kulgera, as well as Angus and Tempe Downs, travelling by truck and car, on which I elaborate more below. From memory, I had sent campaign photos to the organisers so all the brochures were ready spelling out the Australia Party's philosophy and lamenting the melancholia that surrounded the McMahon government. At this meeting I first met Bobby Randall, the writer of the song 'Brown Skin Baby', who supported me without hesitation. After finalising all the political business the delegates left me with Bob.

Bob remembered me as a baby at the Native Institution outside of Alice Springs. He was later one of the Aboriginal children taken north by the Methodist Church to Croker Island at the outbreak of war. This has always been a mystery to me: why a Christian church was allowed to take a large number of Aboriginal children from central Australia to an island off the coast of Australia beyond the battle front, but it happened. What is more, it took Bob 50 years to locate his traditional and blood family. When I spoke at length with Bob he told me he was named after one of the school teachers at Jay Creek because there was nobody able to say where he came from, and who his family was. The name Randall was not a name I was familiar with, and it turned out that his white father was William Liddle, a telegraphist and lease-owner near the South Australian and Northern Territory border. Bob took me to meet all the Aboriginal families in the area, many of whom knew my mother, like the Kerin, Stokes, Palmer and Renner families, who were once babies with me in the Alice Springs Native Institutions. I spoke to them about their rights to legal protection and to a heritage and that 'Land Rights' was something they should vote for. I asked for their support, at the same time lobbying the Labor Party to continue Aboriginal study grants as a way forward for Aborigines.

That night Bob took me to my policy launch at the Dutch Club. There would have been about 200 people there, mostly of European descent, people who had come through migrant hostels around Australia. Some of these people knew me because of my soccer connections and through working in the South Australian Railways. I talked of my background and then focused on the rise of political consciousness in Aboriginal politics. Some asked about their own well-being while most wanted to know how 'Land Rights' might work. I explained that the first step would be an inquiry, and once laws were enacted some kind of body with links to legislation, history and traditions would decide who would get what land, excluding lands already settled by white Australians. They wanted to know about statehood too. I explained that, in whatever form statehood came, it would begin as an interim and a partial arrangement. I covered issues such as education, health employment, transport and security for all. After an hour I took questions on all of the issues I had covered. Fishing was the only issue I did not deal with. I took 15 minutes or so elaborating on how the Territory was a growing business and one that could be built on as a shared relationship with Aboriginal groups in the north of Australia.

The following day two things occupied my thinking: sport and travelling to a number of island Aboriginal communities off the Territory coastline. The issue of sport was a personal one. I had been included in the South Australian

Aboriginal football team to play Tasmania, and they went on to win a place in the Australian finals. But duty won out and I missed the finals! My first ports of call in the campaign were the Tiwi Islands, Port Keats then across to Milingimbi, Oenpelli, Umbakumba, Alyangula and Angurugu and finally back to Gove and Darwin. In Darwin I spent a couple of days on the soapbox outside the Legislative Council's chambers, and at some hotels in and around town before travelling south back to Alice Springs by car.

I stopped off at Katherine, where my brother Bill was working as a painting contractor and spent a few hours with him, then continued on to Tennant and Barrow Creek and passed through Aileron where my mother's sister, Maudie Lake (nee Swan), lived before driving on to Alice Springs. On my return to Alice I went directly to Jim Downing's house to find that Norma had by this time collected the caravan from the railway yards and had moved it to a site at St Mary's children home located on the airport road. The caravan site was located under a huge peppercorn tree in front of the old children's dormitory. We had a roof over our heads! This sight brought back memories of the Bungalow system where hundreds of bush and traditional camp kids had once lived.

The old dormitory was empty and the children at St Mary's now lived in groups of four or five in new Californian bungalow style homes managed by house parents who tried to create as far as possible a 'normal' home. I had mixed emotions about these new developments and methods of solving the half-caste problem but like my mother, they made me an offer I could not refuse, though it was still no choice. I was just grateful my family was safe, and could use the shower and toilet facilities, as well as the swimming pool on scorching hot Alice Springs days.

My sister Sandra and her family lived in Alice at that time. It was an opportunity for Norma to get to know her and the children. Sandra had four children: Tanya, Nerissa, Kerryl and the new baby Andrew. Norma would call in most days to see Sandra and although from different backgrounds they got on very well and remain friends to this day. Sandra later worked at the Aboriginal Tula Artists gallery. This organisation was funded originally by the Office of Aboriginal Affairs in Canberra. Gradually as the Tula art movement increased in popularity and income it formed an independent Tula art movement. Alice Springs was the centre of the Aboriginal art trade with its genesis at Papunya and it gradually spread to Utopia, Urapuntja and the Finke valley. Commercial Aboriginal art was in its infancy at this time and Sandra well remembers sitting talking to some of the famous artists that came out of the Papunya Tula art movement, such as Rover Thomas, Clifford Possum and Billy Stockman.

Like me, Sandra's background was a product of my mother's relationships and haphazard lifestyle. As children, Sandra and my youngest brother Sam inherited my mother's married name by default, although Reginald Wickman had long since gone. Sandra's father Allan Kunoth and Sam's father Syd Kunoth were born on a cattle leasehold called Utopia located on Alyawerre and Anmatjarra lands. Allan was a big man and had spent his youth in the same Native Institution as my mother but later left to work on his white father's pastoral lease. One of Allan's other children Ngala, or Rose, Kunoth gained national fame for her lead role in the film *Jedda*, and later became a political notable in Alice Springs in the 1980s.

Allan and Syd were the sons of Amelia Kunoth, an Arrernte woman born at Kulgera. As a young girl Amelia was a 'day girl' at the first Alice Springs Telegraph Station and lived in a camp on the opposite side of the Todd River. She would go to work each day, have a shower and don clean clothes as an unpaid domestic servant. At the setting of the sun she would leave her clean clothes to return to her camp in rags. As she got older Amelia moved back to town to live with her husband Trott Kunoth in a bungalow on Railway Terrace.

Both Sandra and Sam spent time living at St Mary's Children's home at the time my mother was head cook at the Government's residence, where she had the small servants' quarters that still stands today. Nevertheless, Sam inherited the same background as Sandra, they both lived in Church homes throughout their childhood, mainly because my mother did not have a permanent home for them and they were unable to live with her while she was working.

In October 1972 the Federal election was called for 2 December. Things started to hot up. Australia Party supporters had distributed brochures to a few households and arranged a location to launch the central Australian campaign. In Alice the Reverend Jim Downing organised visits to outlying communities including Warburton, the Finke, Papunya, Hermannsburg, Utopia (Lake Nash) and Apatula. A big ceremony was planned for the hand-over of the Musgrave Park cattle property at Mimili and a traditional ceremony called *inma*, a Yungutjatjara word for a dancing ceremony, was to be held during this process.

Jim Downing flew me to Warburton and Apatula. He was a registered pilot and used this skill mainly in his Christian missionary work. The Warburton leg of the journey was good because I was able to meet up once more with the mostly old men I had worked with on the housing project. Families such as the Bakers also knew my family. At Apatula I met many of my mother's brothers and sisters of full-descent, in particular Fannie and Joker Doolan. Joker was at the Mimili ceremony and was overjoyed that I'd come to Apatula. He introduced me to every family in the community, indicating my relationship to the Summerfield brothers, Injti and Percy. These two men were my mother's blood brothers. They and their wives and children, whom I discuss later, enthusiastically welcomed me.

The campaign leg from Papunya (meaning woman's body) to Utopia and Hermannsburg was piloted by Jim Thomas. This first trip was significant in two respects; my campaigning about Land Rights revealed to Jim the really deep feelings Aborigines had for their home land and the trip was the beginning of a lasting friendship between Jim and me. The single-engine light plane set off from Alice Springs at about nine in the morning taking a westerly route to Hermannsburg. Arrernte people had come in from nine or ten local outstations as well as from Haasts Bluff and Glen Helen cattle stations to meet me. They all gave me a very warm welcome and many said they were either related to me or they knew my mother or some of her sisters. Some of my mother's older sisters had married into the Arrernte community; others had left the mission to live with their families at places like Titjikala, Kulgera or Ernabella. Jim sat unaffected as I gave my electioneering speech at Hermannsburg, but the next stop at Papunya was to be a different matter.

Papunya was a half-hour flight from Hermannsburg and until then I had not had much time to ask Jim Thomas his views on Aboriginal politics or Labor's policy on Land Rights, but he was about to get my perspective when we arrived. We talked about some of the history of alcohol prohibition in the Territory and some of its consequences. Until the war all people of Aboriginal descent had been prohibited by law from drinking alcohol or using opium. However, when martial law came into force during the war all Ordinances were suspended. Some half-caste but not bush people were allowed to drink alcohol. By the late 1960s canteens were beginning to be opened in a few communities; however, Hermannsburg was not one of them. It was under the strict control of Lutheran missionaries like all the other Finke River mission communities. But as history shows us, grog-runners find a way in most communities where alcohol is banned. The Territory was no different.

These musings lead onto to the life of Albert Namatjira. Jim knew about Albert's art of course but knew little of his background or the hardships endured even though he became such a famous painter. Although Albert was granted citizenship, a very rare and highly controversial act by the Territory Department of Native Affairs administration, it came with embellishment from the self-promoting Lutheran Church. The Church saw Albert's artistic success as a product of Lutheranism rather than his own capacities. But things started to unravel when he bought a motor vehicle so that he could go out bush to paint more often. It was rare for Aborigines to own a vehicle; more to the point his relatives placed obligations on him to use the vehicle. Problems arose when he was in town with the vehicle because of these traditional ties. He ended up taking alcohol out to the communities. The end result was catastrophic. He was charged with grog-running, went to jail and lost his citizenship. As an aside, colonial control in the Territory had issued only about six people 'exemptions' from the *Aboriginals Ordinance 1918* (Cth) in the nearly 100 years up to 1952.

It was in this frame of mind that we arrived at Papunya air strip, where we could see transport already there to collect us. In these isolated Aboriginal reserve towns forward arrangements had to be made because according to Jim, Aboriginal people had been left at the airport for days on some occasions to die in the heat. The manager showed me around the reserve fringe camps. The comparison between them and the housing for white employees and the administrative officers was stark. After a short meeting we had an early lunch when the manager told me that there would be more than 100 people coming. He was right. It reinforced my expectations that there would be a lot of interest in civil rights because a number of court cases had come up over the previous two years involving public remarks by local magistrates. As the crowd began to mount I could see Jim at the back. He had possibly never seen so many Aborigines at a political rally, but things were to get a lot more interesting. More than 150 people crowded around a small grassed and treed area in front of the old galvanised Kingstrand government building. I began by telling them that my mother Eileen Briscoe came from this country and was among those taken away and incarcerated in government Native Institutions for many years. I said I wanted their support to defeat a government that had persistently attacked their cultural, civil and political rights. The current member Sam Calder, whom they knew well, had been contributing to the denial of their rights ever since the Second World War.

I outlined the Australia Party's policies for a better deal for Aboriginal cultural, political and economic rights. I told them that the Territory administration had historically removed their mixed blood relatives from their homes and put them in institutions to feed the needs of cattle station leaseholders for labour. These relatives I said had been taken and some had never been seen again: this meant they could not go through the lore. This was, I continued, against old people's lore, their rights and their cultural practices. Ceremonies could not be performed for those missing people and this policy had to be stopped. Communalism was likewise against traditional lore and some way had to be found to stop white governments together with cattle station bosses from breaking down Aboriginal law and culture. I told them I had come back to tell them that although in their minds they had always believed that this country was theirs white people had never recognised their association with their lands. They had been exploited by pastoral interests and given jobs to feed the interests of cattle leaseholders, who had no interest in either their wellbeing or their health. I could see Jim's eyes getting wider as the administrators began moving in, in an attempt to close the meeting. Some white blokes were good people who did help Aborigines.

Others, I said were brutes, because it was the system that kept them in place in government administrations like these at Papunya. I could feel the tension and saw the nodding heads, including Jim's.

The workers' lunch break was ending when the administrators attempted to stop the meeting. I yelled at them that this was a political meeting and they had no right to intervene. I told them I had not completed my policy speech and what I had to say was important to their political interests. I would not be dictated to by bureaucrats, the very people who had been exploiting them since the war. The crowd agreed with me and began arguing wildly with the government bosses. After about ten minutes calm was restored as the Northern Territory administrators backed away. 'Land Rights is the most important issue' I yelled out 'and this is your land. This land is your past, present and future, left to you by your ancestors, ancestors who have given you this land and the stories are your obligation to look after. Cattle, white men and government have stopped you from keeping the country in good health, have stopped you from doing your ceremonies to keep and look after your country'.

By this time I was being asked how these ways of protecting their country would operate. I said the Labor government had promised to give them their land back. They would have an inquiry as to how the law for 'Land Rights' could be worked out. Lawyers and anthropologists would work with the older people to find out about Aboriginal lore, who had the story for that land, and most importantly had that land been passed on to the designated custodian. In short had Aboriginal lore continued to be practised in keeping country healthy? The crowd and Jim were riveted and buoyed up over the prospect. I told them that a big fight by Aborigines in the cities and towns had occurred and governments had now determined that no more stealing could take place. The old people's lore would be restored.

After a further hour, as the clock turned to two-thirty I had completed my appeal to them. The questions eventually stopped and Jim and I came together as the workers went their own individual ways. Jim and I, together with Aboriginal Council members and a few of the white teachers, spent an hour together at the communal canteen – another corrugated iron Nissan building – where afternoon tea and sandwiches had been arranged. After some interested questioning from this group they let me know that I nearly caused a riot. It was a scene that Jim Downing never forgot. On the journey to Lake Nash and later during an evening meal on our return to Alice Springs the issue of Land Rights was a hot topic. I went through the same routine in a number of places.

A break from my routine came when my Uncle Cydica Kunmanara Warri invited me to go to a land handover ceremony at 'Mimili, Punugnka nyinaku'. I had no vehicle so I asked one of the old St Francis House boys, Malcolm Cooper, to take me south across the South Australian border. The route to Mimili was south along the Stuart Highway through Indulkana, which was once called Musgrave Park.

Let me say something about Malcolm Cooper. Coop, as we called him, had completed an apprenticeship in Adelaide, and later took a liaison job, in the late 1960s, in the Department of Social Security. Coop's job was to employ Aboriginal men and women in a special employment program that had been set up between the Department and seasonal fruit growers on the Murray River near Berri. Some years prior to this program, the South Australian government had moved Pitjantjatjara people from the Maralinga and Woomera Rocket Range project area to create a reserve at Barmera, called Gerrard Lutheran Mission – a ready source of labour. As the program developed he was sent to Alice Springs to tap into large pools of surplus labour that existed there. Coop took his wife Aileen and their two children, Michelle and David to live in Alice Springs. Both had traditional ties in the area. Although Coop was born in Alice Springs he was related to people in the Arrernte lands and Aileen was born in Yungantjatjara country near a place called Aprawatatja or Fregon.

Coop's family and my relations set off as arranged to celebrate this important event. About 1000 people, some from as far as Katherine turned up to witness the handing over of the cattle station to a Yungantjatjara group. We had arrived a day early so that Aileen could spend some time with her mother, who came up from Pipulyatjara. She had not seen her since she was taken to the Oodnadatta orphanage in the late 1930s. Coop asked me to go with him to a camp near Aprawatatja to collect Aileen's uncle, a very old man, whom again she had not seen since the 1930s. We arrived at the camp in the late afternoon just in time to experience a most spectacular sunset. The red sun covered the western sky for a good two hours before setting. We had a cup of billy tea from the soakage in a nearby creek and sat drinking it until the sun had set and then prepared for the journey to Mimili a distance of about 120 kilometres. It was a very clear night but with no moon. This coupled with the very tall acacia bushes made driving a very scary operation but the old man knew exactly where to go. He was the only one not frightened of becoming lost. The lights and campfires of Mimili in the Musgrave Park valley were a very welcome sight for all except the old passengers, who knew all the time where they were!

About ten old men who were the native Yungantjatjara land owners (native title had not yet been invented) danced for about two hours in celebration of the return of their sacred places. Yungantjatjara people are the traditional owners of Uluru (also known as Ayers Rock). What does this mean? It means that all stories of the land and cultural knowledge come from the Ngatjutjara, Yungantjatjara, Pitjantjatjara and Marduntjara groups and their *Tjukurrpa* (dreamtime). The story of the rock from the *Tjukurrpa* begins at a hill called Wiputa. From this hill two boys in a dreamtime story created the shape of the rock from wet sand at that time. In the dance the old men performed they re-enacted the building of the Wiputa and sand hills nearby and kept singing as they built a big mound of soil. With special wooden clubs called *tuni* they pounded the dirt solid with sticks as they sang. Later they went hunting for a euro (small kangaroo), made a 'ground oven' to cook the euro and turned the hole into a rock hole. The *wopa* (or tail) broke away from the animal as it cooked and the boys flung it over their shoulders and it came to rest on the sand hill, which turned into the rock that exists today. The big crack in the rock represents the euro's tail. Once they had eaten the euro they went north-east past Puntu Tjapa; my grandmother's birthplace to Alinta, now called Mount Connor, near Kulgera. Their bodies lay preserved, in rock because they had fought over water and died on top of the table top mountain Alinta.

This story has its parallel at Itikawarra, or Chamber's Pillar, that tells how the fire women were struck down by Wati Nyiru (an old man) who was turned into stone. Other stories go deep across the Gibson Desert, as far north to Yuendumu, across in a north-easterly direction near Titjikala and Waltanta (or a place near Alice Springs called Erldunda). Cydica Kunmanara Warri told me these stories go south to Indulkula kutu, which is where my mother's two brothers Intji and Percy, went through the lore. There are many stories, many that tell of sites belonging to women, attached to Uluru, too numerous to recount here. The ceremony ended with Kuna Pibi stories by four men with dijeridoos (or *yidarrki*). This instrument was not known to Pitja Pitja peoples and they laughed calling *yidarrki*, *pipatjara*. This word *pipatjara* was invented by Yungantjatjara people; it was not originally part of their culture. What they did was to take an English word 'pipe' and join a suffix to a Yungantjatjara word, *tjara*.

The next day it was back to politics in Alice Springs with my newly arrived campaign manager Len Smith. Len was a good friend who had offered to take leave to come to the Territory to help the campaign. It is something I will always be grateful to him for. Len stayed 'next door' to us in the old children's dormitory while in Alice Springs. It had not been used for decades. The furniture was covered in dust-sheets and cobwebs and its main inhabitant was a feral cat and her kittens. But it didn't seem to worry Len – we made him as comfortable as possible – and then got to work immediately planning visits to the big Aboriginal populations close to Alice Springs, such as Amoonguna, Santa Theresa and the town fringe-camp areas. A custom had grown up in the fringe camps that bush people from the south like the Mardu and Anangu peoples from the Musgrave and Petermann Ranges camped south of the town, those from Yuendumu camped between Mount Allen and the stock yards while Arrernte people camped at Albert's camp a few kilometres along the Hermannsburg road.

While I was away Jim Downing and Len Smith formed a campaign committee including George Bray, his wife Florence and their young children. The basic task of the committee was to carry out several letter and pamphlet drops around town and to let nearby reserves know which dates I would be arriving to campaign for votes. I covered all the nearby reserves, the temporary fringe-camps, nine-mile and the old Gap police station used since the turn of the century. Len and I went out to Yuendumu campaigning, broke down on the return journey, but limped home safely.

The Little Sisters of the Poor, a Roman Catholic order, had built a small garden on the airport side of the Gap. They welcomed bush people who came there for whatever reason to camp. At any one time there would be ten or 15 people camping there. It was the Little Sisters who took me to both Amoonguna and Santa Theresa to speak about the Australia Party policy and 'Land Rights'. Everywhere I went Aborigines wanted to know what it meant to them and when it would come. Voting day came around and late in the day on 2 December 1972 we heard the news that Whitlam had swept the moribund Liberal-Country Party government out of office. In Alice Springs my family, together with my mother, her husband Henry Styman and Len Smith joyously celebrated at my sister Sandra's home. I spent polling day in Darwin doing the rounds of the local polling stations meeting voters and party officials. Although I had not been confident of winning the Northern Territory seat, I was happy enough with the outcome including the fact that I had achieved enough votes to get my deposit back.

Later in the month after returning to Alice Springs we went north to Aileron as a family to visit my mother's sister, Maudie Lake. Maudie was with my mother at Larapinta, Horseshoe Bend School and later at the Native Institution in Alice Springs. As a young woman she married Hettie Perkins's eldest son Percy Lake. Maudie lived in a typical tin shack near the cattle bore across the road from the Roadhouse at Tea Tree. It was hot even by Alice Springs standards and Norma especially felt the heat. She spent much of the weekend just sitting or lying, which was unusual for her. At night Maudie took mattresses and beds outside to sleep under the stars. She was very pleased that we had travelled up from Alice Springs as she knew I was in the area. Norma knew about Maudie from tales I had told her. She was keen to talk at length with her about our family, especially about their youth in Larapinta. Maudie too, asked many questions about Norma's past, wanting to know about the family, and where we had been living. It was a lovely weekend that followed an incredibly hectic couple of months.

We travelled back to Alice Springs and the following day I borrowed the home's portable cooker and we put on a barbeque at St Mary's Children's home. The day was scorching hot and as I cooked for the family, my mother, my sister and

George Bray's family. I could see a number of people coming directly towards us from the hot, dry Todd River bed. There was a woman of about 50 at the rear of the children who came running up asking for Gordon Briscoe. Mum knew the woman immediately as Percy Summerfield's wife. She was with her own and two of Injti's children. The group had trudged ten kilometres in the burning sun to see me, which was both gratifying and an act that made me feel very humble. They said that Percy had heard that I was in town and wanted the family to come and check out how I was. My mother's brothers had not seen me for over 30 years and yet they had not forgotten me. It was a humbling gesture for which I have the greatest admiration. At the time my mother's two brothers were out of town working on a cattle property called Granite Downs just over the border in South Australia. I had always known about these family connections but nothing could have prepared me for the lump in my throat seeing these relatives walk out of the Todd River on a scorching hot Alice day. Percy's wife must have heard from Cydica, who is closely related to the Briscoe family and the Doolan family from Larapinta (Titjikala and Apatula). Over the next few years I grew to know them better and spent much time with Cydica Warri and the children.

Not long after, the reality of providing for my family began to nag away at my thoughts. I had had lengthy talks with Len about becoming a researcher with him on Professor Borrie's National Population Enquiry at the Australian National University. But at the back of my mind I felt I wanted to reacquaint myself with my bush family, to re-learn my mother's language, a living language. There was something else too; I had made a promise to Neville Perkins to help establish an Aboriginal political body we had registered in Canberra called the Central Australian Aboriginal Congress. This organisation was to be a hedge against the power monopoly created in the region by the Country Party. I stayed in Alice to clear these commitments while Norma went ahead to Adelaide to stay, first with her school friend Elaine and later with Millie Glenn, my mother's sister. We later bought a house in Adelaide; again Norma was very keen to give Aaron some schooling stability. And I took up Len's offer in early February to work with the National Population Enquiry for a year before we all moved to Canberra, and another life, in early 1974.

Chapter 11
A new era in Aboriginal politics, 1974 to 1981

The Labor Party initiated three programs that made life more tolerable for Aborigines when it came to office in 1972. The first was the Woodward Royal Commission into 'Land rights', the second initiative was to grant the Northern Territory some measure of independence that opened up the prospect of Aboriginal people representing themselves, even if as Party members. The third initiative was to implement a ten-year plan to improve Aboriginal health. Events moved at pace. By mid-1973 the Redfern Aboriginal Medical Service had been set up as a democratic and 'self-determining' service with a number of off-shoots in other towns such as Congress in Alice Springs. They were fully funded by the Commonwealth health insurance scheme. These initiatives bought together my two great intellectual passions: political theory and better health outcomes for Aborigines.

Not many people realise, at least in Australia, that, on the one hand, it was Vladimir Ilyich Ulyanov Lenin who first wrote at length about 'self-determination';[1] on the other hand, it was American President Woodrow Wilson who hinted its importance in his Fourteen Points for peace near the end of the First World War. Wilson then spelled out the historic, political and economic importance of self- determination in his opening address to the Paris Peace Conference early in 1919. The term had originated at the London International Conference of workers in 1896. It was later accepted by the United Nations in 1949, as a term supporting colonised peoples' desire to reclaim their heritage, and to rule or to manage their own affairs. In the 1920s it meant 'the rights of nations' and in the 1970s it meant the 'rights of Indigenous peoples and decolonised groups', which is exactly what Aborigines are, and have been since 1788.

In my view Indigenous peoples, meaning a collective national group, are entitled to a national democratic body to build an economy. But this principle is made more difficult by the dominance of the 'national interest' over smaller groups! Multi-national organisations like mining companies act as states in their own interests and will over-ride Aboriginal interests as they do so. As a principle Aboriginal groups must create an unbreakable solidarity with each other. It is a matter of struggling against large business interests and at times national governments. The right to land and to be democratic is paramount to a group's

---

1   Lenin 1975: 567-617.

existence, rights that were absolutely denied prior to the 1970s. Aborigines have that right now, as a central feature of the concept of 'self-determination'. This politico-economic perspective on self-determination is historic and as relevant today as it was in the period of the origins of capitalism in the mid-eighteenth century or earlier.

Aborigines have experienced poor health, to a greater degree than their white counterparts, since first contact. Watkins Tench described how Aborigines suffered from smallpox epidemics.[2] Reports of diseases such as leprosy, tuberculosis, polio, hookworm and blindness together with colonial and Australian apathy make morbidity certain.[3] But what began well for Labor soon hit a hurdle when in early 1974 Archie Kalokerinos scolded the Labor cabinet and its health administrators for not attending to Aboriginal blindness. Archie was a general practitioner whose practice in New South Wales serviced Aboriginal government reserves and fringe dweller camps. He came to prominence through his defence of an Aboriginal woman charged with the murder of her baby. The British derived medical system railed against Archie not only because he was of Greek descent but because he was making researcher's assumptions based on the philosophy of nutritional deficiencies, particularly vitamin C, rather than 'the facts'. It is true that Archie was a general practitioner making assumptions without proper university research backing, but few came to his aid when, in the late 1960s, he was faced with an unknown illness in Aboriginal babies in his medical practice at Collarenebri, New South Wales. The medical and university system failed Archie, and Aborigines too, because they condemned his 'flamboyant' and pioneering approach to the subject and his non-scientific claims appeared to alienate him from the support he needed and had asked for.[4]

Archie was dumbfounded at just how racist and objectionable the Australian health system was after travelling to a number of remote Aboriginal bush communities. In late 1974 he stepped up the rhetoric about the appalling conditions in many communities and attacked the Labor government for its apathy. Not long after I got a call from Fred Hollows to come to a meeting at his new house in Randwick. Fred had recently bought Farnham House following the untimely death of his first wife, Mary. He was rather fascinated by the history of the house, it had once been a brothel for American soldiers during the war and before that a nunnery. The juxtaposition amused Fred!

It was at Farnham House that Fred, Michael Johnson and I sat down and listened to Archie giving his version of what was going on in Aboriginal health across Australia, in particular eye health. He was angry and upset that the ophthalmic

---

2   Willey 1979: 51-61.
3   Moodie 1973.
4   Moodie 1973: 189-190.

profession had let Aborigines down for such a long time. He contrasted this neglect with the treatment that white people had been receiving since the turn of the century, when many of their poor contracted what was once called 'sandy blight'. It was known that Aborigines were subject to this disease in epidemic proportions, yet whites did nothing. Archie, I remember, called them 'racists' for allowing such a wealthy country to shower whites lavishly but practice denial with Aborigines and burden them with the worst eye health in the world. He maintained that whites in rural society competed with Aborigines in the struggle for land. So greedy and so brutal was the backlash of white society against possible Aboriginal success in this area, that they shipped them far away from their homelands and concentrated them on reserves with complicit governments' help, to ensure their dehumanisation. From centralisation they stripped them of their religion, changed their names, and sometimes fed them poisonous food. Fred was stunned at the anger Archie showed. Archie said, 'Fred you have to support me because I've already issued a statement about my trip and I've spoken to the press.'

In late 1974 I was a Senior Liaison officer in the Commonwealth Department of Health. Dr Spike Langsford was the head of Community Health and Dick Walton was his counterpart in the Aboriginal Health Branch. When I arrived back in Canberra I went straight to Spike's office with my colleague Dr Len Smith. As it happened a meeting was in progress and Spike's secretary tried to stop me. Len stood wide-eyed behind me as I burst into Spike's office unannounced. It could not have been better staged as all eyes swung around as I belched forth my anger, to the effect that everyone in the room, including the Deputy Secretary Cyril Evans, was culpable. I said to them, 'You are as guilty of racism as those medical specialists you protect.' I remember saying, 'All of you are men of no consequence, and weak as water (one of Charlie's favourite sayings).' I swung around to Spike saying: 'You, Spike, and you, Cyril Evans, are more culpable because you've known all along since the 1950s that Aboriginal blindness was caused by the filth you forced them to endure'. I wasn't finished yet, and in their usual forbearance they watched on. I still had the floor: 'It has been your fault that you did nothing about preventing concentrations of Aborigines on reserves, centralised missions, reserve hospitals and camps to keep whites from feeling discomfort. Now, one of your own colleagues has revealed your crime and you simply sit back and exacerbate the Aboriginal eye health epidemic.'

Dr Pip Ivil jumped up and supported me, saying, 'Spike, why don't I go and see what this is all about.' And so the next day Pip and I travelled to Sydney to meet with Archie and Fred. We had read in the morning newspapers that Fred had issued a press release agreeing with Archie, saying that he was right and the Health Department's response was culpable. It was particularly amusing that the department counteracted the assertion that Aborigines had the highest blindness rates in the world by citing some small Indian Ocean island that had higher rates. Fred attacked the disingenuous nature of the health officials' deceptive response about Aboriginal blindness rates and doing nothing! A day or so later action replaced deception.

Dr Pip Ivil was the medical practitioner in the Aboriginal Health Branch, and was a New Zealander known to Fred. When Pip and I got to the Prince of Wales Hospital Fred was in the midst of a very big public clinic. The clinic was structured so that when you went to the first floor you went through big butterfly doors of opaque glass. Once through the doors there was a corner reception desk with five or six orthoptic nurses milling around calling out instructions to doctors and patients. Fred's working area was a rather big long thin room, like a very well lit barber's shop with white coated medical staff leaning over chaired patients, looking through records or talking to each other. In short when we arrived it was a scene of high activity. Suddenly things came to a halt as Fred's voice boomed across the room as Pip and I moved towards him. Fred caught hold of Pip's coat, Fred was not a tall man but he was a bigger build than Pip. Patients, other doctors, orthoptists including Gabby O'Sullivan, who was later to become Fred's wife, had to save Pip from Fred's vitriolic remarks and his scathing criticism, coupled with expletives that anyone who knew Fred can only imagine for themselves! The upshot of the public scuffle was that Pip was yelling: 'Fred! I'm on your bloody side!' Fred yelled back: 'Well you'd better pull your finger out now and do something.' The melee ended with Fred yelling for Pip and me to go directly to his office in the teaching part of the University Hospital.

Pip was still shaking after we wound our way to the Ophthalmology Department, where Fred's staff settled him with a cup of coffee and sat us both down. Soon, Fred was up there and looking, as I recall, straight at Pip saying: 'Now Pip, I don't want any bullshit because I don't have time and these people need help, OK?' After that the rest of the discussion went smoothly. Pip said that he would draft a budget to cover what Fred needed for a nationwide survey, screening and treatment program. Fred said: 'Look Pip, I'm on the United Nations health team to eradicate Chlamydia trachomatis blindness and this program needs to fit in with that.' By this stage Pip had calmed Fred down and had him in a better mood. Pip went on to say, 'There are a few things to be covered. First, I have to ask the Minister to talk to you Fred!' which he did from his office. Fred turned to me and said, 'Biggo, could a national survey and treatment program work?' The question sounded very similar to the one he had asked me at the first Redfern meeting of the Aboriginal Medical Service. I looked pensively at him for about ten seconds and then said: 'What about money, Fred?' Pip looked at me and said, 'Leave that to me, because, the Minister, who is waiting for my report, wants to do something and it's going to cost him. We want to know from you whether it can be done.' I said, 'If Aborigines are heavily involved, and if Fred runs it, the program can work! But, we're looking at a good five or six year ongoing project. And, it's going to take that long, particularly if, I hope, Fred means to take medicos to communities rather than forcing Aborigines to come to cities as happens now, and can you guarantee follow-up?' Pip and I left, with Pip's parting words: 'Expect a call from Minister Everingham; and the word is go!'

The call came in June of 1975. Fred rang me at home and the first question was: 'Biggo, would Aborigines support the program?' My response was: 'Will the doctors do what we want?' 'I will organise the ophthalmologists,' Fred said, 'that is, the College and state branches and the microbiologists, the optometrists and orthoptists.' He paused then and said to me, 'I want you, [another pause] to be my Assistant Director.' I never said anything because although I never doubted Fred's sincerity I wanted to see what Fred had in mind. A couple of weeks went by when he rang me to say that a meeting was to be held at the new headquarters of the Royal Australian College of Ophthalmologists in Surrey Hills. The college had resolved to cooperate, but there was no word yet on the branches.

It was now September 1975 and the trachoma program budgets were ready in draft form. Dick Walton sent a copy to Dr Jim Fair, President of the College, to keep him in the loop if things went sour; and things did go sour, with Malcolm Fraser's 'coup' of 1975. The Health Minister had had cabinet approval for the program to go ahead prior to the dismissal of the Whitlam government, but the problem then arose that while the government was in caretaker mode nothing could happen. Spike called me to his room and said that Cyril Evans wanted to see us. Three of us, Spike, Dick Walton and me, went to Cyril Evans' room high in the Albemarle Building at the Woden Valley offices in Canberra. Cyril Evans, the Assistant Director of Health, confirmed that, luckily, Minister Everingham had signed the approval papers prior to the dismissal but nothing could be done then until an in-coming government endorsed Labor's proposal. The government changed on 13 December 1975 and further delays occurred in the interregnum.

In early 1976 the new Health Minister, Ralph Hunt, approved the proposal with reservations. The Minister made a number of changes to the original proposal saying that the program would now be regarded not only as an Aboriginal trachoma project but as a rural eye health program and funded under that heading. He also required that state governments as well as College branches had to be involved through consultation. As time went on the department would review progress. I really had no faith in the new Liberal-National Party government, but, to Ralph Hunt's lasting credit, he saw the proposal through Cabinet once more. Fred had by this time convinced the college members of the value of the program.

By January 1976 the Department of Aboriginal Affairs had allocated $25,000 in their budget to contribute to the National Trachoma and Eye Health Program. To facilitate planning, Fred called a meeting in February of that year. Rosie Denholm was appointed to coordinate the planning, Dr John Slade and Dr Doris Graham, experienced microbiologists, were co-opted onto the committee, now chaired formally by Fred, myself as a Health Department member and state branch College members, as needed. One of my tasks was to arrange for state health department discussions, but of more immediate importance to me was the need to arrange community consultation together with hiring other Aboriginal support staff. Fred asked me if I knew of an Aboriginal person that could be employed as a liaison officer to pave the way for the medical teams as they went into Aboriginal communities, to liaise with its leaders about the benefits of the program and generally gain their goodwill.

I knew straight away that Trevor Buzzacott was the perfect person for the task. Trevor's father was an Arrernte man from central Australia and his mother was an Adnyamathanha woman. Trevor was culturally and socially well suited to work in the area around the Flinders Ranges linking Arabana and Dieri peoples from Kopperamana and Killalpaninna, and possibly Yunguntjatjara from Ernabella. In the 1930s two reserves close to the Alice Springs rail line were set up by a white man named Finniss to coordinate Aboriginal labour in the area; the mission became known as Finniss Springs. The other reserve was at the foot of the Flinders Ranges called Neppabunna. Most of Trevor's people come from this region and many had migrated to Port Augusta, which is where Trevor went to school and learned a trade in the Commonwealth railway yards. He also played football there, representing the regional district side before entering league football in Adelaide for Central Districts. Trevor played for South Australian Aboriginal football sides and was twice selected for the Australian representative side. Trevor had close social and political links with Aboriginal leaders in Adelaide and spoke two or three central desert dialects. His attributes were well suited for the important task at hand. I first met Trevor when he worked in Canberra at the Department of Aboriginal Affairs. He later returned to Adelaide to his position in the State Department of Aboriginal Affairs before moving to a post in the Justice Department, where he is currently employed. I asked Fred to interview Trevor for the position of Senior Liaison Officer. He fitted the bill perfectly.

Trevor came to the program immediately and was at the planning meetings when the other staff, Rose and Reginald Murray, were interviewed and selected for clerical and vehicle maintenance positions. The Murrays were wise and well read in Aboriginal affairs in general. These two were hard to go past as part of the survey and treatment team because of their skills and temperament. Rose came from Western Australia and was removed from her family as a child. She was taken by Native Welfare and placed in Sister Kate's Home for Aboriginal children. This happened to many well known Aboriginal people from Western Australia such as Kate George, and two others who have since died: Gloria Brennan and Rob Riley. Tjilpia Nabaltjari Jones, a trained nurse whose main job was to set up the clinics on the program, was also taken away from her mother as a very small child and taken to north Queensland. Both Rose and Tjilpia found their mothers while working on the program. It was a particularly emotional time for everyone to see these young women united with their mothers for the first time. It still amazes me that in the recent past white people could simply pick up Aboriginal children from camps and take them across the continent without authority – a travesty of justice.

Reg Murray was a relative of a good friend of mine, Stewart Murray, who in turn was a close relative of Pastor Doug Nichols, both from Cumeragunja. Reg Murray's motor mechanic skills made him the perfect person to guide the team successfully around Australia, criss-crossing the country from place to place. With a five or six car convoy in tow it was a hazardous job and mammoth task, for which he earned everybody's respect and love, particularly Fred's.

Susie Bennett came onto the program as field secretary and Jack Waterford as the media representative. Jack took a two-year leave-of-absence from the Canberra Times, where he is now editor-at-large, to work on the program. He still maintains an ongoing passion for Aboriginal issues. Jack and Susie later married and now live in Canberra with their three grown-up daughters. Then there were the many local people that joined the team en route. In the central desert region my sister Jennifer Summerfield worked both as a health worker, team leader and interpreter. Jennifer was born at Titjikala and spent some time as a child at Areyonga. She married an important Pitjantjatjara Wati, Tjinja Mick, and moved west to live with him at Umuwa. While there she trained and became a health worker and because of her language and medical skills was invaluable to the program, travelling throughout central Australia, west through the Mardu desert lands on to Broome and Derby. Jennifer agreed to go further west with the program to interpret trachoma business to communities around the western desert lakes area into Tjigalong on the eastern Kimberley. Another important person on the team was Donald Ferguson who came on the trial program run with me and Dr David Moran. Donald was a Wati from Armata and came to the central desert region to help plan the feasibility route in the very early stages of the program. His skills were crucial in the desert lands and were employed throughout the survey and treatment program. In fact it was Donald whom I worked through to take Fred and Leo Shanaghan out west on the secret business that was the catalyst for the success of the trachoma program in the Pitja Pitja lands. In Western Australia people like Allan Mallard, one of the older men from the large Mallard family, were indispensable team members too.

Many white people were employed too but it was when we got to Queensland that Aboriginal people became invaluable because of the political climate and oppressive state legislation. In Queensland Aborigines had to leave the reserves, deny their racial heritage and meld into a white population to achieve a better life because of the harsh state *Aboriginal Protection and Restriction of the Sale of Opium Act 1897* (Qld). Some applied for exemptions, while others were caught and sent back to reserves like Palm Island. To have an inward sense of self was to be guilty of anachronism: almost a blight on one's character. Aborigines not under government control were deliberately kept out of employment their skills manifestly under-utilised. In the trachoma program we used them. Aboriginal leaders of great regard, both now deceased, Clarrie Grogan and Mick Miller were close friends and crucial helpers. At one time Clarrie was Australasian middleweight champion and following retirement, became a prominent political leader in Queensland. Many years earlier Clarrie had come to the Centre as a boy, living with us in Charlie's mother Hetti Perkin's house, at 'Rainbow Town' near Heavitree Gap in Alice Springs. Clarrie as a young man held boxing nights in the Capital Theatre in Alice Springs, where he held exhibition bouts with Syd and Ted Kunoth. The younger boys, like me, would hold junior bouts to get free tickets to the Saturday picture nights. I used to fight with Richard Bray, who later became a great Port Adelaide full forward, and Kevin Tilmouth. Clarrie used to take us boys running; we would all scramble along like Brown's cows following him out to Jay Creek where my mother had grown up in the Native Institution. It all comes back to me running through that area from Rainbow Town, to Honeymoon Gap then onto the Jay and back to town chasing Clarrie.

The scope and coverage of the National Trachoma and Eye Health Program was immense. In May 1976 field surveys initially began in New South Wales but because of flooding were diverted to Port Augusta where they touched base with government health agencies and local Aboriginal leaders to seek their cooperation for the field clinics. The teams surveyed communities from Ceduna to the Flinders Ranges to establish the extent of trachoma infection and other eye problems. Later medical teams would return to offer treatment, immunise against trachoma and conduct field eye clinics to correct problems. The team then headed north, tracking around the central and western desert region by way of the Pitja Pitja lands and back to Port Augusta by July of the same year. Alice Springs was an important staging point where teams split up to tackle regional areas; the same was carried out at the Katherine staging post to cover the Barkley Tableland, Victoria River, Arnhem Land and Port Keats region. Patricia O'Shaughnessy, the trachoma program's first field secretary, did an incredible job organising the team during this period. It is an understatement to say that the team was shattered when the vehicle she was driving failed to take a corner and rolled inflicting fatal injuries 20 kilometres from Hall's Creek in Western Australia. Just 31 years of age, a tireless worker and full of cheer no matter what was happening around her; local Aboriginal groups still remember her with affection. That tragic event occurred on 26 June 1977, and by Christmas of the same year the team had returned to Sydney still sad but having travelled throughout the Northern Territory, back to Murchison in the west, on to Alice Springs, Darwin, Burketown, Normanton and Croydon in the Gulf of Carpentaria, down to Mt Isa, Cloncurry and Boulia. Other teams went to the Torres Strait, but although people living near the sea have eye problems it is generally not blinding trachoma, but mostly due to the opportunity to swim often.

In 1978, two screening teams went into Queensland with both very expected and unexpected results! It just so happened that at this particular moment Jo Bjelke Petersen, the leader of the Country National Party in Queensland, had called a state election. Petersen was a New Zealand-born farmer who had moved to Queensland to grow peanuts on a farm close to an Aboriginal reserve. He was a rabid assimilationist, believing that Aborigines should have no rights over and above those of white Australians. Petersen took a dislike to the way the trachoma teams were cutting across election boundaries, in his mind unduly influencing as well as aiding and abetting Aborigines to vote for the Labor opposition. Petersen's approach was to attack and discredit the Aboriginal leaders working for the program; in particular, he singled out Mick Miller and Clarrie Grogan. Mick and Clarrie were both political activists and avid opponents of Petersen's Nationalist state government. Jim Fair, the College President, became involved and Petersen demanded that the trachoma team leave Queensland. After much discussion the team withdrew to western New South Wales.

In general, screening across Australia was complete by May of 1978 although there was some rescreening to check that antibiotics such as Septrin were doing their job. The team traversed the zone patterns twice, once to screen people, the next time to prescribe glasses that were needed, check medication, and see whether there were any signs of ear, nose or throat infections in readiness for corrective surgery. Although there is little doubt that Patricia O'Shaughnessy's death affected the overall morale of the program for some time, the team nevertheless managed to lift its spirits and ultimately achieved outstanding results in the field; a feat without precedence.

I was best man when Fred and Gabi Hollows were married in 1980 by Father Frank Brennan. The reception was held at Farnham House where many of their friends and relatives toasted the newlyweds well into the night. Their first child Cam was born in 1982 followed by Emma, Anna-Louise, Ruth and my god-daughter Rosa at regular intervals over the next decade. As Gabi likes to remark, 'There has always been a Briscoe present when a Hollows child is born.' Without exception they have all grown up to be intelligent, very likeable and well rounded young people.

Fred recognised Dr Frank Flynn's pioneering work on Aboriginal eyes. Before the 1940s it was unknown in the Northern Territory just how prevalent trachoma was among Aboriginal people. When Frank arrived he began looking at health issues in Aboriginal communities managed by the Catholic Church, and because he was an ophthalmologist he took a particular interest in eye diseases. In his report to the Commonwealth government he highlighted the incidence of trachoma blindness. As a result of his work he was asked by the Northern Territory administration to carry out wider surveys and treatment of Aborigines under their care. Flynn was the only one working in this area until Dr Ida Mann came along in the early 1960s to begin her research; however, she was more interested in the science rather than the prevalence of trachoma. Regardless of what the reports or science showed, Aborigines remained infected with trachoma. The medical profession knew about this and knew how to treat it, but nothing happened until the 1970s. Even at this stage there was a level of criticism coming from some Aborigines and doctors claiming that the 'mass treatment' was an assault on Aboriginal patients. They, like white society for a century, either thought this approach should wait until Aborigines were trained themselves or that Aborigines should be left alone. All of these were noble thoughts but the overburden of disease, neglect and indifference had then become a crime against humanity.[5]

Although the trachoma program focused on eye diseases we also surveyed living conditions in the communities at the same time. Some of the findings of the program, as I recall, were that housing was inadequate as well as being insufficient living and sleeping areas for extended Aboriginal families. One of the more insidious issues resulting from overcrowding was that water for bathing, cooking, drinking and washing clothes was far from adequate, which in turn promoted pools of infection like trachoma from which re-infection was guaranteed. Poor nutrition, including lack of access to fruit, vegetables and fresh food, particularly in rural areas, was the norm and families found it impossible to ward off infections such as trachoma. Public health issues including the lack of clean water, inadequate sewerage and other inadequate means for disposing of garbage and animal waste all exacerbated the cycle of poor health. The National Trachoma and Eye Health Program report covers much more than I can deal with here, but suffice to say that trachoma is a preventable community disease passed on by sharing mucus through touching and even sexual contact. It hardly needs to be said that poor hygiene hinders a community's ability to ward off dangerous infectious diseases like poliomyelitis, and aids infection when simple practices like washing hands are limited; but this happens when people of hunter-gather traditions are concentrated on reserves and compounds when resources that are taken for granted by the rest of society are not available.

---

5 United Nations 1949. See also United Nations Declaration of the 'International Covenant on Civil and Political Rights': United Nations 1991.

It condemns Aborigines to a life that harbours infections that they themselves have no way of controlling. This is what Archie Kalokerinos saw, and this was what he attacked the incumbent Labor and previous Liberal-Country party governments for.[6]

When the program started Fred Hollows sought to take a broad approach to improving Aboriginal health. What he wanted to do was to give people some capacity to free themselves from being victims and suffering from socially spread diseases like trachoma. However, freedom from social diseases takes more than goodwill and money. It needs political will. Today trachoma and other infections still remain endemic among Aborigines even though better health care regimes are in place and self-determination is government policy. This of course suggests that proper education and training are needed to deal independently with epidemics of treatable conditions such as trachoma. It also means having regular access to people who can monitor eye-blinding problems. Concepts such as self-determination take time to evolve, and Aboriginal medical services have been an important landmark in coordinating the idea of independence and delivery of successful health programs.

The Pitjantjatjara Health Service Council was set up while the trachoma program was in full flight. The program brought together the newly created service for its first meeting where it sought approval to carry out medical screening, and to have a military field hospital placed in the Amata area to carry out eye surgery. This was a first, to take the operating table to the people; it established the protocol that post-surgery treatment was to be carried out in a person's home country. Fred and I, along with many others, supported and actively helped the Pitja Pitja health council and the Central Australian Congress health service get off the ground. My role was convincing the Commonwealth Health Department to create a pilot program that supported both the Anangu Pitjantjatjaraku, and Ngunumpaku health services to commence their operations in the late 1970s and carry on into the future. Fred helped these services, as a promise to the Wati Anagnu Tjuta Tjuta Council to assist them in protecting their traditional culture. While all this was going on I was co-opted by the government to work in Africa for three months to manage a team of Aboriginal participants.

The Festival of Black and African Culture, or FESTAC as it became known, was a project funded by the National Australia Council for the Arts and managed by Bob Edwards. Bob was an Australian Institute of Aboriginal Affairs executive as well as a National Australia Council administrator. In 1975 Bob asked 'Nugget' Coombs to approach Gough Whitlam for funding to send an Aboriginal contingent to the Festival. The proposal was approved. An organising committee of Aborigines was set up to manage the program and because of my familiarity

---

6   Kalokerinos 1974: 1684-1750.

with the project along with my previous dealing with the Nigerians I became the obvious choice to coordinate the Aboriginal contingent. I left for Nigeria in November of 1976 unaware that my time away would spark a watershed in my life.

As a gesture of goodwill the Australian government gave the host nation Nigeria a permanent exhibition of Aboriginal Australia's prehistory. The exhibition was built on the 'Out of Africa theory' in which Australian Aborigines had migrated from Africa, the cradle of human life, across landmasses by way of the Indian continent, down the Indonesian archipelago and on to the Australian continent. Evidence found at Lake Mungo confirms this migration at 40,000 years before the present. Estimates are that the Aborigines arrived as early as 120,000 years before the present.[7] The exhibition went on to explain the peopling of the continent, the 'techno complex', or tool kits used by Aborigines for millennia up until the arrival of European contact in 1788. Professor John Mulvaney, who was then Professor of Archaeology and Anthropology at the Australian National University, bought together the display. The pre-contact display was coupled with live dancing, ground and modern paintings. I oversaw the movement of the exhibition from Australia to Nigeria, managed the 150 Aboriginal dancers from the Territory, scholars, special artists and orators who attended the university as well as the Festival conferences. In all I was away in Africa for more than three months and during much of this time I was on my own and my alcohol consumption increased substantially.

The role of alcohol in my life had gradually built up during the 1970s. In the early part of the 1970s when I was heavily involved in political activism in Sydney, a lot of the dealings with Aborigines were carried out in hotels and places where alcohol was freely available. From this beginning my intake of alcohol gradually increased to a point where it was starting to affect my health, causing problems like aching bones, bad back, knee and digestive problems. Initially I tried to shrug off these ailments by justifying to myself that these were conditions of becoming older and less active. I was drinking regularly, but when I went to Africa my drinking intensified. It became almost a daily habit because I had more time on my hands, money in my pocket and every event that I attended involved easy access to wine and spirits. When I returned to Australia I realised I was doing things out of character such as fighting and getting involved with disputes in hotels and clubs. I was well aware too that my drinking was having an impact on the family and I resolved to try and give up the grog.

But it took a number of steps. The following Christmas we spent with my brother Sam and family in Sydney. My other brother Bill, who was a very heavy

---

7   Bowler and Thorne 1976: 127-140.

drinker, was also there. By New Year's Day I felt so unwell that I was determined to stop drinking. I did there and then, and for a number of months completely stopped, but over that year I lapsed a couple of times. It was not until later in the year that my resolve hardened and I finally thought enough was enough and stopped drinking altogether. And as I write this memoir, I've been true to my word.

Another incentive was that the children were growing up fast and I felt I wanted to be more of a participant in their numerous activities. By now we had three children. Our daughter Lisa was a shy contented little girl who was happiest playing in her room or with the girl next door – as long as she wasn't too far from her mum. Our second son John was named after Norma's brother and followed the Fosters in another respect in that he has green eyes just like those of his maternal grandmother. John was an outdoors boy. He was always looking to play rugby on the front lawn with the neighbour's kids, his elder brother Aaron or me. They were all keen sportspersons, each doing well in their respective sports. Aaron was a very good all-rounder, his main passion was soccer, which he played at an elite level with the Canberra City colts' soccer team, and he was also a competent cricket player during the summer months. Lisa was a one-sport person – hockey. Later she played in the weekly Canberra competition, as well as being an ACT representative player for a number of years. John loved his rugby league. One of my lasting memories is standing on the side-line with John hurling down the side and the crowd calling out: 'Go, Johnny B'. He loved it and he too was a representative player.

My parents-in-law also visited from England about this time and we had some memorable holidays with them on the South Coast. They loved the sun and would while away many an hour sitting in deck chairs as though they were on Brighton beach in England. These holidays were special for Norma; she loved and related well to her parents. A particularly sad time for her on their final visit was finding out that Pop had lung cancer. The journey home for Beatrice and Pop was horrendous because he was so sick. It was only a matter of weeks later that he died.

The trachoma program gave me an enormous sense of worth in my working life and as it drew to a close I found working as a generalist public servant losing its challenge, at the same time I was having to come to grips with my new alcohol-free life. In an effort to revive my interest in the public service I applied for a secondment to the Department of Prime Minister and Cabinet, where they were conducting an inquiry into Aboriginal health. The work there was interesting. I was well looked after but my thoughts were straying towards the idea of going back to university to fulfil my long held dreams, and the early 1980s seemed a good time to do so!

Chapter 12
The education years: 1980s

Governments tend to swallow up people when they gain power. Though some win and some lose, after each government's rise to power, their supporters either profit from the success on the outside, or are brought in to bring a change of political emphasis to the bureaucracy. That is the way it was with me and many other Aboriginal people; the challenges of the Whitlam government were long gone and the realities of conservatism had arrived. I was not the only one struggling with the new reality, and I can recall daily struggles between Barry Dexter and Charlie Perkins over when an Aboriginal person would head up a department to become the most senior public servant. By the early 1980s it was becoming obvious to me that my lack of tertiary qualifications was going to be a stumbling block in gaining promotions. I also felt a sense of alienation from what was happening in Aboriginal Affairs, compounded by the fact that the Fraser government had its own band of policy advisors. In 1981, with this sense of dissatisfaction swirling around in my head, I decided to seek re-entry to the Australian National University. This time I sought advice from student services and chose more wisely a liberal arts degree, majoring in what was then called Australian Studies.

In the early 1980s a number of issues plagued my mind and uppermost among them were the Nookanbah dispute, public health in Aboriginal society and again eye health. The background to the Nookanbah dispute was that a decade earlier the Walmatjirri and Nyinkina groups had walked off Nookanbah Station in a dispute over management's treatment of Aboriginal workers. In 1976, in support of these workers the Aboriginal Land Fund bought the land and handed over the property. But antagonistic miners used their political dominance to register hundreds of mining claims in search of diamonds and other mineral resources on the land and created an access road to a mining site that violated a sacred site. The Yangnara people blocked the road and took the miners to court under the *Aboriginal Heritage Act 1972* (WA). While all this was in process an oil mining company decided to use its legal clout to drill for oil close to other sites of significance. The dispute went to the Western Australian Parliament in 1979, resulting in further government action; the miners subsequently attempted to bulldoze the community blockade under police guard. In hindsight this dispute was local but became both national and international with recall to the United Nations as a political strategy of last resort. By the time the Nookanbah dispute was over the question of 'Land Rights' in Western Australia was as far away as ever, I was beginning to believe that the return of Aboriginal heritage was an impossible dream.

I was feeling quite low, as I am sure other Aborigines were feeling, about the episode at Nookanbah and the fact that health in Aboriginal communities did not appear to be improving worried me. I had just spent six month on a special economic inquiry into Aboriginal health while working at the Department of Prime Minister and Cabinet. Prime Minister Fraser had called for an investigation into spending in this area and also to assess state and federal progress in a budgetary context. The inquiry found that aspects of Aboriginal health, such as primary health, were being funded, but that there was an overburden of public health measures that remained unaddressed. On a personal basis I found the work at Prime Minister and Cabinet interesting in itself; the process was fairly simple: bureaucrats articulated Cabinet discussion with briefing papers, Cabinet discussed the ideas from the briefings, and then bureaucrats prepared written statements of acceptance or rejection along with follow-up advice. Cabinet was divided into two parts: decisions and follow-up. All these processes made me realise that governments made 'paper decisions' prepared and followed-up by bureaucrats. It kept coming back to me how people in the general society looked after themselves, taking public health for granted. The drinking water problems of urban dwellers posed no obstacle, their sewage was taken as a matter of fact, their waste water was out of sight and new technology was something few people thought about. Money for their own maintenance was no object when wide spread disasters, such as floods, affected their way of life.

The Whitlam reform period had raised hopes of better health outcomes for Aborigines, but this did not seem to be happening. More housing had been provided but lack of maintenance caused as many problems as it solved. Run-down housing rendered Aborigines in danger of not just exposure to the vagaries of weather but to seasonal epidemics and poor maternal health. Infant mortality among the babies of Aboriginal women was still much higher than their white counterparts and this coupled with post-natal infections, rampant sexually transmitted diseases and other social diseases meant that the cycle of poverty was ensured. In general, Health Departments across the north failed to properly supervise remote community outposts, they were controlled by a few untrained community advisors, and 'Rafferty's rules' applied.

Periodic ideological policy changes and vacuums, not fully understood either by government agents or policy recipients, were tolerated without review. Infectious and preventable eye diseases remained in epidemic proportions decade after decade. The small political battles that friends of Aborigines or Aboriginal leaders raised in protest came to nothing. I was totally despondent. On my return to the Health Department my mind was awash with political and personal concerns about the administration of Aboriginal Affairs and my own future. It made me question the role I was playing in the Health Department. After three months in Cabinet I returned to the planning section of the Health Department and started preparing my return to university.

In many ways, escaping the bureaucracy was not an easy task for both strategic and psychological reasons. Uppermost in my mind was the notion that I could not simply down tools because I had a family to support. I had to find a means of going back to university with some kind of financial support. From a psychological perspective I failed to see how I could make further contributions in the bureaucracy to improving the way of life for Aborigines; so I looked for a different way of making a difference. And so it came about. I turned to Gloria Brennan, an Aboriginal public servant from Western Australia, for advice. Gloria was born in the Ngatjutjara country of Mount Margaret, part of the western desert communities. She had been removed as a young girl and grew up in Sister Kate's Children's Home in Perth. She later put herself through university in Western Australia, became an active member of the Labor Party and champion of Aboriginal rights. Sadly, Gloria succumbed to a breast cancer that was terminal a little over two years later; but she had made a powerful impact.

Gloria had come to Canberra to work in the public service in the late 1970s. She was close to Gail Redford, a senior bureaucrat endeavouring to work out how the public service could fashion policy options to support Aboriginal bureaucrats. I met them for lunch at the then Forrest Lodge Hotel and talked about some of the problems Aborigines faced in the bureaucracy, not just about promotion but adjusting to the rigours of clerical life. I talked to them about the idea of going back to university, supported by a public service scholarship that would protect my entitlements. They asked me to apply through my department together with a letter confirming my matriculation status to the Australian National University. While waiting to hear whether anything would come of this proposition Norma and I started planning in earnest for my return to academia. We felt the decision had been made regardless of the scholarship outcome, and as a fallback position Norma started work on a full-time basis. However, very early on in the first semester we learnt that my scholarship application had been successful. I was the first Aborigine to receive one of these scholarships and support also came from the Health Department to return to the Australian National University in 1982 to begin my new life as an undergraduate.

I began my undergraduate studies with vigour taking three subjects: history, prehistory and politics. History was a subject I had done very well in at matriculation at Sydney Technical College, and the magic all came back to me when I started attending lectures at the Australian National University; the history lecturers made a profound impact on my intellect. I recall John Ritchie's lectures on Australian history; he was a great lecturer and the only one who wore a black academic gown. His way of organising work was easy to follow and I remember he used things like slides to enhance the reading along with music of the times. John was my first history tutor and John Clanchy was my student advisor. Under the two Johns my writing and capacity to think things through improved out of sight. During those early university days I would on occasions meet up with Jack Waterford, Susie Bennett and Gloria Brennan to catch up on Aboriginal politics, and ask them to read my essays. It was a good time in my life; I worked hard and felt a new sense of maturity that enabled me to cope with subjects like Australian politics as well as prehistory which became a subject of immense fascination. Under Professor Fin Crisp, my lecturer way back in the late 1960s, politics had seemed so difficult and foreign, whereas this time it began to make sense. Through John Mulvaney's Prehistory lectures, the distant Aboriginal and European past began to reveal to me a past shut out by religious ideology.

Professor Manning Clark showed me too that academia was a liberating force. I had three lectures from Manning. The first lecture was about the value and distinction between primary source material and other collections of information as historical tools. The second lecture was an ABC lecture on historiography. One point stuck in my mind and that was about Karl Marx. Manning Clark said 'that no serious person studying and writing history can by-pass Marx's contribution to history'. 'Britain', Clark said, 'gave the world capitalism, France gave the world modern democracy while Germany gave the world modern historiography.' 'Marx', he went on, 'revealed to us the scientific nature of history and helped us to understand the important distinction between "god" and man.' The third lecture was on Alfred Deakin. On this occasion Manning Clark came down the stairs from his office into a lecture theatre known as the Tank with great aplomb, at the same time removing his ten-gallon hat placing it on the cupboard and sitting next to it with his knees facing the students. He spoke non-stop for 50 minutes on Deakin's nature, politics and contribution to the Australian nation. Alfred Deakin, I heard him say, was born on 3 August 1856, in Fitzroy, a suburb of Melbourne. William, his father, and Sarah his mother had migrated from England in 1850 arriving first in Adelaide then because of the gold rush moved to Melbourne in 1852. From Clark we learned of Alfred's early education and influences that came directly from his sister Catherine. As a public person Alfred was known as a statesman, an orator and one of the 'fathers' of the federal system and three times Prime Minister. He was known also as a mystic, a student, an intellect, a nervous, sensitive, egotistical and imaginative person. These qualities, Clark pointed out, were with him at the centre of the political action in the first ten years of the Commonwealth until his death in 1919. Manning Clark impressed me from the moment his first lecture began, and he set me on a history odyssey that has continued.

Nothing will ever surpass the feeling of joy that I had when Norma, Gloria Brennan and I ran up to the result's board at the university and found that I had passed all subjects with a distinction and credits. This opened the door to completing a history degree with honours – I grabbed the opportunity. I dearly wanted to learn to write about the Aboriginal past. The subjects I chose over the following years helped me work towards this goal and gain a deeper understanding about the discipline of history. My second year majors were European history and the history of the Spanish Civil War; both at honours level, with political science as my sub-major. In third year, the final year of my scholarship, I studied the history of Russia and China at honours level and a compulsory honours subject, History and Theory. But the time came when I had to return to the public service, this time to the Australian Institute for Aboriginal and Torres Strait Islander Studies. The Institute gave me time off to complete my fourth year honours requirements, a thesis and a unit called 'Orientalism'. The time at university was one of the happiest periods of my life. I had been successful in gaining a research degree that covered subjects steeped in the discipline of history with my family financially secure. It enabled me to complete a thesis on the effects of capitalism in a region of Australia that my family came from. This exhilarating experience gave me a taste of what life could be about and I knew I wanted to take on more complex studies.

Looking back on my family life it seems to me that roughly every ten years we as a family moved house. There was nearly a decade in Sydney, a short stint in both Alice Springs and Adelaide, then in early 1974 we moved back to the eastern states and settled in Evatt, a westerly suburb of Canberra. By 1983, we were planning to move once more to a nearby suburb called Mackellar. The Australian Capital Territory government had opened up land for auction in a neighbouring new suburb and we liked the idea of building a new house. The agent who sold our Evatt house, Mario Despoja, a stalwart of the local Croatian community and colleague of mine from the Department of Aboriginal Affairs, introduced us to a local builder Andy Rosin. Andy came with us to the Albert Hall where the land auction was to take place. I mention this story not so much to highlight our regular moves but to document the strain of buying land through the auction process. The hall was packed so full that there was standing room only. Andy, Norma and I got there early and chose three middle row seats so that we could see and hear clearly what was going on. We had a list of the blocks that we were prepared to purchase but quickly were outbid on the first few and as our target list got shorter we became more desperate. The land was proving to be very desirable, and at one point I got so worked up that I put my hand up and mistakenly sent the price higher for our new neighbours! But things worked out in the end when Andy was able to secure one of our final choices. My head was both hurting and spinning as Norma and I drove across Commonwealth Avenue Bridge to get the cheque to secure the block.

It was about a year since Norma's father had died and she was feeling a little anxious as to how her mother was coping on her own. We decided that now was a good time for her to visit England, between selling the Evatt house and building the new one. We rented a house in Kaleen and while Norma flew to England I settled in to look after Lisa and John. I felt that this was a great time to get to know the children's routine better as I was able to study mostly at home. Aaron by this time was in Sydney studying for an Arts degree at the University of New South Wales and living with Fred and Gabi Hollows at Farnham House. Aaron had been very popular at high school and College and had shown a great deal of leadership. I had begun taking a closer interest in his choice of studies at college, and suggested to him that physics and computer studies would enhance his prospects for university entry. While my advice was respected the force of his own character steered him closer to an interest in the more liberal arts. Scholarship was not uppermost on his mind until he scored a part-time job at one of the local department stores. He soon realised that customer service was not a long term working option for him but was unsure where his future lay. It was not that he saw working as a shop assistant an unworthy task; it was more that he wanted a more challenging life and started working towards this goal. Our younger son John, who always enjoyed taking his bike to pieces and putting it back, enjoys more mechanical things and working with his hands and became an apprentice boilermaker when he left school.

Once more I imagined that the transition from undergraduate to graduate studies would be easy; I was wrong again. It seemed that I always had to travel the hard road. I was planning to do a Master of Arts in the History Program and assumed that this would be a simple process. However, my biggest hurdle was that I had only achieved a third class pass in honours. To go any further the history fraternity insisted that I complete a Master's qualifying degree. I felt that this was like saying that you are not good enough so do another honours degree. But I struggled on. I knew I had problems in that I lacked a proper grounding in English, mostly due to my education baggage; I needed to re-learn how to write, think and articulate my ideas better.

I had heard on the grapevine that my Honours thesis was one of exceptional quality but a group led by one particular examiner felt that my work could not be judged just on the basis of its voluminous sources! But this snippet of information, or gossip, gave me the impetus to carry on. I always felt that I'd get marked down on my literary contribution but had no idea that both my thesis and topic would be the stumbling block to progression on to research. I accepted my fate and chose to do a Masters qualifying thesis researching primary source documents produced by the activities of the Weapons Research and British atomic testing processes. The Labor government had recently conducted an inquiry into the Woomera and Maralinga tests from which a large collection of documents ensued. Geoff Eames and Dave Colette were the solicitors, and Dr Heather Goodall was the historian on a special section of the inquiry that looked into the impact of these programs on Aborigines. I decided to create a catalogue of these documents based on issues covered. I then computerised the material giving each document a name according to the issue it covered, and also cross referenced each document with those mentioning Aborigines. For example, if a researcher wanted to find any issues covered both by Prime Minister Robert Menzies and Aboriginal security issues then they could narrow the search down from the 18 volumes of bound documents. The project was accompanied by a 15,000-word thesis explaining how to use the database and issues covered.

Following submission of the thesis I heard informally that I could now progress towards producing a 50,000-word Master's thesis. The informal advice was that Dr Geoffrey Bartlett supported my inclusion into the postgraduate program and I should start formalising a research proposal. I took this advice and looked to build on the work I had just completed mainly because it gave me insight into Aboriginal history in the northern area of South Australia. In history books South Australia is mainly a story about Adelaide and its Liberal-Country Party past. I wanted to investigate how Aborigines had been written out of history during the period from the wars up to the Dunstan government's reform period. It gave me the opportunity to investigate my own family's past, how European political economy had shaped the Aboriginal people's past and the role played (or not played) by the Labor Party in creating a more humane way of life for Aborigines. The strategy I would use was to write a social history of an area north of Port Augusta, cover the Woomera and Maralinga projects and show how traditional Aboriginal society had been changed by the forces of political economy from the post Second World War era to the Labor reform period of the early 1970s. This history of South Australia covered the period dominated by conservative forces until the end of the Dunstan reform period.

This saga was part of my background and approaching it from an academic perspective gave me the capacity and opportunity to use my early Aboriginal political involvement as a tool. As a child I remember listening to tales of how the British people had salvaged German rockets that were bombing London, along with the horrifying tales of the bombing of Nagasaki and Hiroshima. After the war Prime Minister Chifley had jumped at the opportunity to allow the British to use the vast Great Victoria Desert as a testing ground for its new atomic bomb. Chifley saw it as a way of sopping up excess manufacturing capacity after the war, at the same time developing Australia's economic potential while playing host to a dominant European military power. I had heard about the atomic bomb testing at Montebello, and the explosion near Oodnadatta, when I was still at school. This was a place I knew well, and not just a childhood memory, it was country I travelled through many times as an adult. Some years later while working at Port Lincoln 'Operation Antler' was carried out at Maralinga; a 25-kiloton bomb called Taranak was detonated. As a young person in Adelaide I remembered demonstrating about the potential negative impact these tests would have on traditional Aboriginal people and on nearby reserves. I was shocked at these events and still feel deeply about the disrespect the British and Australians showed for Aboriginal peoples' land, and the way these desert people were treated. But now I was about to embark on a research project that most probably would bring all these memories flooding back.

The Australian Institute for Aboriginal and Torres Strait Islander Studies gave me a Visiting Fellowship that basically amounted to a room of my own, while the Department provided me with travel and accommodation support funds for research in Australia and overseas. I began my field research and discussed ideas with my supervisor Dr Peter Read, who was at the time a member of the History Program in the Research School of Social Sciences. I put a research plan to him that included a number of trips to Adelaide, the Nullarbor Plains, Flinders Ranges, Marree and Oodnadatta. The narrative covered the idea that capitalism achieved these changes within most living Aboriginal peoples' lives through rail expansion, pastoral, international weapons and coal mining development.

I bought a Kawasaki motorcycle whose purpose was twofold; it was cheap to run and it enabled me to get to lectures and park easily while in Canberra and it gave me the independence and convenience to carry out my social research in South Australia. On a number of occasions it took me back and forth to the Great Australian Bight and Sydney. It was important in my research that I talked to South Australian locals and also to research local newspapers. While in Adelaide I stayed with Vincent Copley and from there would visit the State Records Office at Mile End, the Mortlock Library, the Barr-Smith Library at the Adelaide University and the Elder Smith's pastoral company's records in Curry Street. At the time I was there the Weapons Research body was writing its own history of the weapons and atomic testing and I was unable to access their records. But my earlier research covered this area.

While researching material in the Flinders Ranges area I stayed with Faith Thomas, born a Coulthard. Faith was removed from her family as a child to a Christian mission at Neppabunna. This mission was created in 1931 by the United Aborigines Mission in the northern part of the Flinders Ranges near Lake Frome and near the towns of Leigh Creek and Copley. Creating a mission there caused great conflict with local pastoralists but the mission survived and acted as an advocate for Aboriginal pastoral labour. Faith Coulthard was removed to Dr Duguid's orphanage for girls of mixed Aboriginal descent at Quorn, and later to the Eden Hills' home for Aboriginal girls. There she reached high school, became a registered nurse and played hockey and cricket for the state in the 1950s. Faith went on to be selected as a fast bowler for the Australian women's team that toured England in 1958. I knew Faith from Eden Hills when she and other girls like Malcolm Cooper's wife Aileen Cooper came to celebrate social events at St Francis House at Semaphore. Faith was a long time friend and I stayed with her while I researched material such as the Port Augusta newspapers and the Railway Union journal. Faith gave me a bed and fed me while at the same time telling me stories of the area that I wrote about in my thesis.

Out on the Nullarbor Plains I stayed with another Aboriginal woman, Margaret Laurie, who I knew when she was a nurse at the Adelaide hospital in the 1950s, and again when I worked with her in the Aboriginal health branch of the Commonwealth Department of Health in the 1970s. Margaret made sure I became acquainted with all the Ceduna Aborigines, and those with whom she had lived with at the Koonibba mission Aboriginal Children's Home. I went out into the Maralinga lands under her guidance and fishing at Thevenard for St George whiting, the biggest whiting I had ever seen. I was familiar with this location from my days as a fireman carting wheat to Port Lincoln for the South Australian Railways. It was also the place where my uncle Rupert Maxwell Stuart began his summary trial for the alleged murder of Mary Olive Hattam in December of 1958. Many in the area remembered the trial of Max and were still shocked by the whole affair and I was reluctant to raise the subject while I was there, relying instead on secondary sources.

I met up with Spencer Wheatra who took me on some field trips out bush; he was one of the old St Francis House boys, and a first cousin to Vincent Copley. One of the places we visited was Cook, a railway town owned by the South Australian Railways on the Nullarbor Plains, halfway between Port Augusta and Perth, Western Australia. People at Cook were fascinated at meeting Spencer because he held the dubious honour of being the first Aborigine to become an inmate in the Cook jail some years earlier. This structure was a wooden box with just enough room for two, most frequently used to house truculent drunks who were travelling on the train west from Port Augusta or east from Kalgoorlie. Stations in earlier times tended to be named after Australian Prime Ministers or State politicians. The town struck me as a classic institutional town where people came from urban areas and became changed by the isolation or confronted with the prospects of alienation. The Nullarbor Plain is a featureless salt bush plain interrupted only by a railway line and a road leading to Maralinga some distance away. It was a place from which I frequently rode my Kawasaki motorcycle back to Canberra.

In the process of my research and the long distance travel to and from the southern parts of Australia on a motorbike I sometimes found it physically difficult. On one of my later trips from the western coast to Adelaide I found the cramps and pain in my lower abdomen overwhelming and felt compelled to do something about it. Vincent Copley took me to a general practitioner at

Burnside in Adelaide who saw me straight away. The doctor said I had a bowel infection caused either by appendicitis or a growth. He gave me antibiotics to ease the immediate pain and suggested that I see a doctor in my home town for a more intense investigation. Meanwhile I still had to complete my MA thesis so I worked feverishly on what turned out to be the penultimate draft. My supervisor advised that the content and theory was good but the text itself needed some rewriting. I was naturally distraught at what could have been a long delay. But the turning point came about in an unexpected way. At the time I was also writing my entry on 'historiography' for the *Encyclopaedia of Aboriginal Australia*, and working closely with the assistant editor historian Dr Ian Howie-Willis. Ian sensed my distress and offered to look the manuscript over on the coming weekend, and I agreed. Thanks to his help I was able to ensure that the thesis was better written and more strongly argued. Ian allayed my mental distress but then I had to deal with my more serious physical issues.

The preliminary medical exploration proved to be more painful and uncomfortable than the illness; but I persisted. And just as well that I did because a growth was located that turned out to be cancerous. The surgeon confirmed that the cancer had not spread to any other organ, and told me that if I had to have a cancer then it was the best place to have one! My stay in hospital was comfortable and made bearable by my many visitors. Norma and the children were regular visitors of course. Others such as my supervisor Peter Read, Charlie Perkins and John Moriarty, Fred Hollows and fellow ophthalmologist Hugh Taylor all came to wish me well and a speedy recovery. Peter Read and his wife Jay bought the good news to me that all my thorough research had paid dividends and the History Program had accepted my thesis and all that was now needed was to for the degree be conferred.

It was about this time that I began to re-think the role the Anglican Church had played in pre-and postwar assimilation programs. The more I thought about it the clearer it was becoming to me that their actions were really in bad rather than good faith. Father Smith, to my mind, had promised our mothers that if he took us away he, and the Church, would care for us and give us a better education than we could possibly have had in the Native Institutions! But both he and the Church reneged on their promise when they failed to review in the years ahead what was happening to the children in their care. And by the 1960s, many of these children's lives had turned into calamities. Neither as children nor later in our lives were we able to collectively nor individually articulate our despair. A number of the boys had committed suicide and many had failed marriages behind them. They failed in the pursuits that the Church served up to them and ended up drunkards and misfits of one sort or another. Yet, the paradox is that some of us did achieve success. I was still trying to imagine what my life during this 50-year odyssey would have been and what I might well have achieved in other people's hands.

This was also the time that other family matters were occupying my thoughts. Sam, my youngest brother, had lived with us on and off for a number of years since his early teens. On this occasion when he came to live with us he was particularly low and despondent about his future. He and I spent a lot of time talking about his options one of which was to enrol in a university entrance course at the Australian National University. I knew that Sam had the capacity to do well at university; while living in Sydney with us, as a teenager, he went to the Strathfield South High School and did very well. All he needed was some direction in his life. He gained entrance to the Australian National University and over the period of the next four years completed an Arts degree with honours. Since then he has used his archaeology background as a professional consultant in archaeological finds and native title claims. As a follow on from this work he went back to his mother's Mardu country and began taking an interest in traditional Arrernte art. He now works Aboriginal stories and designs into his glass making, painting and fabric design business. Sam and his partner Nicky have two young boys, Leeroy and Sam who love to come and spend time at the beach with us at Lilli Pilli.

Australia Day 1988 saw the end of a great political struggle between Charlie Perkins, the Minister for Aboriginal Affairs Gerry Hand and Prime Minister Bob Hawke. Gerry Hand had tried unsuccessfully to control his Department head, Charlie Perkins and there was an underlying tension between them. One of the final spats between them centred on travel arrangements for Aborigines participating in the upcoming 1988 Bicentenary protests against Captain Cook's landing in Botany Bay, or Gwea as the Gweagang and Carrahdigang people called it, Phillip's landing at Sydney Cove and colonial expansion across the continent.[1] It was a dispute settled by Prime Minister Hawke who adopted the 'protest policy' allowing Aborigines to come to the mass demonstration.

In the last couple of years of the 1980s decade I tried to adjust to life once more as a bureaucrat in the Aboriginal and Torres Strait Islander Commission, but it had even less appeal than it had ten years earlier. I submitted my Master of Arts thesis to the History Program, and then waited to hear if I had been accepted as a doctoral candidate by the Research School of Social Sciences at the Australian National University. I decided at this point that if I was accepted I would leave the Commonwealth Public Service. Dr John Eddy was given the task of assessing my capacity to complete a doctoral thesis; John was a Jesuit who had been an Ambassador to the Vatican as well as head of the Australian Centre for

---

1   Collins 1798: vol 1; 452-453.

Australian Studies in America. John taught subjects such as 'Peopling Australia' at the undergraduate level, dealing mostly with European migration. John gave me a glowing report on my capacity to conduct and complete a PhD in a subject of my and the history program's choosing. After receiving a letter of invitation from the late Professor Allan Martin, I accepted the offer around April of 1992. Circumstances came together for me to join the history program at the Research School of Social Studies at the Australian National University. When I joined the department there was a full complement of students and scholars, including Professor Ken Inglis and Dr Barrymore Smith, to welcome me. I was given a shared room with Frank Bongiorno, now a leading Australian historian. I could not have been happier!

Chapter 13
The 1990s and beyond

The 1990s bought with it the joy of our first grandchild, Mitchell James Taylor-Briscoe. Mitchell was born on 4 October 1993, a seven pound plus baby with big blue eyes and a beautiful face. He was and still is the pride and joy of us all, including his proud parents Aaron and partner Meredeth Taylor. Meredeth was born in Melbourne where she spent her early childhood years; during which time her father was a fireman with the Metropolitan Fire Brigade. They later moved as a family to rural Victoria, where her mother established, and became Principal of a school for handicapped children.

However, while as a family we were rejoicing in the birth of Mitchell I was still grappling with academia. Writing a thesis is never an easy task however you come to it. For me it was no different, except that I was driven by fear of failure. Some very clever students falter and are overwhelmed when confronted with big works such as a Master or Doctoral thesis and fail to complete their challenges. Others of lesser innate capabilities make things easier by building on their undergraduate or lower degrees as they progress. By the time students get to the final hurdle they have a lot of experience and material to draw on. My capacities fall somewhere between these two approaches. As Norma always comments, my ability to keep going and overcome whatever hurdles that get in my way are my greatest assets. My other more concrete assets were my lengthy involvement in the politics of Aboriginal Affairs which I could draw on. With these two attributes I strode forward to do something that few others have the privilege to achieve.

Father Smith's dream of integrating us into Australian society was unachievable, in spite of the respect many of the children might have had for him, given the meagre support raised from government and the religious community. They both still have much to answer for! Decades later, Aboriginal peoples' protests were something different to Father Smith's dream. The reality was that they wanted radical political change rather than the 'protestant ethic'. The educational journey that I began in 1942 contained all these characteristics. Eventually the journey had taken me to the Research School of Social Sciences at the Australian National University, where I became engaged in my own research and taught students. When I began my doctoral studies I followed the general procedure for students in the history program which is to read, plan and think about their topics; I followed this pattern to a certain extent but in the end I came more or less to my topic by accident. I had written an article for the Oxford University history journal *History Workshop* about the Aboriginal population and identity. The article was published and crystallised in my mind the idea of a thesis on the way institutionalisation and employment had shaped Aboriginal identity. It appealed to me and it got the tick from most people I spoke to, who thought it would be a good historical project. Historians choose their subjects in the way they want to reconstruct the past, but there are particular schools of thought that influence their view of the world. With my racial and employment background I favoured what I thought was a 'leftist' approach. I mistakenly thought that being a doctoral student I had total freedom!

While still thinking and mulling over my topic the Aboriginal poet Kevin Gilbert died. I went to his wake on the site of the Aboriginal Embassy, and then returned to my room in the history program much affected by what I had experienced at the Embassy site. Standing there too I had seen Nugget Coombs and other whites in the front row hogging the limelight. Not that I wanted to take their places, but it looked bizarre. I had known Gilbert from the days of Aboriginal protest in Sydney in the late 1960s. My thinking turned to his early background, probably because it tied in with my proposed writing of a doctoral thesis on Aboriginal employment in rural areas of Australia. This coupled with my enduring *idée fixe* of getting Aboriginal biographies on the radar of academia; informed scholarly biographies not glossy ones with a sense of journalism! I have been criticised for critically writing about a recently deceased person but find this a rather incipient and hollow argument in the light of continued public attacks on the reputation of the historian Professor Manning Clark.[1] Not only has his monumental work been savaged but very intimate details of his private life have been exposed in newspapers, including his relationships with others who are still living. Aboriginal biographies need to be written in the context of what happened, not treated as a protected species where only the noble are written about for publicity purposes rather for inclusion in historic text. In short I used the press coverage of Gilbert's death and obituaries, which I thought were shallow, to critique how white society handles Aboriginal biography.[2] Few others could appreciate the point I had made and so I was damned out of context. Since then, not necessarily because of my work, changes have been made in this area both by the Institute of Aboriginal and Torres Strait Islander Studies, incidentally where the most trenchant criticism originated, and by the *Australian Dictionary of Biography*. The attacks on my critique of Gilbert I let go through to the keeper and focused instead on my studies.

Life took its own sweet turn! Each Friday afternoon history scholars from the research school take a casual walk across the well-groomed lawns of the university to the History Program's weekly seminar. The seminar was normally given by either students, staffers from the department or visiting fellows. As I

---

1 MacIntyre and Clark 2003: 61-67.
2 Briscoe 1994: 13-31.

left the building I bumped into Professors Barrymore Smith and Ken Inglis who were on their way to the same presentation. Ken asked me: 'Have you decided on a topic for your thesis?' I said: 'Yes, I'd like to study Aboriginal employment in rural Australia.' Ken quickly responded with: 'You can't study that because there is nobody to supervise you.' I went weak at the knees and was silent for a moment believing in my despair that they would perhaps have liked to see me leave the department altogether. I waited for a moment or two and said in quick response, 'Well, my second option is Aboriginal health. Barry, [as most people called Professor Smith] can be my supervisor.' Before they could say no, I said I would like that very much.

Barry Smith was an expert on health and had written extensively on the subject. His Cambridge thesis was on tuberculosis. He had been one of the first post-war Melbourne University students to study at such a prestigious institution. Barry's *magnum opus* was a published work called *The People's Health*, in which he outlined the history of tuberculosis in humans in Britain. The following Monday, in his frighteningly boisterous manner, he knocked loudly on my door, stuck his head around the door and boomed, 'I want a 10,000 word dissertation on your plans containing a time table, research costs, a half page synopsis on your thesis proposition together with your primary and secondary source materials!' I thought that was all as I shuddered but he returned a few seconds later to say, 'I also need to know who your other supervisors will be.' My knees went weak again!

The History Department head in the Research School is rotated on a regular basis and at this particular time it was the turn of Dr Paul Bourke, who had just returned from America. Paul, who knew Barry well from Melbourne University, encouraged me to stay with him because he had a great record of success. I took his advice. Others who I had talked to about my work worried that Barry and I would not get on, but the relationship blossomed. Although Barry was gruff he was invariably right and honest in his appraisal. He knew a lot about protecting his students and also encouraged visiting Cambridge and American scholars to talk to students about their approaches, thesis content and titles. At the time the thesis title seemed very unimportant to me but Barry persisted in that it gave other scholars instant understanding of what a student was doing. This issue came up later when Professor Jay Winter, a renowned Cambridge scholar of Jewish background, asked me at my first seminar the title of my thesis. I was unable to give him an answer mainly because I was focusing on convincing the audience that Aboriginal health was a legitimate subject.

But the discussion about the title was not over. It was traditional for seminar givers in the history program to be taken to lunch at University House, 300 metres from the Chancellery lecture room. On this day Jay culled me out from the moving crowd and focused on my title. As we moved along he said, 'It is the events about the past and the people that can pull your work together. Health itself hides the history.' He went on to say, 'But, the story is about how people organise health, how people get sick, what is done about them, together with some of the contradictions you have already presented to us here today. You have a great project dealing with many things other than health, so what do you think of the idea of "Aspects of Aboriginal health: 1900 to 1940?"' Right then I thought the idea most helpful and I warmed more to the suggestion as time went on. Most students, Jay indicated, struggled with these problems and I was no different. After that run-in I always acted on Barry's advice.

By the beginning of 1993 I had pared down my topic to study disease patterns affecting Aborigines. I wanted to investigate how bureaucratic structures in the Australian colonies dealt with emerging patterns of health and how diseases themselves 'have a life of their own'. A major part of the thesis would examine Aboriginal epistemological ideas about sickness and wellness. Finally, I wanted to investigate how traditional Aboriginal and European health systems dealt with the historical events they created. Aboriginal societies used memory, superstition and the power of spontaneous thought coming from secret society to explain ill health, whereas for Europeans health has been built on science and ideology. Europeans, like Aboriginal health ideology, kept patients deliberately ignorant as a means of control. All this I passed across Barry Smith. At the traditional morning teas I would make sure that I sat next to Barry and discuss most of my ideas with him. Barry wanted to have a very clear notion of my proposition: preferably as compact as one sentence, which I gave him. He was happy with what I had done and he was interested in an atavistic approach to try, if the sources existed, to get inside Aboriginal healers' heads, and I did that through the sources of Daisy Bates, Walter Roths and JHL Cumpston.

Daisy Bates had spent a very long time collecting Noogali and Bibulman languages as well as compiling data on what Aboriginal healers knew about health, diseases and healing. Roth, in Queensland, collected data on sickness, diseases and Aboriginal pre-contact actions in dealing with the sick. Finally, Cumpston began collecting data on Aboriginal illness and wellness when he was appointed head of Customs in the Commonwealth government from as early as the first decade of Federation. Barry himself had also taken a keen interest in dangerous pathogens associated with diseases like tuberculosis, influenza and leprosy and together we produced a sound 10,000-word document as a first step to compiling the first draft of the thesis some time later.

Barry advised me that one of my first tasks was to establish an estimate of the Aboriginal population in my study areas of Queensland and Western Australia in the period from 1900 to 1940 as a determinant of rates of illness and wellness. This proved to be a much harder task than first imagined. Since Federation Aborigines had been excluded from published census counts and it was only through sheer persistence researching Commonwealth archive material, and other original sources, that I came across a mother lode of information in the form of previously unpublished yearly Aboriginal counts. These censuses were carried out from 1921 until the Second World War.

Aborigines' knowledge of health rested mostly on feelings, such as the nature of body heat, superstition and magic. These aspects of Aborigines' knowledge are still powerful, and are not far removed from what the British knew throughout the nineteenth century when little was known of infection and the biology and virology of diseases. However, there were important differences: the colonists bought with them the knowledge of science together with a broad understanding of diseases and organised care regimes while Aborigines had none of these advantages. Smallpox, venereal diseases and a large range of social infections soon began to take effect on an unsuspecting Aboriginal population. Horrendous pathogens such as tuberculosis were endemic along with other diseases like leprosy, coupled with parasitic diseases caused by living in one place too long. And then of course there was the loss of cultural beliefs and practices, along with contaminated food and drinking sources, all of which amounted to British imperial conquest.

Aborigines were concentrated into service depots, reserves and managed missions for convenience, while all the time colonial administrations blundered through on the assumption that they were invited guests rather than an invading force. By the 1901 Federation of colonies any hope of an evenly balanced relationship had evaporated, and in the main Aborigines were left out of the narrative. As a result we had no names, no characters, no lives; they were shadowy figures. This is what I wrote about.[3]

Somewhere in the maze of writing up my thesis Norma decided it was time to move again! Perhaps that statement is a little harsh since the move came about in part because the family decided that I was getting too old to ride a 1,100cc motorbike. This threw up the problem that we only had one car; Norma had to get to work and I had to get to the uni. The alternatives were buy another car or move closer to the university. We chose the latter. Again we embarked on the option of an auction when we saw a Canberra red brick house in O'Connor (an inner suburb) that appealed to us. The house was ideally located a 15 minute walk from the university and also was much closer to Norma's work in the city. We moved in during the spring of 1995. The O'Connor house became a favourite with both of us, in part because of its central location, and in part because of its beautiful leafy garden and oak tree lined street.

---

3 Briscoe 2004.

The O'Connor house also became memorable because not long after moving in Mitchell started school, and we began picking him up in the afternoons. It was a time when we developed a close relationship with him, which became very special to both his grandparents. From the start I would play winter rugby and summer cricket in the back garden with him. As he grew older it became quite competitive at times and we both loved it! Even as a young boy I could see his sporting potential, particularly in cricket, and I determined from then on to coach him whenever the opportunity presented itself. For me these times spent with Mitchell were a welcome distraction from academia.

I completed my thesis in mid-1996 and my PhD degree was conferred in 1997. This turned out to be a family double in that Norma's degree was also conferred at the same time. Norma had started a degree part-time in the late 1980s. She has a very practical side to her nature and chose subjects that would enhance her work opportunities. She majored in political science, applied statistics and population studies. She graduated with a first class honours degree and we as a family are immensely proud of her achievement. Her thesis analysed sex differential trends in infant mortality from 1964 to 1993. A complex study but one that was made easier because she built on her undergraduate studies as well as her work experience in the field of data analysis at the Australian Institute of Health and Welfare and the Australian Bureau of Statistics. It proved to be a lovely day with our now grown-up children, my brother Sam and all their partners there at the graduating ceremonies to wish us both well.I stayed on in the History Program to prepare for a post-doctoral project. My interest in historical demography had intensified and I conceived the idea of a gathering of international and Australian scholars interested in Aboriginal historical demography. My good friend and colleague Len Smith and I called for papers from those interested in the field. The conference was held in the student meeting room at the Jabal Aboriginal student centre where Neville Perkins, in his role as Director of Indigenous Students at the university, opened the conference in December of 1999.

I have a soft spot for Neville, not only because we are related, but because I have known him since he was a baby. He spent his early years being cared for by his mother May, Charlie's sister, and his grandmother Hettie during the time my mother lived with them at the cottages, known as Rainbow Town, near Heavitree Gap. My lasting memory of Neville is of him and my brother Sam swimming in a bog hole on the road in front of Hettie's place after a rainstorm. When I next saw him he was in a grey Newington College suit at Charlie's Bondi unit on my return to Australia in 1964. Years later a 'grown-up' Neville played guitar with Max Silver and Tommy Williams in the 'Black Lace' band at the Foundation on Friday nights. Neville showed early potential leadership as a member of the University of Sydney student body. He gave encouragement to the Aboriginal students campaigning for funds to create the Aboriginal Legal Service, as well as the Land Rights campaign and later raising funds for the Aboriginal Medical Service, which he gladly supported. As the FCAATSI protests intensified Neville was both a delegate and a leading ideas man, utilising his study of Australian government and law. In the early 1970s, Neville returned to the Territory where he was involved in the Australian Labor Party, working feverishly to enrol as many Aboriginal people as possible. It was during this time that he and I came together to create the Central Australian Aboriginal Congress and medical service, later expanded to Papunya, the Pitja Pitja lands and Urapuntja (Utopia). In his role as both Congress director and delegate for Stuart he was a powerful advocate for Aboriginal political representation. He was elected to the Northern Territory House of Representatives and led the Labor Party in opposition. Neville came to Canberra in 1994; I encouraged him to apply for the position as the Director of the Jabal Aboriginal Student Centre. While there Neville and I were successful in creating a greater focus on Aboriginal scholarship which ultimately led to a review of the Australian National University's Aboriginal education under Professor Peter Read.

At the conference I was keen to raise issues that stimulated scholars in the study of ethno-archaeological and Aboriginal pre-contact populations. Historical and local questions were raised by the late Dr Elspeth Young in her paper on alternative approaches to understanding population. Sad to say, Elspeth was one of two presenters at the conference who have since died. The other was Professor Alan Gray who came from Japan to speak on an underutilised topic, 'The future history of Aboriginal families'. Alan Gray died relatively young and his passing was a great loss both as a friend and colleague. I first met Alan when we worked as public servants in the Department of Aboriginal Affairs in the late 1970s. He later became one of my early thesis supervisors before leaving to teach in India and Japan. Over the years he was known and liked by many Aborigines who had a very high regard for both him and his work. Alan believed that, 'statisticians are the fabricators of reality but do so within the ideologies of society'. Like Alan Gray, Elspeth had a long struggle with cancer and just as it seemed that she had beaten the tumour she had a relapse and succumbed, leaving behind a valuable scholarship for Australian National University Aboriginal students.

Dr Helen Ross in her paper on 'town camps' highlighted a new way of looking at contemporary living sites as being part of Indigenous culture, and places where Aborigines themselves are more comfortable than whites expect. Other papers were presented by Dr Anna Schnukal on migration in the Torres Strait, by Dr John Taylor on Indigenous identification and enumeration in the late twentieth century and Professor Jack Calwell on Australian Aborigines and global population questions. Professor John Mulvaney presented his highly speculative work on how long Australia has been occupied from first known data on living sites and the size of the population in 1788 when the British arrived.[4] Len Smith built on Mulvaney's final argument on the number of people living in Australia before the European colonists arrived. As pointed out in the proceedings of the publication, given Mulvaney's standing, his estimates might now be accepted as definitive!

Len Smith and I presented a paper together in which we examined the period between the two wars, a time when native populations in Australia were thought to be in terminal decline. We showed that the Aboriginal population was already shifting from decline to recovery. The collection of papers was bought together and published under the title of *The Aboriginal population revisited: 70 000 years to the present* by Aboriginal History as the tenth in their Monograph series in 2002.

About this time, due in part to the badgering of Neville Perkins, myself and Professor John Richards, a Pro-Vice Chancellor, a review of Indigenous education was initiated on campus and as a result more funding became available for Indigenous initiatives. Len Smith and the head of the History Program at the time Barry Higman approached the new Vice Chancellor, Professor Ian Chubb, with a proposal to create a new Centre for Indigenous History. Funds were allocated and Professor Ann McGrath was appointed head of the new centre. I was appointed as a Research Fellow for three years.

One of the projects involved in the new centre was collaboration between our centre and the Universities of Yale, Ontario and Virginia. The overall program was called 'Frontier Histories'. As part of the project a series of conferences were held at the National Museum of Australia and the Australian National University, later it involved taking a large group of the American academics to the Northern Territory. While there, we gave lectures at many of the academic institutions and visited various tourist attractions. Later Anne McGrath worked in partnership with the National Museum of Australia to produce a documentary video 'A Frontier Conversation'. The film on one level is a simple and watchable account of a group of historians visiting the Northern Territory, but it has an underlying message about the complex problem of the different uses that history is put to in different cultural settings and over long periods of time.

In the process of touring many of the American academics wanted to know about my background and this stimulated me to give a number of lectures both on my biography and my perspectives of the Aboriginal past. In hindsight it was this interest in my life and knowledge of Aborigines that gave me the inspiration and enthusiasm to start thinking about writing this memoir. The

---

4   Briscoe and Smith 2002.

thought crystallised more as time went on and I spent most of my remaining research time preparing for this task. Following the Northern Territory project a number of ideas became clear in my mind: that I should write about my own past and the boys I grew up with together with my family's origins and experiences in the face of European expansion.

I continued with my research as a Visiting Fellow in the department after my tenure in the centre finished. This time as a Fellow which gave me a chance to research my own and my family's — Aboriginal and non-Aboriginal — pasts. It also helped me to look more closely at the creation of the 'Native Institutions' in which my mother and I were interned as 'wards of the Commonwealth government'. At the same time I became involved with the planning of a conference on children's history organised by the Charles Darwin University. I presented a paper on the origins of 'The half caste problem' and its effects on my and other peoples' lives, from the 1870s to the late 1960s,[5] it gave me the opportunity to think and write about my background and prepare for some of the complexities the memoir would no doubt throw up.

I feel that almost as a footnote to my working life I was awarded membership of the Order of Australia in the second highest grade of Officer, or 'AO' on Australia day in 2004. The citation mentioned my work in establishing the first Aboriginal Medical and Legal Services in Redfern in the early 1970s, as architect of the National Trachoma and Eye Health Program and my academic attainments. I later learnt that it was my friend Ian Howie-Willis who nominated me. The award was presented to me that April in a ceremony at Government House, Yarralumla by the Governor General, Lieutenant-General Michael Jefferies. As much as anything I was gratified that my long-standing friend Dr Tom Gavranic received an award at the same time for his work in the Aboriginal and Croatian communities over many decades. The two families celebrated at the Government House garden party following the award giving ceremonies.

Later in 2005 my connection with Alice Springs grew stronger in a much unexpected way. Our second grandson Jack Jonathon Wilde was born on 30 October 2005 in Alice Springs. That made him Umbartuwa, an Arrernte word for 'born in this place'. Lisa and her partner Shaun lived in Alice Springs at the time and it was particularly pleasing to me that Jack was born in my place of birth. Jack was a healthy seven pound plus baby with very dark eyes and hair just like his father. Shaun is a Kalkadoon man from Mount Isa where his extended family still lives. Jack was named after his maternal grandfather, Jack Wilde, who came from Sudan Station near Lake Nash on the Northern Territory/Queensland border, where Shaun is a Native Title Holder. Lisa and Shaun lived in Mount Isa for a time; Shaun as a public servant and Lisa as a

---

5   Briscoe 2008:7-22.

lawyer with the Aboriginal Legal Service. For Lisa it was an insight into rural life as she represented people on the court circuit in outlying areas around the Isa. It meant flying to small communities such as Mornington Island, Cloncurry, Dajarra and Boulia on a week-on week-off basis. An experience I am sure she will never forget. In Alice Springs Lisa's work focused more on child protection that has now become her preferred area of work. She claims that work-related visits to the town camps have opened her eyes to the abject poverty that many of the children live in.

As a father it has been particularly satisfying that Aaron and Lisa have both spent time in Alice Springs as working adults. While Lisa's social focus has been more on the in-town relatives and old friends of mine, Aaron's love is the bush people. He is never happier than when he picks up a four-wheel drive in Alice and goes out bush to meet up with family at places such as Oak Valley Station where my cousin Mary, Robert and family live. More often than not he continues south to Titjikala and Umuwa where more of my mother's relatives live.

During the mid-1990s we bought a fisherman's shack on the south coast of New South Wales. The South Coast is often called 'Canberra's playground' and is a manageable two-hour drive from the capital, with pristine beaches and unspoilt natural beauty. We found ourselves enjoying the coast more and in 2004 started to think about making it our permanent home. The original house on the block was fine for holidays but was badly affected by damp, making it unliveable on a permanent basis or to extend. Plans were drawn up; we started building in 2006 and moved to the South Coast on a permanent basis in early 2007.

As this memoir draws to a close I reflect on my original intentions, clarified by one of my learned history colleagues who advised me early on that: 'You should begin by telling the story from when you were born, tell us what your life was like, who were the people who influenced your life and what events took up so much of your life that you couldn't escape them?' One of the things I've tried to do in this memoir is to give those Aboriginal men and women most important in my life a character and a biography upon which others can build – an historiography of, inclusion.

This memoir has not necessarily been a diatribe to evaluate and criticise those who were drawn into becoming involved in what is now called 'The stolen generations' but more what was once called the 'half-caste problem'. My aim was to place the context of my life in the overall polity of the last century of Aboriginal affairs. As a young man I could not escape my family's background, nor could my mother's people escape those forces in society that shaped them. However, my interpretation of those people involved in my life, I believe, has been assertive but fair. Then of course there were those people that my earlier life crossed who will want to see themselves in the text: either because they had a similar time at the House or because they ended up at another institution. However, this story of my life, like most historical accounts represents a selective process where limitations on the text, the importance of parallel events of my own family, my education and my involvement with many people have shaped the narrative. Some people I have known have entered my life significantly through family members and they will know who they are and why they have not entered the text while others have entered fleetingly and earned a mention. I have tried to stick closely to the political text because I think this story is one of significance, and that Aboriginal emancipation, as CD Rowley so clearly stated in his monumental trilogy of the history of 'Aboriginal Policy and Practice', is the history of Aboriginal politics.[6] And, finally as Hobsbawn, the historian puts it so eloquently whereas: 'Biographies end with the subject's death. Autobiographies have no such natural termination'[7] but perhaps the natural termination of this memoir is one for others to follow on with as I enter my three-score years and ten.

---

6   Rowley 1970, 1971a, 1971b.
7   Hobsbawm 2002: 411.

Epilogue

This memoir covers my family's reach across the twentieth century and in so doing is a story that covers race relations policy development and implementation throughout this period. The beginning of the twentieth century was chaotic for Aborigines and policies were made without much thought. On the one hand half-castes were institutionalised as useful labour, on the other people of full descent were concentrated on reserves and missions. By the 1920s the Federal government began to take an interest, albeit ambiguously, in Northern Territory Aborigines, on the one hand retaining aspects of the old protection policy while on the other changing protection to assimilation.

Following the election of the Whitlam government the idea that Aborigines were to run their own affairs descended into a bureaucratic nightmare. Australian nationalism meant something to white society but it seemed that Aborigines were never to be placed on the political agenda without a fight. Self determination as a policy meant people taking control of their own lives as individuals and collective institutions. Equally it meant people working towards developing their own economies in partnership with pastoral and urban capitalism. Institutions for improving the lot of the Indigenous peoples, such as health clinics, general practitioner services, community schools, libraries and sporting activities, run by Aboriginal leaders and community participants, were envisaged. Such activities would help to ward off poverty, unemployment, raise community consciousness and help develop democratic structures that fitted into the wider Australian political system. Aboriginal communities would have a surplus from their own products and that surplus capital could help them plan the future. Continuing community education could be bought in from institutions such as universities, business institutions and education structures such as tertiary training institutions and local schools. Institutions dealing with legal and human rights questions could form part of the community structures. Commonwealth governments created the funding and the ideology but states had only policy guidelines rather than legal ones to follow.

In general, however, state governments objected to funding gravitating directly to Aboriginal groups and communities and failed to work out or prescribe how their race policies were to be implemented. If their factionalised governments would not cooperate, nothing would happen. For decades Commonwealth funds were spent on bureaucratic solutions that neither of the major political parties cared about. 'Human rights', the post Second World War 'brave new world' for all based on international laws, were treated with contempt. As Australian national and state governments changed so too did race ideologies. These ideologies were built on the prejudices that Aboriginal heritage, material culture, belief systems and languages had no basis in the face of Australia's national interests. Huge amounts of the national wealth was spent and wasted on European and British cultural institutions that both destroyed and codified Aboriginal ideologies. For example, St Francis House and other bodies were created along the lines of British workhouses and children's reformatories that changed the culture of people of mixed descent to that of middle class Christian ways of self-perception. Both self-management and self-sufficiency stood as barriers to Aboriginal democracy, human rights and equality. Employment strategies such as the Community Development Employment Program (CDEP) acted as a bar to participation in the Australian capitalist economic system. Returning Aboriginal lands stolen by European expansion was an absolutely unacceptable notion in the face of the shibboleth of private property. Land rights, a major concern of Aborigines, was resisted by Australian governments and was depicted as an affront to the national interest, meaning that it prevented the economic development for the whole nation. Uranium mining, mineral extraction for iron ore, oil and aluminium were all seen as more important than Aboriginal rights, heritage, reparation and welfare.

Of course things have changed, albeit slowly, but much of the accounting of that change I leave to others. Every few years as self-determination policies took effect so new issues arose where confrontation seemed inevitable at every turn. Some sites of significance were returned while material objects, the plunder of colonial dispossession such as grave sites, were sporadically returned but large ceremonial caches were refused and retained in state and national museums. As Aboriginal political institutions such as the National Aboriginal Consultative Council grew in the 1970s and 1980s Australians lost patience with Aborigines as demands for reparation of material culture grew. When the new Aboriginal and Torres Strait Islander Commission came into existence, greater powers flowed to that body to implement, more intensely, self-determination policies. At the same time a ginger group called the 'Council for Reconciliation' was situated within the Department of Prime Minister and Cabinet under Bob Hawke and later Paul Keating. This body was established in 1991 and quickly monopolised current ideas such as 'Deaths in Custody', borrowed from the South African revolution of the 1970s and 1980s. Influences also came from the Northern Lands Council and possibly the Aboriginal Treaty Committee, coupled with Eddy Mabo's legal lobby on 'Native Title'. These groups also had links to the National Aboriginal Land Rights lobby and the supporters of United Nations issues; it took some years to fashion an ideological position on 'Reconciliation' policy.

As a historian it is easy to understand that propaganda has always been an ingredient of traders of power and those involved in Aboriginal politics are no different. Propaganda is equally familiar to those involved in the scripting of the 'Reconciliation policy'. Beginning with a legislative cover the Council for

Aboriginal Reconciliation Council including Torres Strait Islanders had a ten-year sunset clause from 1999. It aimed to improve relations between Aborigines and Australians, but nobody was quite sure who was to say sorry to whom or for what. Many people simply said sorry but had no knowledge why they were doing so. Others began by blaming all the aggravation on Aborigines who were demonstrating without saying what their slogans meant. Reconciliation gradually came to mean to increase understandings of Aboriginal culture, history (their disadvantages and how their lands were taken) and a commitment to address issues in the timeframe leading to the anniversary of Federation in 2001. The exercise was not simply to produce 'motherhood' statements that would pave the way for a political 'compact' or bi-partisan approach to Aboriginal affairs but to gain the support of both left and right of Australian politics.

At first, the Prime Minister's Reconciliation policy section fashioned ideas of 'Social Justice' for Indigenous Australians in 1991-92. Their statement covered every aspect of the Aboriginal Affairs portfolio anointing the ideas of fairness, needs, social disadvantage in health, education, law, employment and dependency, deaths in custody and the removal of Aboriginal children. However, in the end most of what 'Reconciliation' stood for failed and went by the wayside. Reconciliation policy became murkier than ever as Labor was replaced in 1996 by John Howard's Liberal-National coalition government. The Council was left without a bureaucratic arm when the sub-branch in Prime Minister Howard's office was disposed of.

The twentieth century began under conservative rule and ended the same way, beginning as a century of racial discrimination and ending with the dismantling of the Aboriginal and Torres Strait Islander Commission, Labor's Aboriginal democratic structure. This latter process began with John Herron the Minister for Aboriginal Affairs when he launched a book by a South Australian academic, Geoffrey Partington lauding Australia's British identity. Partington attacked ideas built by 'Nugget' Coombs and blamed him for dismantling the Liberal-Country Party's assimilation ideology. This set in train the process of the denouncing 'Black Armband' history. Left historians wanted a more scholarly revision of Aboriginal and non-Aboriginal history of dispossession that reflected the conquest of the continent and its first peoples by British and Australian colonialism: the depiction of colonial violence, cultural genocide of Aborigines and their past. Of course, all governments attempt to rewrite their own perspective of their nation's past and John Howard entered the debate to defend his British perspective of Australia's past. All who were critical of his position were branded 'the thought police' and agents of 'political correctness'. As the debate heated up, who could ever forget Howard's disgraceful outburst in Melbourne at the Reconciliation Convention on 26 May 1997, where Howard proclaimed that his policy was to be called 'Practical Reconciliation'? From this point the Howard government resisted all suggestions of direct Aboriginal democratic participation as a special group. The Aboriginal and Torres Strait Islander Commission was suspended and the new Minister for Aboriginal Affairs Mal Brough dismantled all bureaucratic structures for providing policy advice, choosing to fill that role himself along with chosen advisers.

However, there are still reasons to be optimistic on the history front. The first development had its genesis in a Fred Hollow's fund-raising night in the late 1990s. Among the invited guests was Nigel Milan, the then chairperson of SBS television. Nigel was generally praising SBS for its approach to Aboriginal politics and social coverage, though on some points I disagreed. As the evening progressed, Nigel came back to me and said, 'What can I do to provide better SBS resources for Aboriginal development?' To which I replied, 'Nigel, you can give Aborigines back their history. Australia has diverse media institutions that could produce either film or television documentaries depicting the historic dispossession of Aborigines beginning with early Macassan contact, European contact up to Captain Cook and the various wars of resistance from Captain Phillip to the political resistances such as the 1967 referendum, the Aboriginal Embassy and the Redfern riots leading up to 1988.' I felt that perhaps I had been too harsh on Nigel as he shook his head. However, he never forgot that conversation! Some two years later at another Hollows Foundation annual general meeting Nigel came up to me with a great smile on his face declaring that he'd convinced the SBS organisation to produce a series of documentaries on what he called 'black white relations'. He had appointed Charlie Perkin's daughter Rachel as the director who was fresh from directing the highly praised film *One Night the Moon*. [1]

The production of *The First Australians* went to air in 2008 as I reached my 70th birthday. It was an important achievement because for the first time Aborigines reclaimed their history, interpreted to a wider national audience in the most engaging of communications – television. This ground-breaking documentary series covered the entire 200 years of Aboriginal/European contact. The chief Aboriginal presenters were Marcia Langton, Bruce Pascoe and me, along with other historians of note. The series was able to put forward Aboriginal people's points of view to the wider community in a way never before attempted. Widely acclaimed, the series helped many understand the impact of colonialism on the first Australians.

There are also happenings in a different but equally important media. The *Australian Dictionary of Biography*, the classic publication by the History Program of the Research School of Social Sciences at the Australian National University, is beginning to show an interest in broadening its Aboriginal

---

1   Perkins R 2001.

biography. The Dictionary began some 40 years ago and until recently retained an out-dated criterion of only including those who had been dead for at least 20 years. I would like to see this clause modified, along with a special program to include prominent Aboriginal people guided by a committee of Aboriginal scholars.

Where to now? Aboriginal health has been a continuing theme and interest throughout my adult life and is documented extensively throughout this memoir. It is therefore not surprising that much of my current intellectual thinking revolves around the ongoing debate and impact of poor Aboriginal life expectancy. Historically and with good reason, infant mortality has been seen as the biggest contributor to the poor life expectancy of Aborigines. During the 1970s work by epidemiologists such as Len Smith documented the chasm between the outcome for babies of Aboriginal mothers and those of their non-Aboriginal counterparts. However, more recent studies show that although Aboriginal infant mortality continues to be high, the very real problem lies in the excess of deaths of Aborigines in the middle age groups from 35 to 50 years of age. Just when non-Aborigines are generally in the prime of their life having overcome the excesses of youth, Aborigines are dying of potentially preventable diseases such as heart disease and complications from diabetes.

It is probably too early to say whether the Labor government's Apology to the Stolen Generations will herald a new era of political inclusion for Aborigines. Now however, Aborigines themselves must do some soul-searching to articulate what they mean by the slogans they use in political rallies, in the daily press and in their literature and publications about themselves as a people. In concluding my writings I hope, for my part, that the twenty-first century, in which my children and grand children live, will be the era of greater liberty, equality and fraternity for Aborigines rather than the despair and anguish of the twentieth century.

References

Bandler, Faith 1989, *Turning the Tide*, Australian Institute of Aboriginal and Torres Strait Islander Studies (AIATSIS), Canberra.

Berger, Peter 1963, *Invitation to Sociology, A Humanistic Perspective*, Penguin, USA.

Berndt, Ronald and CH Berndt 1987, *End of an Era: Aboriginal Labour in the Northern Territory*, Australian Institute of Aboriginal Studies (AIAS), Canberra.

Bleakley, W 1961, *The Aborigines of Australia: Their History, their Habits, their Assimilation*, Jacaranda Press, Brisbane.

Bowler, J and A Thorne 1976, 'Human remains from Lake Mungo: Discovery and Excavation', in *The Origins of the Australians*, R Kirk (ed), AIAS, Canberra: 127-140.

Briscoe, Gordon 1994, 'The Struggle for Grace: An Appreciation of Kevin John Gilbert', *Aboriginal History* 18: 13-31.

— 2004, *Counting, Health and Identity*, Aboriginal Studies Press, Canberra.

— 2008, 'Assimilation and Indifference: The Paradoxical Treatment of Indigenous Children in Central Australia, 1914-1951', in *Contexts of Child Development: Culture, Policy and Intervention*, Gary Robinson et al (eds), Charles Darwin University Press, Darwin: 7-22.

— and LR Smith (eds) 2002, *The Aboriginal Population Revisited: 70,000 Years to the Present*, Aboriginal History Monograph no 10, Aboriginal History Inc, Canberra.

Bucknall, Graeme 1990-1996, 'Isabella Violet Price', in *Northern Territory Dictionary of Biography*, vol 1, D Carment, R Maynard and A Powell (eds), Charles Darwin University Press, Darwin: 171-173.

Collins, David 1802, *An Account of the English Colony in New South Wales*, vol 1, Reed in association with the Royal Historical Society, Sydney: 452-453.

Cook, Cecil 1925, *The Epidemiology of Leprosy in Australia*, Australian Government Publishing Service, Melbourne.

Corris, Peter 1991, *Fred Hollows, An Autobiography with Peter Corris*, John Kerr, Sydney.

Duguid, Charles 1963, *No Dying Race*, Rigby, Adelaide.

Duncan, Allan, 'Jobs Project', in *Senate Standing Committee on Social Environment: Reference, Aborigines and Torres Strait Islander: 1971-1976, Official Hansard Transcript of Evidence*, vol 3, Australian Government Printing Service, Canberra: 1150-1174.

Dunn, Margaret 2004, *The Captain, the Colonel and the Bishop*, Crawford House, Adelaide.

Fraser, Ros 1993, *Aboriginal and Torres Strait Islander People in Commonwealth Records: A Guide to Records in the Australian Archives, ACT Regional Office*, Australian Government Publishing Service, Canberra.

Fredrickson, George 2002, *Racism: A Short History*, Scribe, Melbourne.

Gale, Fay 1972, *Urban Aborigines*, Australian National University Press.

Hill, Barry 2003, *Broken Song: T.G.H. Strehlow and Aboriginal Possession*, Vintage, Sydney.

Hill, Ernestine 1933, 'Half-Caste – Australian Tragedy', *Sydney Sun*, 2 April 1933.

Hobsbawm, Eric 2002, *Interesting Times: A Twentieth-Century Life*, Abacus, London.

Horner, Jack 1994, *Bill Ferguson: Fighter for Aboriginal Freedom*, Australia and New Zealand Book Company Limited, Brookvale, New South Wales.

Horton, David 1994, 'Kamilaroi', in *The Encyclopaedia of Aboriginal Australia*, David Horton (ed), AIATSIS, Canberra: 530-531.

Howie-Willis, Ian 1994a, 'Bark Petition', in *The Encyclopaedia of Aboriginal Australia*, vol 1, David Horton (ed), AIATSIS, Canberra: l00-101.

— 1994b, 'Blackburn, R', in *The Encyclopaedia of Aboriginal Australia,* vol 1, David Horton (ed), AIATSIS, Canberra: 130.

— 1994c, 'National Tribal Council', in *The Encyclopaedia of Aboriginal Australia*, vol 2, David Horton (ed), AIATSIS, Canberra: 764-765.

— 1994d, 'Newfong, J' in *The Encyclopaedia of Aboriginal Australia*, vol 2, David Horton (ed), AIATSIS, Canberra: 774.

Jaspers, Karl 1932, *Philosophy*, vols 1-2, Oxford University Press, London.

Kalokerinos, Archie 1974, 'Aboriginal health is bad by all standards', in *Senate Standing Committee on Social Environment: Reference, Aborigines and Torres Strait Islander: 1971-1976, Official Hansard Transcript of Evidence*, 25 October 1974, Australian Government Printing Service, Canberra: 1684-1750.

Kierkegaard, Soren 1976[1936], 'Philosophical fragments', in *The New Encyclopaedia Britannica*, vol 7, University of Chicago, Chicago: 73-79.

Lenin, VL 1975, *Lenin selected works,* Progress Publishers, Moscow.

McCorquodale, John 1987, *Aborigines and the Law: A Digest*, Aboriginal Studies Press, Canberra.

McGlade, H 1994, 'Foley, G', in *The Encyclopaedia of Aboriginal Australia,* vol 1, David Horton (ed), AIATSIS, Canberra: 374.

MacIntyre S and A Clark, 2003, *The History Wars*, Melbourne University Press, Victoria.

Markus, Andrew 1990, *Governing Savages*, Allen & Unwin, Sydney.

Moodie, Peter 1973, *Aboriginal Health, Aborigines in Australian Society*, Australian National University Press.

Moriarty, John 2000, *Saltwater Fella*, Viking, Sydney.

Mulvaney, John (complier), with A Petch and H Morphy 2000, *From the Frontier: Outback Letters to Baldwin Spencer*, Allen & Unwin, St Leonards, New South Wales.

New Encyclopaedia Britannica, 1976, 'Eugenics', in *New Encyclopaedia Britannica*, vol 6, William Benton Pub, Tucson, USA: 1023.

Perkins, Charles 1975, *A Bastard Like Me*, Ure Smith, Sydney.

Perkins, Rachel (director) 2001, *One Night the Moon,* Australian Broadcasting Corporation, 54 minutes.

Read, Peter 1990, *Charles Perkins: A Biography,* Viking, Melbourne.

— and J Read 1999, *Long Time, Olden Time: Aboriginal Accounts of Northern Territory History*, 1999, IAD, Alice Springs.

Rowley, Charles 1970, *The Destruction of Aboriginal Society: Aboriginal Policy and Practice*, vol 1, Australian National University Press, Canberra.

— 1971a, *Outcasts in White Australia: Aboriginal Policy and Practice*, vol 2, Australian National University Press, Canberra.

— 1971b, *The Remote Aborigines: Aboriginal Policy and Practice*, vol 3, Australian National University Press, Canberra.

— 1986, *Recovery: The Politics of Aboriginal Reform*, Penguin Books, Melbourne.

Smith, John 1999, *The Flower in the Desert: A Biography of the Reverend Canon P. Mc.D. Smith, MBE*, Copy Master, Adelaide: 13-74.

Smith, LR 1980, *Aboriginal Health Bulletin*, No. 1, Australian Government Publishing Service, Canberra.

Spencer, Baldwin 1896, *Horn Scientific Expedition to Central Australia*, and *Through Larapinta Land: A Narrative of the Horn Expedition to Central Australia*, Melbourne.

— and FJ Gillen 1968[1899], *The Native Tribes of Central Australia*, Dover Publications, New York.

Stanner, William 1972, *After the Dreaming: Black and White Australians – an Anthropologist's View*, The Boyer Lectures, 6th printing, Australian Broadcasting Commission, Sydney.

Stevens, Frank 1971, *Racism, the Australian Experience: Prejudice and Xenophobia*, vol 1, Australian and New Zealand Book Company, Sydney.

— 1974, *Aborigines in the Cattle Industry*, Australian National University Press, Canberra.

Strehlow, TGH 1969, *Journey to Horseshoe Bend*, Angus and Robertson, Sydney.

Taffe, Sue 2005, *Black And White*, University of Queensland Press, St Lucia, Queensland.

Tavan, Gwenda 2005, *The Long Slow Death of White Australia*, Scribe, Melbourne.

United Nations, General Assembly 1949, *Universal Declaration of Human Rights*, Australian National Committee for United Nations, Melbourne.

United Nations, Office of the High Commission for Human Rights 1991, *Fact Sheet 16, The Committee on Economic and Social and Cultural Rights*, UN Office of the High Commission for Human Rights, Geneva, October 1991.

Willey, Keith 1979, *When the Sky Fell Down: The Destruction of the Tribes of the Sydney Region, 1788-1850*, Collins Pty Ltd, Sydney: 51-61.

Wilson, Bill and J O'Brien, '"To Infuse a Universal Terror": A Reappraisal of the Coniston Killings', *Aboriginal History* 27: 59-78.

Windshuttle, Keith 1994, *The Killing of History: How Literary Critics and Social Theorists are Murdering our Past*, Macleay Press, Sydney.

— 2000, 'The Myths of the Frontier Massacres in Australian History. Part I: The Invention of Massacre Stories', *Quadrant* 44(10): 8-21.

Primary sources

National Archives of Australia, Canberra

Commonwealth Record Series (CRS) A1, Correspondence Files, Annual Single Number Series, 1903-1938

CRS A1, item 1926/5350, Half-Castes in NT re Training and Employment of, 1925-1927.

CRS A1, item 1933/479, Apprentice (Half Castes) Regulations Nth Australia and Central Australia, 1929-1934.

Half-Caste Apprentice Regulations, folios 1-10, 53-55 and 291.

Letter from Chief Protector CE Cook to Government Resident, Darwin, 22 March 1930, folio 55.

Letter from Secretary NTPLA to Minister for Home Affairs, 18 February 1930, folios 1-10.

CRS A1, item 1933/243, Ministerial Visit to Stuart – 1933, 1932-1933.

Visit by Minister for Interior, JA Perkins and Secretary, Department of Interior, HC Brown to Alice Springs, folios 218A-219.

CRS A1, item 1936/2765, ...Reported murder of in NT, 1936.

CRS A1, item 1936/7846, Half Castes Employed outside NT, 1924-1936.

CRS A1, item 1936/9959, Inspection of NT Schools by Supervisor, 1936-1937.

Half-Caste Institution.

CRS A1, item 1937/1718, A.X. Herbert, Appt Dispenser Dresser NA, 1929-1937.

CRS A431, Correspondence Files, Annual Single Number Series, 1946-

CRS A431, item 1947/2348, Northern Territory. Population Statistics. NT, 1918-1953.

Report on Hermannsburg. NT Annual Report, 1913.

CRS A431, item 1950/2768, Attacks on White Men by Natives – Killing of Natives – Central Australia [parts 1 and 2], 1928 and 1929-1950.

The Findings of the Board of Inquiry into Coniston Killings, 1928-1950, parts 1-2.

Commonwealth of Australia Gazette, No 138, dated Friday 4 December 1928 and signed by Governor-General Stonehaven and Mr CLA Abbott, folio 445.

Attachment 'Finding of Board of Inquiry with Exhibits 1-13', part 2.

Article 'Aborigines, Recent Shooting', *Sydney Morning Herald*, 10 May 1929.

CRS A659, Correspondence Files, Class 1 (General, Passports), 1939-1950

CRS A659, item 1939/1/996, Half Caste Home, Alice Springs. NT [File no. 2], 1928-1939.

Half-Caste Home, Alice Springs, NT, folios 174-182.

List of inmates; including Eileen Briscoe, 31 August 1929, folio 403-405.

Letter from Reverend W Morley to A Blakeley MP, 23 November 1929.

Freeman's Report, 26 March 1932, folios 403-405.

Letter from PE Deane, Secretary Department of Home Affairs to The Secretary Commonwealth Treasury, Canberra, February 1929, folios 70-79.

Letter from J Bleakley to Secretary Department of Home Affairs, 14 February 1929. Article 'Scandal of North', *Adelaide Mail*.

Letter, HA Parkhill, Minister for Home Affairs, Canberra.

CRS A659, item 1945/1/2493, Transfer of Half-Castes, NT to Racecourse at Balaklava, S Australia [Part II], 1942-1946, 1957.

Transfer of Half-Castes, NT to Racecourse dated 4 June 1942, folio 9. [This file was opened in 1942 but added to in 1945 following a number of women, including my mother, myself and Bill, being sent from Sydney to Balaclava, after hostilities ended in Europe.]

Letter from Department of Labour and Industry to Mr EWP Chinnery, Director Native Affairs, Department of Interior, Canberra, 24 January 1945, folios 14-15.

www.ingramcontent.com/pod-product-compliance
Lightning Source LLC
Chambersburg PA
CBHW060929170426
43192CB00031B/2873